CL16

Gloucestershire
COUNTY COUNCIL

D1139262

GAVIN HENSON

MY GRAND SLAM YEAR

GAVIN HENSON
MY GRAND SLAM YEAR

Gavin Henson
with Graham Thomas

HarperSport
An Imprint of HarperCollins*Publishers*

First published in UK in 2005 by
HarperSport
an imprint of HarperCollins*Publishers*
London

© Gavin Henson 2005

3

A CIP catalogue record for this book
is available from the British Library

ISBN-13 978-0-00-721686-6
ISBN-10 0-00-721686-6

Printed and bound in Great Britain by
Clays Ltd, St Ives plc

The HarperCollins website address is
www.harpercollins.co.uk

Contents

Acknowledgements

I would like to thank the following people for making 2004–05 such a memorable year: Alan and Audrey Henson, Sarah Henson, Trevor and Megan Watkins, Glyn and Marian Henson, Charlotte Church, Matthew Williams, David Norman, Stuart Bevan, Adrian Durston, Simon Homeyard, Jack Hayes, Robert Williams, Jamie Griffiths, Hywel Jenkins, Peter Underhill, Matt Ginvert, plus all my team-mates and coaches.

In helping Gavin write this book, Graham Thomas would like to thank Peter Underhill, John Pawsey, Tom Whiting, Nigel Walker and Catherine Thomas.

CHAPTER ONE

Can I Kick It?

As soon as the referee blew his whistle for a penalty, I knew I could kick it. Forty-four metres out from the posts and two or three in from the touchline, it was my kind of distance. Go a bit closer and everyone watching *expects* the kicker to score, rather than hopes. Sometimes that expectation can get to the kicker. From 44 metres out, and by the touchline, I could sense the hope of 70,000 people in the stadium and the millions more watching on TV, but I think the only person who truly *expected* it to go over was me.

Firstly, though, I had to be told to give it a go. Stephen Jones was our first choice goal-kicker and took all the short-range kicks. That's how we had practised all week in the build-up to the match. He took short and medium-range kicks and I practised long ones. This was 44 metres and at an angle, but it had to be out of Stephen's range for it to be in mine. I looked across and saw Stephen signal to Gareth Thomas that I should have it. There were four minutes left on the clock and this was very likely to be our last chance to win the game. But Stephen didn't hesitate. 'Give it to Gav,' he said and walked off. The skipper backed up the decision and then it was down to me.

After the match, after we had beaten England and were back in the dressing room, Mike Ruddock, our coach, told me he couldn't watch. 'Why not? I knew I was going to kick it.' And it wasn't bravado. I did. *I really did.* I had spent all week practising kicks from that kind of distance and when I concentrated, and got all my preparation right, they had all gone over. All I had to do was repeat it. That's what I was thinking as I was lining up the ball on the tee. I wasn't thinking about the match, or the result, or the time that was left. My mind was clear of all that stuff. Believe in your technique ... don't hit it too hard ... you've got the legs ... and keep your head down.

To be honest, I did have one small seed of doubt. But that was nothing to do with me or my abilities. It was the pitch. The Millennium Stadium is an incredible arena, but the pitch can sometimes be a problem. Because precious little sunlight gets to it, it is regularly re-laid and sometimes it can cut up badly under pressure. Put it under a lot of pressure – like 16 huge guys scrummaging against each other in a Wales-England Six Nations match – and it can cut up very badly as it did that day. All over the field there were mounds of turf where the pitch had been churned up by the twisting force of 16 sets of studs. What about one set of studs? When it really mattered? In the back of my mind was the fear of slipping if that top inch of turf gave way. If my non-kicking foot slipped just before impact then the ball would go off line. Remember David Beckham's missed penalty for England in Euro 2004? Stay nice and light on the left foot . . . be flexible . . . strike it down the middle.

There had been a roar when Steve Walsh awarded the penalty, but now there was just silence. I didn't mind that as it helped clear my head. I stepped back, kept my rhythm through the run-up, and struck it just as sweetly as every other kick I'd put over on the training ground. I didn't need to wait to see it go over, I knew it was there from the moment I struck it. I always do. It must be like that if you're a tournament golfer and you hit a putt you've practised a thousand times. You know from the connection, just from the feel of the ball as it leaves the putter or your foot, whether or not it's going through the posts. Normally, I have a quick look just to convince myself it's on line and then I run back before the touch judges signal, while the ball is still travelling towards the posts. Only if it's a windy day, and I don't trust the breeze not to blow the kick off line, will I keep looking until it's through. There was no wind in the Millennium Stadium that day as the roof was closed. It was blowing a gale outside but under the protection of all that steel the wind was never a factor. From the moment I struck it I knew I'd scored. I turned away, threw the tee back to the touchline, and raised my finger in the air. Thanks for coming.

A few of the Welsh players shouted and screamed but I can't remember what was said. I was in my own little world. But I snapped out of it when someone demanded we re-focus and win the ball straight from the re-start. We did better than that, we won another penalty and were able to pump the ball back into their half. It was 11–9 to us and England were running out of time. John Yapp made a burst and I tried a drop goal but it was charged down. A 14–9 lead would have given us a little more breathing space, but there was no time for England to get back into range and win it with a drop goal of their own or another penalty. Time had run out for England. This was our time.

There was a huge amount of pressure on us going into that game. We felt confident we could win it, but the circumstances had changed from Wales-England matches in previous years. We still weren't the bookies' favourites but the Welsh public certainly expected us to win. You could sense that from talking to fans and it was reflected in the media coverage where all the talk was about this being our best chance of winning for years – perhaps the best opportunity since 1993, which was the last time Wales had won against England in Cardiff, and certainly the best since 1999 when Scott Gibbs's famous try had won the same fixture at Wembley.

I felt we could win and would win. So did the rest of the squad. But the expectation from outside added to the nerves we all felt and looking back now it was an edgy performance, definitely our most nervous display of that championship.

To me, it felt as though almost all the pressure was on us rather than on England. Okay, they were the world champions but this was a very different team to the one that had lifted the trophy against Australia just 15 months before. Sir Clive Woodward had gone and there was no Martin Johnson, Lawrence Dallaglio or Neil Back. Andy Robinson had come in as coach and although England had beaten South Africa the previous autumn, the Wallabies had taken their own revenge at Twickenham a week later. Also – and most importantly for us – they looked vulnerable because of lots of injury problems. Jonny Wilkinson had been missing since the World Cup, but other key guys, like Mike Tindall, who I would have been up against in the centre, were also crocked.

But there was pressure coming onto us from another direction, too. It was coming from within. We knew we needed a big scalp to give us that confidence boost. It was crucial if we were going to go from being an improving side, in the second tier of world rugby, to a team who could not only rub shoulders with the big boys, but often beat them. Before the Six Nations championship had begun there were plenty of pundits who felt talk of a Welsh revival was just hype. Keith Wood, the former Ireland captain, said as much on TV, and so did Jeremy Guscott who laughed out loud in one interview when Jonathan Davies suggested Wales could be about to take some big scalps. I suppose you couldn't really blame them. It's hard to claim a genuine revival when you are basing it on matches that ended in defeat, even if those defeats were extremely narrow and accompanied by some superb performances. Heroic defeats may be exciting at the time, but they are always followed by massive feelings of frustration instead of a satisfying glow. You can dress it up, you can put a spin on it, you can talk about encouraging progress until you're blue in the face; but a defeat is still a defeat.

We had suffered two such defeats in the previous autumn. The first was against South Africa when we came from a long way behind to lose by just a couple of points, 38–36. Then we suffered an even greater agony by being edged out by New Zealand by just a single point. That defeat, 26–25, was harder to take because we had not only been ahead but we had chances late on to win it. Both those results were very much in all the players' minds going into the game with England. We were very proud of our performances against the Springboks and the All Blacks – and we felt the supporters' pride – but we didn't want to suffer like that again. We wanted to get that first big win under our belts because we all felt the confidence it would generate would provide huge momentum for the rest of the championship.

Although I felt the pressure, I wasn't really nervous in the few days before the match. I felt confident and I wasn't afraid to say so. The trouble is that some people take that as arrogance. I don't see it like that. If someone asks you if you think you are going to win, what's the point of saying no, or you're not sure? What's the point of pretending? I've never been into all that stuff when players offer no opinion of what the result of the game might be. For me, you might as well speak the truth, and the truth is that I felt we would beat England. If I build myself up, and my own team, then it makes me feel confident. It also puts pressure on me to go out and prove my point and I don't mind that either. I'd rather that than spend time talking up how great England are and how they might do this or that to us. For me, that would just fill my head with doubts because I would be thinking about those opposition strengths instead of those of my own team. Anyway, in the days before the match the Welsh team management decided I should be put up before the media. I didn't ask to be there. It was purely their call. But when I said that we would win it was taken as being a bit too cocky in some quarters.

I didn't care. I wanted to carry that complete self-belief with me onto the field on the Saturday and I wanted to put myself under pressure because that's when I feel I respond. So that's why I said it.

The journey from Wales' team headquarters at the Vale of Glamorgan Hotel to the Millennium Stadium is always one of the highlights for me of any international match. But as this was my first Six Nations game and we were playing England, the old enemy, I took time to savour it and soak everything in. As the bus made its way to the centre of Cardiff there were thousands of supporters out on the streets even though it was still a few hours until kick-off. They all waved and shouted good luck when they realised it was the Wales team bus and as a player that makes you feel very special. It really gives me a hell of a buzz and I think it provides a massive advantage compared to the away team. By the time I got to the Millennium Stadium I felt ready to take on the world. The other boys were all in the same frame of a mind and we felt we couldn't wait for the game to start.

It's at this stage that some players get quite emotional about the whole occasion and what it means to them – especially as we were playing England. But I was determined not to let that happen to me. I just wanted to treat it as another game. I'm not one of those players who likes to use outward emotions to psyche themselves up. I prefer to be a bit more controlled and stay relaxed.

I knew if I allowed myself to get caught up in the whole occasion then it would be a waste of energy – and I'd need every ounce of that.

The match began well for us and I managed to put in a solid early tackle on England's Mark Cueto. Jason Robinson had thrown the ball into midfield, we chased up in a line and I got in a good hit on Cueto. That allowed me to settle. Suddenly I was able to concentrate harder and felt really into the game. I felt good about myself physically – strong. Then, Mathew Tait cut back inside towards me and I dumped him, although he managed to keep hold of the ball. It was his first touch in international rugby and I was aware of the crowd reacting to my tackle which gave me a big lift. Now, I felt settled and after another good tackle on Julian White I was flying. This is going to be okay, I thought. It's going to be a good day.

Stephen Jones missed an early penalty, but within 10 minutes or so we scored a try through Shane Williams. I had a hand in the build-up but the crucial pass was the one delivered by Michael Owen, a lovely floated one that opened up enough space for Shane to dart over in the left corner. Michael is a wonderful rugby player and I really admire his handling skills and his vision, which so many other forwards just don't have. It's like having another back standing in the line so I had no hesitation about giving him the ball when he was calling for it. Stephen couldn't add the conversion but we were 5–0 up and playing some good rugby. Nothing tight or anxious, just a nice flowing game, and the truth is that we should have got at least one more try in that opening 15 minutes or so. We had our chances.

Charlie Hodgson then struck a penalty before I put in another big tackle on Tait which got the crowd excited and led to all kinds of questions after the match. Mathew was an 18-year-old making his debut for England as a consequence of all those injury problems. Andy Robinson, the England coach, had paired Mathew in the centre with his Newcastle clubmate, Jamie Noon. Obviously, the thinking was that as they knew each other well the nerves might not feel as acute for Mathew as they might have been if he was next to a stranger.

I didn't know much about Tait, although I had heard through the grapevine he had showed a lot of promise for Newcastle and our injured flanker Colin Charvis, a clubmate in the North-East, had singled him out before the game as an exciting prospect. Alun Carter, the Welsh team's notational analyst, and the man in charge of finding video footage on all our opponents, had done well to find me some clips of Tait which I watched on the Friday. I could see that Tait was a quality player with quick feet and good hands. I also couldn't help thinking about his age. Eighteen! I was still used to being described as a youngster myself and yet I had turned 23 at the start of that week. Here was a kid five years younger than me. I've always had a strange feeling about coming up against players younger than me. It creates an extra little competitive edge in my mind. It's almost as if they are a bit of a threat to me and at the back of my mind a little voice is telling me to put them in their place. Or at least *try* to put them in their place. I suppose it's a desire to try and set the standards rather than allow someone new to come along and set them for you.

We had been defending well and I was feeling confident when Tait tried to run straight at me. It meant I had to make a head-on tackle which is the type I have always enjoyed, right through from my earliest days as a kid playing age-group rugby. I like the aggressive side of the game and those tackles give you the chance to get right in someone's face. When a player runs right at me, I don't have many worries about the contact, I feel comfortable making that form of tackle and I must admit I enjoyed that one on Mathew. I managed to stop him and pick him up at the same time. Suddenly, his momentum was gone and it was me moving forward with him horizontal in my arms. Someone said afterwards it looked as though I was moving a shop-window dummy but at the time these things happen so quickly you don't imagine that they will become a talking point. After the game, I was asked if I'd planned to embarrass Mathew but that was rubbish. It had nothing to do with the fact that he was 18 and making his debut. It was just that he was running straight at me and I was the

Gavin Henson

one who had to stop him. It wasn't as if I had singled him out or anything because I had also put in those solid hits on White and Cueto, too. But I'll admit that tackle on Mathew did feel good. I liked the surge of adrenalin it gave me because this was a player we had talked about before the match as a possible danger man. Mathew had been bragged up in the Zurich Premiership and is quite a physical player himself. I had seen one try he had scored for Newcastle against Sale where he had bumped off Jason Robinson so he obviously had strength to go along with his general sharpness and good feet. So we did our homework on him and it paid off.

In the days afterwards there would be T-shirts printed with the picture of me holding Mathew in mid-air with a few mildly insulting captions on them. I don't suppose Mathew minds too much. He shouldn't. He's a lot younger than me, he's going to be a very good player for England, and I know that one day he'll get his revenge. In fact, later in the game he made a tackle on me that denied us a try. I had made a break on the outside of Mathew and thought I had got away from him. But just as I tried to accelerate away he stretched out and got a hand on my jersey to pull me down. That was careless. Next time, I thought, I'll make sure my shirt is fully tucked into my shorts.

We increased our lead to 8–3 at half-time thanks to a penalty from Stephen Jones. People have often asked me whether I mind having to share the goal-kicking with

12

Steve but I'm more than happy to do so. A lot of people might view me as an individualist, a loner, and in many ways I suppose I am. But what I most want from playing for Wales is to be part of a successful team. That's the priority. It always has been for me. I want to stand out but I want people to look at me as someone who catches the eye within a winning team. Stephen is a fantastic kicker, one of the best in the world, so there's no way I would resent it when he's asked to kick at goal. A lot of people don't actually realise that kicking can be tiring because you are the only player on the pitch actually doing anything for 90 seconds while everyone else is having a rest. The nice thing about having Steve take all the short and medium-range kicks is that I get to have a breather like everyone else.

Shortly after Stephen kicked his penalty, Danny Grewcock and Gareth 'Alfie' Thomas both ended up in the sin bin. Grewcock decided to plant his foot across Dwayne Peel's head at a ruck and Alfie came running in to try and chin him. They both ended up in the bin – something for which Alfie was very apologetic about afterwards – but this was a Wales-England game after all and you don't get many of those without a few sparks flying. With Alfie off the field, and both sides down to 14 men, I was moved from inside centre to cover for his loss at full-back. I felt perfectly comfortable with that. It's a position I'm happy with and I'd played there lots of times before. I like to kick the ball out of hand because

I know I can send it a long way – further than most players. When I managed to put England right back on their heels with two big kicks to touch then I started to feel really confident about the way things were going.

Sitting in the dressing room at the break, I felt a bit disappointed and so did most of the other boys. We had scored the only try but we hadn't really played much rugby other than that. We hadn't taken the game to them as we had planned. We promised ourselves that we would keep the ball in hand and run England around more in the second-half to try and stretch them and tire out their forwards. But it didn't really happen. I think the occasion got to us and the match became quite scrappy. England dug in and found they had gained a territorial advantage which we didn't seem able to do much about. Hodgson kicked a penalty to make it 8–6 and then with the game going into the final stages he slotted over another and suddenly we found ourselves 9–8 down. I have to admit a little bit of panic set in. Everyone became quite nervous, there were too many mistakes being made, and there was also the added factor of worrying about the clock. Back in the autumn against New Zealand there had been a mix-up over exactly how long was left in the game. The clock was being halted every time for stoppages so that while we all felt there was some injury time left to play, the referee blew up when the exact 40 minutes was up. When you are losing, although you should be able to remember whether it's a stopped clock or not, that kind of thing goes flying out of your mind in the general panic that takes over. There was part of me that also realised England were much more used to holding out and winning tight games than we were. But as a team something gave us that little bit of calm in the final moments that day in February and I think it was this. We had all believed in the days before the match that we would beat England and I think every Welsh player on that field still believed it as the seconds counted down. We had the individual players and collectively we had the character. All we needed was one more chance. And then it came.

Gareth Cooper, who had come on at scrum-half for Dwayne Peel, made a break from a scrum and rolled a kick into England's half. Jason Robinson tried to tidy up but got swallowed and when he was unable to release the ball quickly enough the penalty was given.

That kick changed my life and I'll remember it forever. But I'll also remember those feelings as the seconds were counted down to our victory. We were playing with a freedom we hadn't managed since the opening few minutes of the match. We were back in the lead and the confidence came flooding back, helped by the crowd who lifted us higher again. We could easily have scored another try – perhaps we should have – but it was obvious we were not going to lose. It felt to me as though that last four minutes could have turned into 25 and

England still wouldn't have come back. It was our day and we knew it.

When the final whistle went, and we had won 11–9, the excitement I felt couldn't be diverted into running, kicking and tackling anymore. So I ran about, jumping in the air. So did everyone else. We all went nuts. It was an amazing feeling and an incredible atmosphere, the best I had ever felt.

I did my utmost to savour those feelings, including later on in the evening when we were among the Welsh supporters. To see so many happy faces on the streets and around the stadium, to know that you can have that effect on people, made me feel fantastic. It was awesome. Like the players, the fans had been through so many bad times they deserved this moment – and they were going to make the most of it.

We spent quite a while celebrating before coming off the field, which was understandable given that Wales had not beaten England for six years. Eventually the rest of the boys headed down the tunnel and turned left towards our dressing room but I was grabbed by the BBC for an interview as I'd been given the man-of-the-match award. By the time I got back to the boys, Alfie had given his post-match chat to the squad but I did catch him giving the call that no-one was to go out that night to celebrate. We had another game in seven days against Italy which would mean flying out to Rome on the Thursday. Alan Phillips, the Wales team manager, backed him up, but I was on a real high by now so I shouted out: 'No way! My fans are expecting me.' It was half meant as a joke but the serious half was that I really did want to go out and let off some steam. It's very hard when you have been in camp all week and everything has been extremely tense and serious. The idea of just going back to the hotel, and trying to get some sleep before getting up and going to a recovery session didn't really appeal.

In the end a good few of us did go out with the management's blessing although no-one was going to push it by sinking too many drinks. The centre of Cardiff was awash with thousands of fans and none of us really had the energy to deal with it for long. In fact, by the time the official post-match dinner had finished at the Hilton Hotel I was starting to feel tired. Mathew Tait was presented with his first cap, which was a proud moment for him, but there was no hiding the disappointment on his face that night along with the rest of the England players.

Secretly, I was also a bit disappointed that evening. I was hoping that a couple of hours spent in the centre of Cardiff might mean bumping into Charlotte Church. I had met Charlotte for the first time after our previous game in November against Japan. I knew she would have watched the England game and was probably out celebrating along with thousands of other people. I didn't have her phone number, but even if I had then

I probably wouldn't have rung it. That's just not me. I think I would have wanted her to make that first move. There was also the fact that she was still seeing her previous boyfriend at that stage. But she was certainly on my mind, and, if I'm honest, I'd been thinking a fair bit about her. I knew she would be watching that afternoon and it provided me with another reason for desperately wanting to do well.

An hour or so after the end of the official dinner, though, I was flagging and there was no sign of Charlotte. I met up with a couple of my mates from Bridgend and then took a cab back to the team hotel. As I was heading back I checked my text messages. There were loads from friends congratulating me on the win over England and the kick, but as I scrolled through I realised there was nothing from Charlotte. One stood out, though. It was from Lyn Jones, my coach at the Neath-Swansea Ospreys. There were no congratulations. It just said: 'Next time, tuck your shirt in.'

CHAPTER TWO

Away Days

It's a strange thing about being a professional rugby player that I find it a lot more difficult to sleep the night of a big game than the night before. On the eve of the match I rarely feel nervous. I'm usually quite calm. I have my routines and once I've gone through those then I can normally nod off without too much of a problem. But the night of the game itself is a different matter altogether. It can take me hours and hours to get to sleep and even then it's quite normal for me to need a sleeping tablet from the team doctor. I normally lay in bed and go through the entire game minute by minute, replaying every move and every tackle. I'll analyse what I did during the 80 minutes and think about any mistakes I might have made and what I would like to do differently next time. Sometimes I can go over the whole game again and again. I think it must be some sort of combination of my own character in searching for the perfect game and all the energy drinks we take in during the course of a match day. The result is that long after most people who attend a game have forgotten all about it and are sound asleep, my brain is working like a video player on automatic rewind.

That Saturday night of 5 February 2005, the sensible thing to have done might have been to celebrate like three million other people. A good few beers alongside friends who are all in celebratory mood is normally more than enough for ordinary people to sleep well into Sunday morning.

Whenever Wales beat England there is cause to celebrate. Had Cardiff not been so manic that night then I might have partied for longer, but, like the rest of the boys, I was very aware that this was only the first match of the championship. We were still in camp at our Vale of Glamorgan base just outside Cardiff and our second game – a trip to Rome to play Italy – meant we would be flying out in just five days' time. I also think we were far too excited about our rugby, about what we were now capable of achieving on the pitch, to waste much more time toasting one victory. You could feel the confidence of the group. Everyone looked relaxed but very determined to keep things going on the course we had set for ourselves. We were a young bunch of players who had only been together for two or three years. I had come in at the end of that period but most of the others had been through some really bad times when they had been absolutely slated by people in the street as well as the media. I know that during the 10-game losing sequence suffered under Steve Hansen a lot of the players used to dread stepping out of their houses.

We now had three away matches – against Italy, France and Scotland – followed by the last match of the championship at home to Ireland. The Irish game always looked the big one to me. Before the tournament began I felt we would beat England, have enough to win in Rome and Edinburgh, but maybe come unstuck in Paris. Even if we lost to the French, though, I felt the Ireland game would still be the critical one, the match where the championship would be decided. As it turned out, I was wrong about France and that, for me, was the game of the championship – the day we came of age.

Bur first stop was Rome, where Wales had lost 30–22 under Hansen two years before and a game I had watched on TV during the time when I was very much out of favour. That defeat was a real low point for Wales as they went on to suffer a Six Nations whitewash and Colin Charvis lost the captaincy. I was viewing it from the outside but the team of 2003 seemed to lack all the things we now had in bucket-loads – self-belief, confidence, faith in all the systems drilled on training fields and a general level of contentment throughout the squad.

We all felt we could beat the Italians this time but recognised they were a physical team who played with a lot of commitment, as they had shown the week before when they had run Ireland very close. I felt the important thing for us was to play with the same freedom and fluency that we had shown in those opening 15 minutes against England. If we did that, I felt sure that our skills would be too much for the Italians and we'd score plenty of tries.

The first thing that struck me at the Stadio Flaminio was the number of Welsh supporters who had made the trip. Rome can't be a bad place to spend the weekend, even when the weather's not great, but the victory over England appeared to have given more impetus to the numbers who had made it over. When we ran out before the kick-off there were Welsh flags everywhere and red jerseys seemed to be outnumbering blue ones in every part of the ground. Maybe that gave us a feeling we wanted to put on a show because we soon got into our stride and played some lovely stuff. Shane Williams was as lively as he had been against England and within five minutes his run allowed Tom Shanklin to create the position from where Michael Owen put Jonathan Thomas in for the first try.

The Italians were unable to get near us. We were all over them. In fact, we should have scored two more tries before my mistake gave them a way back into the game. I took a pass and drifted wide past a couple of players but I was running out of space. I decided to try and chip the ball over Luciano Orquera, the Italian No.10, but he got his hands to it. Suddenly, instead of creating something that might have given us a try, I was watching Orquera run back from where I'd just come and he kept going all the way to the line. If it had come off then I think I would have been more or less clear to the Italian try-line and either scored myself or put someone else in. But Orquera jumped early and snatched the ball out of the air. Maybe I should have dummied to kick at the last moment and run around him, just like Joe Rokocoko did to us in the previous November when New Zealand beat us by a point in Cardiff. I suppose it was a bit careless on my part, but sometimes these things will happen when you try and take risks and that was always the style that Mike Ruddock and the other coaches had encouraged. So, although I was annoyed with myself for not lifting the ball over Orquera, I wasn't down on myself for trying. If people criticise my game because I like to take chances then I don't really care. That's just the type of player I am and that's the way I think rugby should be played. From the point of view of Wales, our rugby is high speed and high risk, but as Mike always stresses, it's also high reward. And I knew our reward would come later in the game.

By half-time Italy hadn't added to their five points, while we were up to 19. We had them pinned back at a scrum and when I spotted the support in the corner I knew this time my kick would cause them problems. It may not have been the best option, but it worked.

Tom Shanklin jumped to catch it. 12–5. I had a go with a penalty from much further away than the one against England, but it fell just beneath the crossbar. I was happy with that attempt, though. I remember I struck it well but they use a different type of ball in Italy and it behaves slightly differently. In Wales we use the ball manufactured by Gilbert, but in Italy they are provided by Mitre. I don't feel the Mitre ball travels quite as far as the Gilbert and although I hit it really well, and it stayed dead straight, it just dropped beneath the bar. It was a difficult kick, but it wasn't a bad effort. No worries. Just before half-time I put Hal Luscombe through to cut inside their defence and a brilliant piece of quick-thinking from Martyn Williams gave us a third try when he touched the ball against the foot of the post. Stephen Jones converted and we went in with a 12-point lead.

They pulled back three points with a penalty early in the second-half but they still couldn't lay a finger on us when we really flowed. Shane tore them to pieces with another of his fantastic runs and the space opened for Brent Cockbain to go over. Two minutes later we scored an even better try. Alfie and Kevin Morgan wrecked their defence again and Shane ran it in. 33–8. It was all over even though there were 25 minutes left. We eased off after that although Rob Sidoli scored our sixth try in the last few minutes. It finished 38–8, a thrashing by Six Nations standards and proof that we could now live with our own reputation and the expectancy it had brought. We had shown confidence and plenty of ability. Mike Ruddock calls it 'licence to thrill' and we had certainly done that.

Italy are probably the weakest team in the tournament but the pleasing thing was that there had never been a hint of complacency on our part. We had kept our feet on the ground, even though we were coming off a victory over the world champions. I think the fact that Wales had lost in Rome two years before helped us in some ways because it was mentioned as a kind of warning whenever we discussed the Italians. We paid them a lot of respect, but at the same time we knew that we had not really performed that well against England. We were capable of much better and we delivered it in Rome.

I had enjoyed the whole day. The Stadio Flaminio may not be the biggest international rugby ground in the world but it's got character and creates plenty of atmosphere. We had gone there and put on a show and it felt good to come off after a job well done. The team management were happy enough, so were the players, and I could tell the fans were very glad they had made the trip. Once again, the call from the management was for everyone to go back to the hotel after the official post-match dinner and once again it didn't quite work out that way. After the dinner had ended, we were chatting to some of the Italian players who were great company. They invited us to jump on their team bus rather than go back to our hotel on our own and myself, Shane Williams and Jonathan Thomas didn't need to be asked twice. There are some traditions in rugby that I still feel are very valuable and relaxing with the opposition when you occasionally get the chance is definitely one of them. I got on well with Aaron Persico, the Italian flanker, who is a really good guy. He's from an Italian family, but he grew up in New Zealand. He and our own Kiwi, Sonny Parker, knew each other well from their younger days. Aaron and his mates showed us a little bit of Rome, a city which, unlike Cardiff, is comfortably big enough to lose yourself in if you want to escape the rugby crowds for a while. We stayed out until around two or three in the morning, but again the main purpose was to avoid a sleepless few hours laying in bed rather than go on a drinking session.

We flew back to Cardiff on the Sunday morning and discovered the feel-good factor produced by the victory over England had now gone into overdrive. Everyone wanted to talk to us and the newspapers were full of reports stating the significance of our win in Rome. It was the first time Wales had begun the championship with back-to-back victories since 1994, they said, the last year when Wales had actually won the tournament even though they lost their final game against England. Some of the papers actually speculated on our chances of winning the championship, while one or two even mentioned the Grand Slam. There was an air of disbelief about the coverage, though, as if they couldn't quite believe it. For me, there had been nothing at all odd about our two results so far. I felt we would beat England at home and I was equally confident we would do the Italians in Rome. The next game, though, a fortnight later, was against France in Paris and I have to admit I wasn't so sure about that one.

The two-week gap in between suited us down to the ground. It gave us an opportunity to really work on things in training but also to get plenty of rest before the trip to the Stade de France. We watched a few videos of the French and most of us came to the conclusion that they had actually been playing pretty poorly. Like us, they had won their opening two matches of the championship but they had been no better than average. They had won 16–9 at home to Scotland but only thanks to a late try and they had been saved from a shock defeat by a few dodgy decisions that went in their favour. After that game, the Scotland coach Matt Williams had gone nuts about the referee and it was hard not to feel sympathy.

France had then gone to Twickenham to play England a week after we had beaten them. Once again, the French played virtually no rugby but they somehow managed to win by a point, 18–17. They were 17–6 down at one stage so you had to admire their resilience but there was nothing very stylish about them. They never looked like scoring a try in the whole game and had to rely on six penalties from their scrum-half Dimitri Yachvili. So long as we didn't give away too many penalties it was obvious that we would be in with a chance.

The Stade de France in Paris is one of my favourite stadiums and I was really looking forward to playing there. It's an awesome place, like some gigantic space-ship from the outside and just as stunning when you are in the middle of the pitch. It's intimidating. But some things were in our favour. It was very cold that day, which was fine by us. You don't want to be playing France in Paris when they have the sun on their backs.

We came out for the warm-up and the noise was unbelievable. The crowd sounds mix in with horns, a French brass band, a manic French voice on the stadium speakers, and firecrackers going off. The French national anthem also really fires things up. I have a confession about our own Welsh anthem, 'Hen Wlad fy Nhadau', or 'Land of My Fathers'. Part of the reason I don't sing along before the game is that I want to remain in control and a little bit detached from things. But partly, it is because I don't actually know the words. It sounds terrible but I was never taught them in school for some reason and I've just never felt the need to learn them. The foreign players in our squad, Sonny Parker, who grew up in New Zealand, and Brent Cockbain, who's an Australian, probably know all the words backwards, but I've never made a point of learning them. I've been tempted at times to join in for a couple of lines but I never do. I like to have set routines and as I wouldn't sing the national anthem before a training session, why do it before a game? It certainly doesn't mean I'm not patriotic because I am. I'm fiercely proud to be Welsh and I think it's great that we have our own language. It's part of our identity as a nation. But even if I sat down and learnt the words then I still wouldn't join in, either at home or away. For me, the pride comes from looking out at the crowd and recognising the passion on the faces of the Welsh supporters. I like to take all that stuff in. I get a buzz from seeing what it means to them but I don't want to be like that myself just before I play a rugby match. I want to be in control – calm and cool. It's at that stage that I really focus on what I'm about to do and that was how it was in Paris.

No matter how much any of us had focused, though, I don't think we could have done much about that opening 15 minutes of the game. France were on fire. They were all over us. Things actually started off quite well. I put a kick in along the ground and the French had to defend. But our pressure lasted about 60 seconds. After that we just couldn't get the ball and they came at us in wave after wave of attack.

We were on the rack and they scored a try after just four minutes that had been building and building. It ended when Dimitri Yachvili crossed under our posts and he then converted it to make it 7–0.

The French coach, Bernard Laporte, had recalled their

powerful wing Aurelien Rougerie and it was obvious the idea was to run at Shane Williams and do some damage physically. Rougerie caused us lots of problems early on and it was he who scored their second try which made it 12–0 after just 12 minutes. That try, though, angered me because they shouldn't really have got away with it.

Serge Betsen, the French flanker, took me out off the ball by stamping on my foot. I've still got the scar, a little reminder of the day that will probably take some time to fade. Betsen is renowned for being a tough character, although as this was the first time I had played against him I didn't really know what to expect. I'll know next time, though. France had possession and Betsen came on a dummy run. I could see that he wasn't going to be given the ball so I tried to slip off marking him to take the next player. As I tried to step across, though, Betsen stamped on the inside of my foot. My boot came off and my foot was trapped under his studs. I had to hand it to him. He did it perfectly. There was just a little glance to see where I was, then his foot came down hard on mine. But just before the impact he looked away to make it appear as though it was an accident. It was judged so perfectly that the referee, Paul Honiss, and his touch judges all thought it was just an accidental collision. Fair play to him, I thought. He's done that well.

The other thought was how close he had been to breaking my ankle. My foot turned straight over but, luckily, my ankles are pretty flexible. I've stretched the ligaments so often that I've now got quite a lot of give in that area – enough to avoid a serious injury on this occasion, anyway. I was on the ground, in quite a bit of pain, but what made me angrier was looking back to see Rougerie scoring France's second try. Betsen had done his job so well that the hole created by my fall had opened up the space for France to score. The ironic thing is that Betsen had come very close to missing this international. He was expected to get a big ban for tripping Stuart Abbott during a Heineken Cup match between Wasps and Biarritz. Abbott had been left with a broken leg. Somehow, Betsen had escaped. I hadn't – but maybe in one sense I was fortunate that my ankle was still intact. The skin was cut, but the bone was only bruised and fortunately there was no damage to the ligaments.

I put my boot back on as France missed the conversion but at 12–0 down in as many minutes it already looked a very long way back for us. France were flowing, the crowd were loving it, and we were defending for our lives. They came again in sweeping attacks from one flank to the other. They were awesome. When French teams are in that kind of mood there's not much you can do except try and ride it. Thankfully, although we couldn't get our hands on the ball, we defended really well and made our tackles. Gareth Thomas, in particular, was magnificent. Unfortunately, in making one of those tackles, Alfie broke his thumb and had to go off. I could see it was a bad injury and was starting to think that maybe this wasn't going to be our day. We were being completely outplayed . . . stuffed. Rougerie looked about seven feet tall every time he had the ball and Shane was getting run over. Julien Laharrague was a big threat every time he came into the line from full-back, Yannick Jauzion and Damien Traille were powerful in their midfield, and our pack was being out-muscled. Traille went over our line again, but luckily, they were called back for a foot in touch.

Somehow, during all this pressure we got out of our own half and Stephen Jones kicked a penalty to make it 12–3. Then, Yachvili kicked one. 15–3 to France. More pressure, more bouncing around as we tried to take down their big men with the ball, but amazingly we survived without conceding another try. In fact, we had the last word in the half when Stephen put over his second kick to make it 15–6.

I can remember sitting in our dressing room at half time thinking, 'This is bad. This isn't supposed to be happening. They are meant to be a poor, out-of-form team and we're supposed to be super-confident. We're losing, more than that, we're being over-run, and our captain is in the room next door having his thumb put back together.' Doubts were definitely starting to set in. And yet we were only nine points behind when, from the balance of play, it should have been about 30.

Those players who weren't too knackered to speak made the point that we were still right in the game and that we hadn't played. If we could just keep hold of the ball and get into the match then it was still there to be won. Mike Ruddock had his say and kept it brief and to the point. 'Three Ts,' he said. 'Turnovers, tackles, territory. Don't turnover the ball. Make your tackles. And make sure we stay in their territory when we kick.' It seemed like a fair summary.

Alfie's thumb turned out to be broken in five places, so Michael Owen, our No.8, took over the captaincy and gave his own little pep talk before we went out for the second-half. There was mention made of doing it for the skipper. Kevin Morgan moved from the wing to full-back to replace Alfie and Rhys Williams came on to take Kevin's place on the wing. We needed something to spark us straight away and it came just a minute into the second-half. I made a tackle on the French centre Yannick Jauzion deep in our half and he spilled the ball. Stephen Jones got hold of it and I think all the French team expected him to just hoof it downfield. Instead, Steve ran and made a fantastic 50-yard break. The attack continued and when Shane Williams skinned Rougerie on the outside, to get a bit of revenge for the first-half, then Martyn Williams was on hand to score our first try.

Now, we had some real belief and the French looked a bit shaky. Stephen had put the conversion over so there was only a two-point gap between the sides. We attacked them again and they didn't like it. You could see there was a bit of panic in their body language. When we were given a penalty, a few of the French players seemed to freeze, and so Martyn tapped and ran and forced his way over for another try. Suddenly, from being under the cosh at 15–6 down, we were 18–15 ahead. It was incredible.

Of course, a mature team used to winning would have kept on attacking at that point. They would have gone for the jugular and scored a third try to demoralise the opposition. But we weren't a mature team. We were still very naive in our approach in many ways and so we started to defend. It was as if there were only two minutes left in the match and we had opted to try and hang on to our two-point lead. In fact, there were actually still 34 minutes left and it was a ridiculous idea to think we could hold what we had. We stopped playing positive rugby and went into a negative frame of mind, just as we had done against England.

It took them awhile, but France eventually drew level through a penalty from Frederic Michalak, who had been sent on to try and win them the game. It was now extremely tense and came down to a battle of nerves. Steve, as ever, kept his and kicked another penalty and then struck a superb drop goal to put us six points clear at 24–18. That was a crucial kick because it meant the French felt the need to go for the try and the conversion to try and win the game, rather than kick three times for goal. They put us under loads of pressure but we kept them out. John Yapp, our young prop, had come off the bench and really did well as part of a great forward unit. A year before I remember watching the Welsh scrum being crushed by France and the turf at the Millennium Stadium being churned up as we were driven back. But in those last 10 minutes in Paris the boys up front were so solid. Martyn Williams had an immense game and so did Stephen at half-back. It was fitting that Steve should have the last word when he booted the ball over our own dead-ball line, although there were a few anxious glances until Honiss put the whistle to his mouth and blew up.

I'll admit there were a few moments during that last five minutes when I thought things looked bleak. They were mounting attack after attack and scrum after scrum. As a back it was out of my hands. I was just hoping the forwards could hold out. And they did – magnificently.

I love playing against French teams. They combine strength and power with great skill and flair. When you beat them, it's very satisfying. I had found Jauzion and Traille very difficult opponents in the centre because of their size and their pace, but to come out on top against them felt great. I looked at the scoreboard. France 18, Pays de Galles 24. We were all on a massive high and I think it was then that we really believed we could not only win the tournament, but also do something very special with a Grand Slam.

This time they would have needed to put road blocks around the hotel to stop us from going out, but the strange thing was I felt a bit subdued. I went over the road to a quiet bar with a couple of the boys but it never developed into a big night. Maybe we were all just too exhausted. Or perhaps we were just too stunned by what we had done in the space of three games.

I had a load more text messages on my phone, from family and friends, but this time there were also some from Charlotte. My rugby career had really taken off in a new direction over those few weeks of the Six Nations, but life off the field was changing, too.

CHAPTER THREE

Get Lost, Gav

Stephen Jones is the happiest man I've ever met. He may even be the happiest man in the world. It doesn't matter what the situation, the weather or the workload he never stops smiling and being upbeat. He must have his own supply of happy pills and they must be a better brand than anyone else's.

I was rooming with Steve at our Vale of Glamorgan Hotel on the night we beat England. When I finally got back there in the early hours, I was still on Cloud Nine but Steve was somewhere way beyond that. We chatted for a long time before finally getting some sleep and I must have still been smiling from ear to ear when I went downstairs for breakfast the following morning. I was part of a Welsh team that had beaten the world champions and my kick was the moment that had clinched it, a moment I had prepared for all my waking hours and dreamt about when I was asleep.

Nothing, absolutely nothing, could bring me down. Or so I thought.

Then, Alan Phillips, the Wales team manager, came over with a newspaper in his hand. It was the *News of the World*. Splashed all over one page was a story about Charlotte Church and me. The headline was something like, 'CHARLOTTE TELLS GAV TO GET LOST.' The story made me out to be some kind of stalker and quoted Charlotte describing how I had 'pestered' her for her phone number the night of the Japan game. I was gutted.

Of course, the other boys in the squad had all read it and thought it was hilarious. What made it even funnier for them – and much worse for me – was that I had told them all how I really liked Charlotte and wanted to see her again. In fact, I hadn't seen her since that night in November and now this story seemed to be saying she thought I was a pain in the arse. Once the boys clocked on to my reaction, as I sat there like some sad loser staring at the paper, their mood changed. They started ripping into me, good and proper. To the real dealers in mickey-taking – guys like Tom Shanklin, Rhys Williams, and Ceri Sweeney – this was as if all their Christmases had come at once. They were queuing up to give me a good kicking. All I could think was, 'The bitch!' My 'pestering' her consisted of me giving her mother, Maria, *my* phone number as she had asked me for it that night I had met Charlotte. Oh well, I thought. That's that. Might as well take it on the chin, let the boys have their fun until they get bored, and get ready for the next game against France.

On the following day, Monday, we were back in training when I was told by Hal Luscombe, our wing from the Newport Gwent Dragons, that some bloke had rung him in a bid to track down my phone number on behalf of Charlotte. The details sounded a bit sketchy to me, though, and I thought is was probably part of another wind-up. Probably, the hand of Shanklin was involved somewhere along the line. I didn't really want to hand over my phone number to someone I didn't know, so Hal gave the guy the number of another handset he happened to have on him. Sure enough, a message came through that appeared to be genuinely from Charlotte. She apologised for the story and claimed her mother had been set up by someone who had then spoken to the press.

We arranged to meet up the next day and she was still very sorry about what had happened. Once again we seemed to hit it off and our relationship developed from there. It was a strange time to start dating a high profile girlfriend, one match into my first Six Nations campaign, and I did have a few concerns that it might prove to be a distraction. There were plenty of people who were also worried and a few of them sat me down and told me to drop the whole idea. Peter Underhill, my agent, who was in the middle of re-negotiating a great new deal for me with the Ospreys, was concerned this might mean I took my eye off the ball. Scott Johnson, Mike Ruddock's assistant coach, took a tactful approach and carefully spelled out some of the dangers that might lay ahead. Scott's like that. He really thinks deeply about the welfare of every player under his responsibility. Alfie, our skipper, was a bit more blunt. 'Listen, butt,' he said. 'You want to steer clear of all that crap. She might just be out for a bit of cheap publicity.' As captain he had a perfect right to be alarmed. The last thing he probably wanted was for me to go off the rails and for the team to be badly affected. I listened to all their advice, but I didn't take it.

It was the same with my parents. It hadn't taken long for the newspapers to catch on that I appeared to be Charlotte's new boyfriend. Neither did it take them long to trace where my parents lived and they were soon outside their door. 'What the hell is going on?' said my Dad. But he wasn't too concerned about the cameras outside his house. He could deal with that. He was far more worried that my rugby career – something he had helped me build since I was old enough to walk – was in danger of going down the drain. 'Don't worry, Dad. It's all under control.' But I don't think Mum or Dad were too convinced early on.

I was happy, though. Charlotte had come to my house to explain all about the newspaper story and we had got on really well. I dropped her back home at around 11 and was keen to see her again. I gave her a goodnight kiss and as I drove home I thought, this is great. She's a really nice girl. I feel comfortable with her and I can handle what comes with it – the press, the photographers, even the stick from the rest of the boys in the squad. It'll be fine.

And it has been. We sent each other loads of texts after that night and things just progressed from there. If Charlotte had not been a famous singer, then I admit we probably would not have gone out with each other. That's not because I wanted to be seen with someone famous, but because of the kind of person I am. I'm basically quite shy. I would probably have been too shy to approach her in a bar and come out with all the chat to find out about her. But as I knew a little bit about her anyway, I didn't need to go through all that. It sort of broke the ice. I knew who she was. She knew who I was. There was also an aura about her which I felt comfortable with. She's fun to be around.

But it was a weird time to start a relationship. In a sense Alfie and Scott Johnson were right. I did find it hard to focus. I had never really had a serious girlfriend before, not since I was at school, anyway. Rugby had always come first and I hadn't given much time or thought to relationships. But Charlotte and I just seemed to hit it off. She has an image in the newspapers of enjoying a good night out and a lot of drinking. She does like to party sometimes, but there are lots of different sides to her and her drinking isn't as bad as they make out. She's just a normal 19-year-old, enjoying her life.

So that was how I came to be sitting in a bar in Paris a few weeks later, exchanging text messages with my girlfriend after we had just beaten France. We had just won our third match of the Six Nations and had already beaten the two overwhelming favourites for the title. On and off the field, life felt good.

Financially, things were improving for me, too. I had come into professional rugby at 18 years of age and joined Swansea. It was the right decision from a playing perspective and I'm very glad I chose such a great club. But within a couple years the place was in financial meltdown. The club went into administration, wages were halved overnight, players left, and no-one knew what was around the corner. Thankfully, for me at least, the Neath-Swansea Ospreys lay around the corner and some much needed financial stability in my life. But by the time I went to Paris in late February 2005 my first contract with the region was drawing to an end and I had to decide on my future.

Talks about extending my contract had first begun back in the previous November but I had left it all with Pete, my agent, in order to concentrate fully on my rugby. My relationship with Pete is a good one and I trust him to look after my interests. He certainly seemed to have pulled off some pretty good deals for two of his other clients. Gareth Thomas was very happy at

Toulouse and Colin Charvis had seen his career resurrected by joining Newcastle. Pete isn't everyone's cup of tea, but then most agents in the game quickly divide opinion. But I was impressed by the fact that he soon realised my priority was to remain with the Ospreys in Wales rather than simply try and get as much money as possible from a move to England or France.

I was anxious to get things wrapped up so that I could focus fully on playing, but I was also aware that my standing in the game was changing. I had become a regular in the Wales team and there was interest in me from clubs in both England and France.

I could certainly have taken more money by leaving Wales, but so long as I felt the new deal from the Ospreys was a fair one I was more than happy to stay.

The Ospreys were having a very successful season. We were top of the Celtic League and more importantly I was enjoying my rugby there under the coaches, Lyn Jones and Sean Holley. I had no real desire to leave, even if I could have got maybe £30,000-a-year more by linking up with a French or English side. I felt very settled with the Ospreys and keen to remain there.

Eventually, an agreement was reached and I signed a new contract with the Ospreys. Pete had come over to Paris and I put pen to paper in a room in the team hotel. It was a four-year contract which ties me to the region until I am 27. A few of my team-mates, who had only signed two-year deals, were amazed I had committed myself for four years. But for me, it was relief. I don't have to worry about my future for a while. The Swansea experience taught me that is much better to be in work and secure, than out of work and worrying about where your next pay packet is coming from. I also wanted to show my commitment to the region by pledging my future to them. They had shown a lot of faith in me by giving me regular rugby and I wanted to repay that trust.

After we had beaten France, we flew back to Cardiff on the Sunday and life could not have been sweeter. I was in the middle of this incredibly exciting journey with Wales, my regional future with the Ospreys had been sorted, and I was seeing Charlotte. Even without the half a dozen boys who were on Wales duty, the Ospreys continued to win during February and into March. They beat the Borders 34–10 at The Gnoll in Neath, gained an impressive 16–12 victory away in Dublin against Leinster, and then hammered the Newport Gwent Dragons, 30–0, at Swansea's St. Helen's ground. But while the Ospreys were homing in on one championship, most of my thoughts were on another. If we could beat Scotland, then we would be in a really strong position to face Ireland at home in what most people expected would be a Grand Slam decider for both countries.

We had a 15-day gap between the game in Paris and our trip to Murrayfield to meet Scotland which gave us all plenty of time to recover. All, that is, except

Alfie, whose broken thumb had ruled him out of the remainder of the championship and cast something of a shadow over his Lions chances. Thankfully, though, Alfie stayed within the group as a non-playing captain and he remained a massive influence.

Scotland were going through a rough patch which they showed few signs of emerging from. They had been white-washed in the 2004 championship and although they had gained credit for their spirited performance in Paris in the opening round of 2005 the game had still ended in another defeat. The following week the Scots had been badly beaten at home by Ireland and even though they managed to scrape past Italy in round three the match had been an absolute stinker. We all knew, though, that Wales had a pretty poor record at Murrayfield in recent years and those of us used to going up to Edinburgh and Glasgow in the Celtic League had often found life difficult.

In the build-up, the big stress from the coaches and the management was that Scotland always came out with a big first 20 minutes. So long as we could contain their fire in that opening period, we felt we had the superior skills and extra fitness to win the game. As it turned out, we were just oozing confidence after beating France and in the opening minutes at Murrayfield almost everything we tried came off. Instead of a raging fire the Scots weren't able to create a single spark. The truth is that we had won that game by half-time. We were 38–3 up at that stage and most of us switched off and started thinking about the Ireland match.

We had the best possible start with a try after just four minutes. It was a cracking one, too. Ryan Jones started it deep in our own half when he burst between two Scots – Stuart Grimes and Scott Murray – who tried to tackle him. The move was taken on by Kevin Morgan, Gethin Jenkins and Rhys Williams before Martyn Williams did brilliantly to put Ryan in for the touchdown. I was just behind Ryan and could tell we were going to score. But I was half-hoping he might get tackled so that I could claim the glory. That's how confident we all felt. As it was, Ryan finished off what he had started.

It proved to be the start of something really big for Ryan. He not only ended the season turning up on the Lions tour in New Zealand as a replacement, but played in both the Second and Third Tests against the All Blacks. He had a storming game against Otago just after his arrival and his whole impact on the tour was massive – huge enough to make him one of the biggest successes on the trip.

But what people probably didn't know that day in Edinburgh was that just a few minutes before Ryan was charging over for the try, he was being violently sick in the changing rooms. Nobody batted an eyelid because he does it before almost every game. I have never seen a guy get so nervous before matches. It doesn't really make much difference what the game is, either. It can be a fairly routine Celtic League match for the Ospreys and Ryan will still be spewing. What makes it even worse for him is that he doesn't really eat anything on the day of the game and yet he's still spewing! It can't be good for him. It's nuts.

Now that he's a big star for the Lions, I'm wondering whether or not Ryan will be able to control his stomach movements. I teased him a little bit after he made his Wales debut by asking him whether or not he was still planning to be sick before Ospreys games. It was the same after he played for the Lions. 'Don't you think you should stop spewing before Wales games now?' He agreed it was overdue. But he's a great guy, a fantastic back row forward, and despite all his pre-match nerves he's an extremely confident person about his own ability.

Scotland actually put us under a bit of pressure after Ryan's try. We were well stretched down our left-hand side but their outside-half, Dan Parks, chucked out a wild pass to no-one in particular. Rhys Williams snatched it out of the air and almost had the time to jog up their end to score under the posts. 14–0 to us and we knew we were still only warming up. Poor old Parks had a nightmare match, one of those days when every-thing he touched finished in a horrible mess. He was eventually substituted and I remember feeling very sorry for him as his own fans were booing him when he touched the ball and cheering when he was taken off.

It's not nice when you hear that kind of treatment given to any player. I've got to know Dan from chats after matches and he's a sound guy who gives his all. You would think supporters would be aware that an international player is not going out of his way to be deliberately awful. In fact, I've never liked to hear players get booed when they are off their game. It happened towards the end of last season for my Wales team-mate Ceri Sweeney at the Newport Gwent Dragons. Ceri was going through a bad patch and the Dragons fans turned against him. I just don't understand that. What kind of benefit does it give your team if you boo one of your own players every time he touches the ball? If that happened to me one day with the Ospreys, it would be the day I would consider moving on.

That might sound a bit extreme, but it's true. The fans are the reason I like playing rugby in front of big crowds, rather than just for my own amusement before two men and a dog. It's entertaining supporters that gives me a real buzz. If I'm thinking of watching Manchester United then I like to check the line-ups to see whether or not Cristiano Ronaldo is playing. If he is, then I get excited. That's how I would like people to react to me as a rugby player. I would love it if fans of the Ospreys or Wales think that way about me – that my name on the team-list makes a big difference to how they view the game. I want to have the reputation of an entertainer, like Ronaldo. I want people to have the urge to watch me because they are not quite sure what I'm going to do next. If my own fans booed me then I don't think I'd be able to cope.

I was actually having a quiet game in that first 40 minutes in Edinburgh. There was no need to do much else than master the basics. We were so slick in our passing and so instinctive in our movement that Scotland were left chasing shadows. After Rhys had scored, we added a penalty and then created another eye-catching try for Shane Williams with Martyn Williams' handling skills again prominent in the move. Chris Paterson, another of the Scottish guys I get on well with, put them on the scoreboard with a penalty, but we were only midway through the half and it was already 24–3.

We went straight back onto the attack and Tom Shanklin ran through Rory Lamont to set up a fourth try for Kevin Morgan. Now the Scots looked very panicky every time we ran at them. Dwayne Peel, who creates so much danger when he suddenly takes off from around the fringes, left the Scottish defenders in his wake with another darting run and Kevin had a second try and our fifth. It was 38–3. It wasn't even half-time. It was all over.

I was aware that my input had been fairly minimal. I hadn't scored and I hadn't had to do that much. Not that it bothered me, it really didn't. Sometimes you just have to accept that you're not going to be the main attraction. Of course, I'd love to make the headlines every week but rugby isn't like that. It's a team game and when you're part of a team as good as we were in that first 40 minutes then you're just happy to go along with the ride. I did what I needed to do, but the other players around me were doing plenty of damage on their own.

We came out for the second-half and scored a sixth try quite soon on. Dwayne, who was tearing Scotland to pieces, created space for Rhys Williams to stroll over. We didn't manage any further tries, but I think the Scottish comeback had as much to do with our own wandering concentration as with any big improvement on their part. Scotland came back and scored three tries as we slacked off. I was replaced by Ceri Sweeney with about 15 minutes to go and watched the last moments from the sidelines. It was obvious we were tiring a little after our first-half efforts, but to be fair to the Scots they did play some good rugby in that last half hour. I think there's a lesson in there for them which they need to take on board. They took a leaf out of our book and became willing to take risks in attack. They came at us from different areas of the field and they looked to try and keep the ball in hand, something we always strive to do. I think that has to be the future for Scotland and the basis for any recovery. They have the type of players who need that more adventurous approach and when the likes of the Lamont brothers, Rory and Sean, ran at us in that second-half they cause us problems. Not enough problems to ever threaten the result, though: it finished 46–22 to us.

The Scottish newspapers had been full of pictures of Charlotte on their front pages on the morning of the game, a Sunday. She had flown up to Edinburgh to watch the match with a gang of mates and they all seemed to be wearing cowboy hats with the words 'Girls On Tour' printed on them. But it remained a girls-only weekend. Within a few hours of the match finishing we were at Edinburgh Airport boarding our flight back to Cardiff. Our final game of the tournament, against Ireland, was just six days away and as the Irish had played the previous day then the Welsh management wanted to try and lessen the advantage the Irish had of an extra day's training.

Ireland may have had an extra 24 hours of recovery time for their bodies, but on that Sunday it was probably their minds that needed more attention. Their own Grand Slam dreams had bitten the dust. Despite carrying victories over Italy, Scotland and England under their belts they couldn't cope with France who had won 26–19 in Dublin on the Saturday afternoon. Not even a brilliant individual try from Brian O'Driscoll – who would go on to be my Lions captain – could save them. The Irish could still mathematically win the Six Nations title, but as far as the Grand Slam was concerned, it would either be ours or nobody's.

'Nobody in the squad is talking about a Grand Slam.

We're just treating the build-up as if we were playing any other game,' claimed Mike Ruddock in the papers on the Monday morning. All I can say is that Mike must have flown home on a different plane. Everyone was talking about the Grand Slam. In fact, it's *all* we were talking about. The management may not have uttered the phrase to the players for fear of breaking the spell, but everyone from 1 to 22 chipped in with their own thoughts of what it would mean if we pulled it off. We imagined what the reaction might be among the fans and the media, how the hype and the level of coverage would go through the roof. Someone also rightly pointed out that it might mean an end to people banging on about the old days of the Seventies.

I don't want to appear disloyal about this. What the great Welsh teams of the 1970s achieved for the country was unbelievable. To win three Grand Slams in eight years and five Triple Crowns was an incredible achievement. But I was born in 1982. I have no memories of any members of that side outside of the re-runs I've seen on television. Gareth Edwards, Barry John, Phil Bennett, JPR Williams, Gerald Davies – these were obviously brilliant players – but they are from my father's generation so it's hard for me to feel the same kind of connection as my old man does. The same goes for all the other players in the present day Welsh squad. Even Gareth Llewellyn was just a kid back then!

All the current squad have massive respect for what

those guys did. But what has annoyed us in the past is when those players from previous eras slag off the current ones. They have questioned our desire, our commitment, the way we have played the game, and lots of other things – often when they themselves have lost touch with the modern game and rarely even watch it. That is when you lose respect. I have to say I don't want to name names and I don't even know if those kinds of criticism have been directed at me. I tend not to read the coverage of Welsh rugby in the newspapers or watch much of it on TV. But I have much more time for the ex-international who actually comes up to you, face-to-face, and tells you what he thinks of your performance – good or bad. I put Jonathan Davies in that category. He's always been honest and straight about my performances, but also constructive. I just about remember Jonathan as a kid before he went to rugby league but he is someone I have a lot of respect for. The same goes for Ieuan Evans, someone I loved watching on the wing for Wales. Mark Ring, who played for Wales and Cardiff in the late 1980s and early 1990s was another of my favourite players because of his attitude. He was an outrageous entertainer who was willing to try anything.

The bottom line, though, is that former players – even those who were your heroes – are in the past. Players live in the present. They want to make their own history and that was all that mattered to us as we touched down in Cardiff on that Sunday night.

CHAPTER FOUR

Slamming It

I was thankful it was a short week. Having played in Scotland on the Sunday, it basically left us with only five days to get things right before we met Ireland. That was enough. I don't think any of us could have coped with more than that and a two-week gap between matches – as used to be the norm – would definitely have sent us all completely nuts. As it was, everywhere we went in those five days, everyone we bumped into at the Vale of Glamorgan Hotel, people around our training base, anyone who had an excuse to come up and talk . . . it was all, all about the game. The *Western Mail*, the national newspaper of Wales, was giving the match a level of attention I had never seen before. Day after day there were pages and pages of stuff about the players, the fans, the number of pints that were going to be sold, historical stuff about previous games between the sides and all the rest of it. I looked at the copies where they were left laying around the hotel. But I didn't pick them up.

Two facts became unavoidable, though, however much I tried to ignore the newspapers and not listen to the radio or watch TV. Wales had not won a Grand Slam for 27 years and we had not beaten Ireland at home for 22 years. If we won this game, then the impact would be massive and the party afterwards would be awesome. What more incentive did we need?

For me, personally, there was an extra edge in this match as I would be up against Brian O'Driscoll. Like me, O'Driscoll is a centre and someone who seems to enjoy being the centre of attention on the field. Unlike me he had been a permanent fixture in his side for the past five years. He was their best player and although he was playing at outside centre and I would be inside, I knew that when our paths crossed I would have to be at my very best in order to contain him. He had scored an incredible try against France the week before and I knew from own experiences against him how difficult he was to play against. I'd been up against him twice before. The most recent time was earlier in that season for the Ospreys against his Irish province, Leinster, at St. Helen's. I had suffered an absolute shocker with the boot, but felt I had handled O'Driscoll and his centre partner, Gordon D'Arcy, quite well. The time before, though, at The Gnoll, O'Driscoll had been the big difference between the sides. The Ospreys matched Leinster in most aspects that night but O'Driscoll was world class and he had won them the game. I wouldn't say I was worried about O'Driscoll before that Ireland game; we were all trying hard to just concentrate on our own strengths. But I was aware of how good he could be and how we would all need to be fully alert.

Before the Scotland match a lot had been discussed within the squad meetings of what the Scots might offer. There was a different approach in the countdown to Ireland. It was far more about us, rather than them. We felt they were under far less pressure than us because they had lost to the French and their Grand Slam had gone. So our aim was to concentrate on ourselves and encourage each other to go out and play our normal games. We were not that bothered about Ireland. We were far more concerned about avoiding the effects of all the hype and expectation that built up during those five days. We felt that if we played with the same freedom and fluency we had shown at Murrayfield then the result would take care of itself and so would the Grand Slam.

I woke up at 7.30am on Saturday, 19 March 2005. Nothing unusual in that, it's the time I always seem to wake whether it's match day or not. I pulled back the curtains in my hotel room at the Vale of Glamorgan and felt the full force of a perfect sunlight. The sky was also a perfect blue and there wasn't a cloud in sight.

It was the perfect setting for a final match in the Six Nations championship; it was a perfect day for a Grand Slam.

As our coach advanced through the centre of Cardiff towards the Millennium Stadium it seemed to me as if the whole population of Wales was out on the streets. There were fans everywhere; far more, it appeared, than were out and about even on the day of the England game. Everyone seemed to be wearing something red, either a replica shirt, or a T-shirt, or else they had dyed their hair red for the occasion. There were banners hanging outside the pubs, put there by our shirt sponsors, Brains, featuring players from our squad, while people underneath them were walking along wearing the identical shirt. Young, old, men, women, when they saw our team bus they became frantic – waving and cheering and pulling on their mates to catch a look. I just gazed out of the window and drank it all in. We all did. Most of the players I spoke to after that day agreed with me that the journey to the stadium was one of the real highlights of the day. The buzz you feel from the fans' cheering and clapping is hard to describe. It makes you desperate to get out there and play.

One of the stories that had appeared in the newspapers that week was about Charlotte and her role that afternoon. She had been invited to sing the anthem before the game, alongside Katherine Jenkins. The idea had come from Rupert Moon, a former player with

Llanelli and Wales, who was now employed within the marketing operation of the Welsh Rugby Union. Most people seemed to think it was wonderful idea, but I had been angry and amazed from the moment I'd heard about it. This was a massive game and the stakes were about as high as you could get. If things had gone wrong, then I'm sure her singing beforehand would have been highlighted as a distraction. I didn't want that to happen – for both our sake's. Maybe, at the back of my mind, I felt it really was a distraction. It was an added complication at a moment of the build-up when I really like to go into my own little world and think purely about my performance. It also struck me as a strange decision on behalf of the WRU. On the one hand, the team management were doing all they could to play down my relationship with Charlotte and trying to get the media to stick to the rugby. On the other, they were asking Charlotte to take centre stage before the biggest match we had played for years – something they knew would be a huge talking point. It somehow seemed to undermine the management. Charlotte, though, was pretty excited about the whole thing so I decided it was best to keep my own doubts to myself.

When it came to it, I think I glanced across to Charlotte as she sang in front of 75,000 people, but only the once. Like everyone else in the squad, I felt well prepared for the task ahead and fully focused on what I had to do. My worries over being distracted didn't materialise and the anxieties I had about the game itself turning out badly soon melted away.

Michael Owen, who had taken over the captaincy from Gareth Thomas after Alfie's injury in Paris, gave a rousing team talk before we left the Millennium Stadium dressing rooms. Nothing too tub-thumping or over-the-top, but he just hit the right note by calmly reminding everyone that we needed to forget the prize and concentrate on our own performance. He told us that we were a good side . . . a fucking good side and we weren't about to lose. He wanted us to play with the same sense of enjoyment and excitement we had shown against the Scots. Of course, there was massive expectancy but he reminded us that we needed to put that to one side and just play our normal game. In other words, 'Go out and enjoy it.' That's always the best message you can hear as a player before a game.

I knew Michael pretty well even before I'd got back into the Wales squad earlier that season. I had played with him at Wales Under-21 level, although he was a little older than me. Mike is a top guy, very genuine but extremely dedicated. He takes the game exceptionally seriously and can remember every detail about every match he has ever played in – and some that he hasn't. Quite often, two of the boys in the squad might be discussing a game and one will remind the other of an incident during the match. If they are struggling to remember some small detail then Mike will step in to remind them of the date, the result, who scored, and maybe even what minute the crucial try came in. He's a walking encyclopaedia. With a bit of effort, I can usually recall most of my goal kicks – the ones that went over as well as the ones that missed. But Michael not only remembers everything he did in every game, but what all the other 29 players did, too.

So you don't pick an argument with Mike about rugby and no-one would question his credentials as an international captain, either. He may have taken over the job because of injury but he wasn't fazed by it and he had the respect of everyone in that dressing room. Rather like Martin Johnson, Mike leads by example. He is probably the most skilful forward out there and the way he enjoys playing a passing, running, handling game is perfectly in keeping with the way this Wales team try and play. He was absolutely the right choice to take over as skipper once Alfie was ruled out. Some of Mike's offloads in the tackle are just stunning to watch – so athletic and precise. He may not be the most forceful back row forward in the world but he has fantastic hands. It's noticeable to me that opposition backs are often caught out by Mike when he's in the back line. They look up and see a 6ft 5 inch, 18-stone forward in front of them and think he won't be too skilful. So they try and get away with rushing up to make the tackle, only to find he's floated out a perfect pass to someone in space. England were guilty of that in the opening minutes of our match against them, when Michael set up Shane Williams for the try. Later on in the year, I would be sitting down chatting to England's Mark Cueto during the Lions tour of New Zealand. He admitted he had been badly caught out by Michael in that match. He had seen it was a forward in midfield and thought there was no way Mike would do anything other than charge forward or throw a flat pass outside him. Mark said he rushed up to cut down the space and couldn't believe his eyes when Michael casually floated the ball over his head and into Shane's arms.

Of course, there are times when it doesn't come off. On the Lions tour, in the final few minutes of the match we lost to the Maoris, Mike tried an outrageous pass behind his back and the ball was spilled. If he had thrown that pass for Wales then I reckon a team-mate would have anticipated it, but the Lions were locked into a much more pragmatic approach. The chance was lost and I think that cost Mike in terms of his future selection.

By the time the captain had said his final words, the knock came on the Wales dressing room door and it was time to go. We walked out of the door and turned left towards the tunnel entrance. Then, it's a 20 yard walk along the windowless corridor to the mouth of the tunnel. You can hear the noise of the crowd long before you run down towards the pitch, but as you come out into the air it's the noise that hits you first, right between the eyes, even before the sunlight. On this day, Grand Slam day, the noise was deafening. But it didn't worry or unsettle us. We felt calm and we felt ready. I wasn't nervous and I think that went for the rest of the boys. So many of them had been through the bad times, and I'd had my low points, too, just trying to get into this team, that we were just determined to enjoy this moment. Whatever was going to happen over the next 80 minutes, the outcome was not going to be as bad as some of the dark days we'd all been through. I honestly feel the fans were more nervous than the players that day. The bad omens of so many home defeats to Ireland weighed far heavier on their shoulders than on ours.

CHAPTER FIVE

Rat Attack

The singing during the anthems was loud and passion-ate and there was a real sense of anticipation inside the stadium. The weather made it feel like a summer's day. We kicked off but it was Ireland who looked more comfortable in those opening few minutes. They were methodical and direct, as they always are, and for a while it looked as if it was going to be a really tight game. Ronan O'Gara kicked a penalty to give them the lead and Stephen Jones missed with his first effort. I was on the end of a big hit from Kevin Maggs early on and it seemed to go down particularly well with the rest of his team-mates – particularly O'Driscoll.

I didn't really know Brian at this stage and it wouldn't be until the Lions tour that I would appreciate the real person behind the rugby player. But that tackle from Maggs seemed to be the signal for Brian to unleash a lot of pent up frustration – rage, perhaps – over the defeat to France and the loss of the Grand Slam Ireland had been chasing since 1948. Maggs tackled me and I lost the ball in contact. It was probably going to be a knock-on, but I re-gathered to try and set it up. As I was on the ground, O'Driscoll came in and tried to 'jackal' – a term we use to mean the stealing of the ball from your opponent on the ground . But instead of just trying to rip the ball clear, he also decided to pull my hair and tried to gouge my eye for good measure. 'How do like that, you cocky little fucker?' There was a real flash of anger in his eyes. It was intense. I still don't really know what had wound him up. It may have been something I'd said in the build-up. I'd probably been asked the question, 'Do you think you'll beat Ireland.' To which I'd probably said, yes. I can't be bothered with all that nonsense of playing down your own team and building up the opposition – still can't.

Whatever it was, Brian seemed to lose it. I know he takes a lot of the paper talk very seriously. I saw it on the Lions tour, well before all the business with the Tana Umaga incident had kicked off. Piri Weepu, the All Blacks scrum-half, was in the Maori side that beat the Lions early on in the tour. Afterwards, Weepu had said something which Brian felt was disrespectful and it obviously rankled with him because it was mentioned in the build-up to the match against Wellington, where Weepu was involved again. It was like a red rag to a bull.

Rat Attack

I ended up getting on well with Brian in New Zealand and discovered him to be a really good guy. But like many players, he seems to take on a different personality when he steps onto the pitch. I can never really understand that. I just don't go in for it. I would rather try and stay relaxed and focused than get wound up by an opponent. If someone has a cheap shot at me – a punch, a stamp, tugs my hair or tries to gouge me – I'm more likely to just say, 'What's your problem?' than rise to it. Sometimes, that makes them even more wound up. But I'd rather get my own back by scoring a try or kicking a goal, or making a big legitimate tackle, than something sly. The players I really can't stand are the ones who act like dicks on the field – cheap shots off-the-ball all the time – and then try and be your best mate when the game's over. There are a few about.

After O'Gara's penalty we were behind, but there was no panic. We built an attack in the 11th minute but it wasn't really going anywhere. I could sense we had lost momentum so I stepped back ready to receive and try a drop-goal. Fair play to Dwayne Peel, he's always so aware of what's going on around him, and he spotted my move straight away. The ball came back to me, about 40 metres from the posts, and I drop-kicked for three points to tie the scores. The Ireland prop, Reggie Corrigan, who's a big lump, tried to charge the ball down but only managed to deflect it. Instead of altering the line of the ball, though, it just made it spin end-over-end as it went through the posts. On other days the deflection might have knocked it off course, but not this day. I watched it spin its way over and I thought, 'This is it. It's going to be our day.' I felt I had struck it well, anyway, and if Corrigan hadn't got a touch then I think it would have gone over. But you can never be quite sure with drop goals and that's where they differ from place kicks. Everything has to be spot on with a drop goal and you can never feel straight away that you've scored as you can with a place kick. A drop goal is a difficult skill and not many players master it.

It was my first drop goal for Wales and it had taken me until my 16th cap to get it, so I felt pretty happy as we ran back for the re-start. It was 3–3 and still very tight. We just needed something to spark us, something to put us on our way. It came when O'Gara had the ball on his own 10-metre line and took a fraction longer to clear the ball than he should have. Gethin Jenkins, one of the fastest and fittest prop forwards in the world, only needed a fraction and suddenly the ball had smacked into Gethin's outstretched arms and was flying off behind the Irish back-line. Gethin got there first and hacked the ball on towards their line. 'Please don't mess it up. Please watch the bounce.' But I never really doubted him. He's a superb player. He showed great skill, composure and patience and scored the try.

Gethin has two nicknames. The first is Melon-head. Believe it or not, it's because his head is shaped a bit like a melon. The other is Nightmare-head. This refers to the fact that he's always 'sapping' – draining the energy and enthusiasm from others. There's always something wrong, according to Geth. Either we're training too hard, or too long, or we're having too many team meetings, or he doesn't see what this or that meeting is for, or why do we have to attend this dinner. Whatever's happening, Gethin won't like it and won't be happy. If Stephen Jones was put on the earth to make everyone feel good about life, then Gethin is here to bring everyone down.

But what a player. He has to be the best prop forward in world rugby right now, or very close to it. He's certainly the fastest and the fittest in the Six Nations. He's got it all. There were a few question marks about his scrummaging at one time, especially when Steve Hansen was playing him on the tight-head. But since he's become an established loose-head, he's never looked back. Gethin trains really hard and always has the best fitness results among the forwards. He's also the strongest man in the squad. When you add in his natural speed, then it's a pretty awesome package. He's a real character, likes to go out, and with his new found fame he's out there doing some real damage with the ladies.

I have to say, I do feel sorry for our own loose-head prop at the Ospreys, Duncan Jones. He was up there alongside Gethin not very long ago and looked just as likely to go on the Lions tour. Unfortunately, Duncan got injured at exactly the wrong time and it cost him a trip to New Zealand.

Melon's try was converted by Stephen Jones before we were awarded a penalty about a yard inside our own half. It was a re-run of the England kick in a sense. Stephen looked at it but quickly signalled for me to have a go. It was longer than the England kick, but easier as this was more or less in front of the posts. Again, all I had to tell myself was not to try and kick it too hard. The Millennium Stadium is a good one for goal-kickers because there is hardly ever any wind. So long as you strike it well, there's no room for excuses. I had been kicking well in training that week and felt confident. It was a long way – over 50 metres – but it clipped the inside of the post and went over. Suddenly, we were 13–3 ahead and the crowd were already singing.

The burst of scoring was vital. It not only opened up a gap between the sides, but it settled our nervousness and allowed us to play with freedom. Ireland attacked us, but we defended well and little mistakes began to creep into their game. O'Gara, in particular, started to look frustrated. On the rare occasions they did manage to get the ball to O'Driscoll, Tom Shanklin and I coped well and made our tackles. We were not doing anything particularly fancy; there was little of the spectacular handling style we had shown at Murrayfield. But we were doing enough. We had taken our chances and hustled Ireland into blowing theirs. When Ireland made another error at a ruck, Stephen struck his first penalty and the lead was extended to 16–3.

O'Gara kicked a goal himself before half-time but we went back to our dressing room with a massive roar of encouragement from the crowd. They were now sharing our confidence and the anxieties that were apparent on their faces before the kick-off had given way to smiles. Mike Ruddock and Michael Owen both stressed the need to keep playing on the front foot and not to sit back. The feeling was that the next score would be critical. If we could get it then the Irish would feel it was a long way back and their self-belief might suffer. Most all we knew we were just 40 minutes away from winning a Grand Slam.

Just as we had wanted, we gained the first score through another penalty kick from Steve. O'Gara missed again and I could tell from his face the doubts were setting in. Rugby at this level is all about belief. There is an abundance of ability in a Test match but it comes down to which players feel confident enough to play at the very top of their game. We certainly felt on top of ours even if we had not yet scaled the uppermost peaks.

We should have added a second try soon after O'Gara's miss but Martyn Williams dropped a pass. It was probably the only one he put down in the whole of the Six Nations because a couple of days later he would be voted the player of the tournament. When Ireland gave away another penalty, and Steve put it over, we had pushed our lead up to 22–6. It hadn't been the same flurry of tries as against the Scots. We had needed to accumulate our points more steadily. But the effect was the same; the match was going away from the opposition and we felt in control.

Our forwards were now well on top and when Ireland did try and run at us I felt strong in the tackle. We knew another try would kill them off and when it came it was a good one. We drove through a couple of phases and then the call was for me to have the ball from Stephen. But fair play to Steve, he noticed the Irish defence had drifted early and so instead of picking out me he gave the ball to Tom Shanklin. Ireland's midfield were not anticipating that. They thought the ball was coming my way. Tom had picked such a great angle – really straight – that he just burst through them. If a defence is on the drift and you blast through on a hard angle it causes panic. That's what happened. Shanks went through and had the presence of mind to off-load to Kevin Morgan who raced over.

It was an awesome try and maybe the one moment in that match when we created something off the cuff that was more typical of the way we like to play. I was so far behind play after the dummy run I could see the hole opening up for Shanks. He gave it to 'Rat' and there was no stopping him. Steve's conversion made it 29–6 with 20 minutes still to go. I think it was also a significant try for Tom. He had been talked about as a possible Lions tourist before the game but it was that try which probably clinched his trip. I really enjoy playing alongside Shanks. He's very solid, reads the game well, and I felt he had a superb championship. He would certainly have been in my Lions party, regardless of that break. But it was such a great moment it had everyone talking about him.

I was also really pleased for Kevin Morgan. Rat had gone through a terrible time with injuries but showed great courage and determination to come all the way back. No-one was more deserving of a championship medal. He was very unlucky not to go on the Lions tour as he is an excellent full-back and he seems to be even quicker now than he was before his knee problems.

Ireland then came back at us, but I think we took our foot off the gas. Their prop, Marcus Horan, who had come on as a replacement, went over as we slacked off a bit in defence. There was no panic, though. We went straight back on the attack and Steve kicked another penalty to make it 32–13. But we did drop off a little in the last few minutes. It's somehow inevitable when you think you've got the game won. At Test level you only need to drop your efforts by half a per cent and teams will make you pay. It happened in the last half hour against Scotland and it happened in the final few minutes against Ireland. With four minutes left they scored a second try through their full-back, Geordan Murphy, another player I would get to know on the Lions tour later that year.

That encounter was a strange one, though. Murphy had the ball and I thought he was going to dive early so I slid in to try and make him dive on my legs, in the hope he might spill the ball. Instead, he kept on running and scored anyway. He stumbled a little and it must have looked from some angles as though I had tripped him. In fact, we hadn't made contact. Murphy was fine about it, and didn't make a meal of things, which I was grateful for as I feared I might get a yellow card. But O'Driscoll came running over and started shouting abuse again. 'You're a fucking wanker!' Weird. They'd just scored a try. I just looked at him and he carried on swearing and pointing over. Then, just as suddenly as he'd come over, he was off again.

It didn't really make much difference – the try or the reaction. We were still 12 points ahead and there was no way we were going to let it slip. But we did slack off, no doubt about it. And that's something we have to work on. Against England we stopped playing, we relaxed against the Italians after building up a big lead, in Paris the French came back because we sat on our advantage, we allowed Scotland to save face, and now Ireland had given us a little scare because of the same problem. That's the one thing I really admire about the All Blacks. They are totally ruthless. They are far more likely to rub your nose in it than slack off. We haven't got the same attitude. Maybe it's because quite a few players in this Welsh squad are not used to winning against the better teams. When we are in a winning position, we tend to reflect on it during the match itself, rather than concentrate on increasing the winning margin.

I know I'm guilty of it. I'm hoping that I'll become more ruthless as I get more used to success.

But I don't think Ireland really threatened to upset the outcome in those final minutes. We had no real concerns. We won 32–20. The final whistle went and I felt a weird combination of intense relief and uncontrollable excitement. All the pressure I'd felt all week seemed to flow out of me and I felt quite tired. Incredibly happy that we had won the Grand Slam, but tired, too. The match had been all about winning. It had been a long, hard campaign and we had come through a lot together as a group. If it had ended on the wrong note then it would have been so deflating.

We hugged each other and smiled. We'd done it. All the questions asked during the week-long build-up had been answered. I was keen to get on with the presentation. I wanted to lift the trophy. I wanted to see the fireworks and watch the champagne corks pop. When it came to the moment, it felt really good. It felt as though we were Manchester United and we had just won the Champions League. I'd watched that kind of thing and always wondered what it felt like. Now, I knew. Michael Owen and Gareth Thomas picked up the Six Nations trophy together – the match day captain and the tournament captain. We got our medals, each got our hands on the trophy, and did a lap of honour. The fans were ecstatic and so were we. It's difficult to describe what a high I was on. We went back to the dressing rooms and there were photographers and more champagne. It was quite a scene. Everyone was hugging and shaking hands, but there were a lot of tired bodies as well. Even so, I think all the boys showered and changed just a little more quickly than usual. Then, some of the players' family members came in to say well done.

I met up with Charlotte at the after-match dinner before all the players, plus wives and girlfriends, went to a function laid on by Brains, the brewers who had become our shirt sponsors. Needless to say, the beer was on them. We enjoyed a great night and it felt good to be together in celebration with the same guys I had been alongside for so many weeks. Like the rest of Cardiff, and the rest of Wales, we made sure the party went on long into the night and I eventually made it back to the team hotel at about 5am.

The next morning I had hoped to spend recovering from the night before. But after doing all the media interviews there was a call from the team management to be ready to board the bus by noon. It appeared the celebrations were still in full swing. I had a horrible hangover but managed to get my head together after a few bottles of water and limped onto the team bus. I was wrecked. We were driven into the centre of Cardiff and dropped at a bar called The Yard, a pub owned by Brains on the site of their old brewery headquarters. Downstairs were punters who looked as if they hadn't been to bed from the night before, but we were ushered upstairs and into another private party.

I'm not really a big drinker. In fact, I can comfortably go for a couple of months without a single drink. Every once in a while, I like to let my hair down a bit with a few mates, and then I'll be back into strict training mode and I won't touch another drop for the next few weeks. So, two heavy sessions in successive days is not something I'm very used to – or much good at. It wasn't long before all the players were playing drinking games to get in the mood and not very long at all before I was completely smashed. This was a players' only deal. No wives. No girlfriends. So it was all a bit macho and a bit excessive to say the least. The trouble with stupid drinking games is that if you lose you have to drink more. Then, you are even more drunk and so you lose again. After a little while, I was gone – completely steaming. I dropped a glass and everything after that is a bit of a blur. I was told everything else the next morning as I don't remember any of it. It was suggested I go home – not a bad idea, all things considered – but as I left I verbally abused a couple of bouncers. Some pictures were taken by a woman who seemed to have gate-crashed the party, there was a bit of a scuffle, and I ended up being given a lift home by the police. Luckily, one of my mates had turned up and he was able to look after me.

The next morning, after I'd cleared up the mess in my bedroom, I realised I'd lost my mobile phone and it wasn't long before there were stories in the newspapers about pictures of Charlotte being sent around the world. To cap it all, I was summoned by Alan Phillips, the Wales team manager, to go and have a private word. Apparently, there had been some damage caused in the pub toilets, although my own memories of anything that may or may not have happened were extremely sketchy. A senior police officer turned up to tell me how lucky I was not to have been arrested for being drunk and disorderly. It could have meant a night in a cell, a court case, he said. It could have meant missing out with the Lions. Fair enough, I thought, I was out of order. But if I'd been left to myself I'd have spent a quiet Sunday recovering from the night before. I was only in the pub because I had been told to go there and encouraged to spend all day drinking. I hadn't behaved very cleverly, but it was one of those situations where the whole atmosphere takes over and affects your behaviour. It had been an amazing 48 hours and I hadn't had much sleep. I'm not trying to make excuses. There's certainly no excuse for causing damage in a toilet, but all the booze and the back-slapping meant I lost my senses. I certainly lost my common sense, that's for sure, and it's not an evening I can look back on with much pride.

As well as the sobering experience of hearing about my behaviour from the police, I also made a visit to see one of the senior Brains people to apologise. They had enjoyed brilliant publicity from their sponsorship of the Wales team, but this was the kind of stuff they could do without. I told them how sorry I was and offered to pay for the damage. It was a strange end to an amazing weekend. It's not every day you are invited to take your fill of what was, literally, a piss up in a brewery. But then it's not every day you win the Grand Slam.

Looking back, I think the key word in what we achieved was excitement. We play an exciting brand of rugby that gets us excited as players and that feeds into our fantastic support. The fans get excited watching our style of play and that, in turn, gives us an extra lift again. Basically, our game-plan is to attack from anywhere on the field. There are no rules. No restrictions. In my view, it's the best way to play rugby and it's great to be involved in a group with that mentality. With the Ospreys, and with most of our rivals in the Six Nations, things are more structured. The players are programmed to kick in certain areas of the field, to drive it through the forwards in other parts, and to only attack when they get into the danger areas. It's how most teams play nowadays. But with Wales we are encouraged to attack from behind our own goal-line if we feel there is an opportunity.

It's the type of rugby I always wanted to play as a kid, with the emphasis on running and passing. But because I've always been able to kick the ball a long way, most of the teams I've been involved with over the years have wanted me to use that ability – even when it often went against the grain. Of course, I love kicking the ball because it's one of my strengths. But given the choice, I'd far rather be part of an adventurous running side that keeps the ball in hand.

A huge influence on this Welsh style is our skills coach, Scott Johnson. Scott's an Australian but he has blended his own methods from his background with the traditional Welsh strengths of handling and passing to produce a very fast, very fluid style of rugby. I think Scott is a revolutionary thinker on the game, someone ahead of his time and it's vital that Welsh rugby hangs onto him for the future. If he was lured away from us then it would be a massive blow.

We train with the same approach and that means when we play Tests we are not afraid of making mistakes. It's a style of rugby that requires both good skills and a high level of fitness throughout the team. Every player has to be able to time his running onto the ball, be able to give and take a pass, and have the endurance and stamina to keep doing that up and down the field for the full 80 minutes. In some teams, counter-attacking feels un-natural to the players and they tense up instead of opening their shoulders and really going for their passes. With Wales, there is a fluidity to it all that makes it very effective and hard to defend against.

As regards the future, then I think Wales simply have to carry on playing this way in order to build on our success. We haven't got the players to win against the major teams by playing a tight, slow-paced game and hope to grind teams down through our forwards. It has to be high tempo and high risk.

In so many of our Grand Slam matches we won because we attacked from deep and got in behind teams. Once we broke their first line of cover then it meant their forwards were not able to make heavy collision tackles on our forwards. Instead, they were having to turn back and scramble. If the opposition isn't able to make those heavy, aggressive hits then we have the momentum and with our good handling we can keep movements going by passing in contact until we score. It's simple, really, but not easy to get right. For a start you need players with good hands and big lungs. Each player has to support on the shoulder of the player ahead of him and then be able to use the ball wisely when he gets it. That goes for all the forwards as well as the backs. If you can't keep up, then you can expect to get a row in the team meetings. No rules. No restrictions. But no hiding places, either.

CHAPTER SIX

Ball Boy

I had dreamed about playing rugby for Wales ever since I was little kid and part of that dream was winning the Grand Slam. The dream became reality on 19 March 2005 when I was 23 years old. It was the first Welsh Grand Slam since 1978 and although many of the supporters in Cardiff on the day of the Ireland game could remember 1978, for me it was something I had only read about, or seen the clips on TV. When Phil Bennett led Wales to that previous Slam, my father, Alan, was 20 years old and my mother, Audrey, would have been 21. I was born four years later on 1 February 1982 at the Princess of Wales Hospital in Bridgend.

I was their first child and two years later my sister, Sarah, arrived. Dad has always led a very active life. He played rugby and since he left school he has worked as a felt roofer. It's his own business but he began working for my grandfather, Glyn, until my grandpa's knees went and forced him to pack up. That allowed me to have a go when I left school. I managed to stick it for six months but that was long enough. Rugby's a breeze compared to laying felt roofs which is proper work. One of my main aims in being a professional rugby player is to earn enough money to allow my dad to retire, in order to save his knees from giving way as my grandpa's did.

Rugby has always run through the family. My grandfather on my mother's side, Trevor Watkins, played rugby for both Maesteg and Bridgend as a centre and was part of the Maesteg 'Invincibles' of 1949–50. My dad started his rugby career with Heol-y-Cyw and then got picked up by Maesteg, where he arrived as fifth-choice prop. He was a bit small for a prop, but powerful, and within a year he had fought his way through to become first choice. He went on to become the club's captain between 1990 and 1992 when they had a decent side. My mum was also into her rugby. But then as one of nine children, with six brothers, I don't suppose she had much choice.

My parents were both from the village of Pencoed, just outside Bridgend. It's where I started out until we moved to St. Bride's Major, a much smaller village near the beaches of Southerndown and Ogmore, when I was two. People say Welsh rugby is very tribal and parochial and they're not kidding. Pencoed is only a couple of miles from Bridgend, whereas Maesteg is eight miles up the Lynfi Valley. But as my old man played for Maesteg, I was brought up to consider Bridgend the enemy. It's a rivalry that was played out during my childhood in an annual Boxing Day fixture that was as heated and brutal as any local derby you can imagine.

My earliest memories are of going to Maesteg three times a week with my father. From around the age of five or six, he would take me to the Saturday games and to training nights on Tuesdays and Thursdays. On Saturday, I would be ball boy at the home games but he'd never take me to the away matches. He probably wanted to enjoy a post-match drink without having me around.

It wasn't very long before I was allowed to go into the dressing rooms on match-day. I used to stand and cower in the corner, dressed in my kit, while dad gave his team talk before the game. He was a really good captain. He'd never stop talking, gee-ing everyone up all the time and he was very passionate. In fact, he was the exact opposite of me and how I am in the dressing room before a game. I like to stay quiet and sit with my own thoughts. I've never been captain of any side I've ever played for and never wanted to be. The idea of being captain and having to give team talks to a large group of players frightens me to death. I don't mind being a leader on the field through my game. But leadership off the field isn't really for me.

Dad was a good talker, though, and it came naturally

to him. He wasn't ridiculously over the top, but he got them fired up. I would stand there and take it all in and none of the others played seemed to mind that there was a little kid in the corner. After a while, they let me join in some parts of their training sessions. I was especially keen on being allowed to join in with the kicking. Brett Davey – who went on to become a very good goal-kicker for Caerphilly and Pontypridd – was there as a young player and I'd try and keep up with him. Sometimes, I'd beat him, too.

There was a centre playing for Maesteg at the time in the early 1990s. His name was Huw Woodland and he was good enough to get into the Wales squad. But it was a measure of the rivalry between clubs that when he left to join Neath he suddenly became hated at Maesteg. That's what it was like – very close-knit. You were either part of it or you weren't.

I desperately wanted to be part of it, so I kept going along with dad and watched every game I could. But Maesteg wasn't my home-town club, it just happened to be where my father played. My local club was Pencoed and so that's where I started playing my mini-rugby for the under-8s when I was five. Mum and dad would come along and mum actually coached my school team at St. Bride's Major Primary. Dad would often buy me rugby jerseys as presents, but he always refused to get me a Wales one. 'You don't get given that one,' he'd say. 'You have to earn it.' It seemed a long, long way off.

There would be a rugby match to go and see every weekend. When Maesteg were away, my grandpa Trevor would take me to watch Bridgend. At an early age I could appreciate that Bridgend were of a slightly higher standard than Maesteg. But it didn't alter the rivalry. I still wanted them to lose. They had some quality players like John Apsee, Aled Williams, who went on to play for Wales, and a young promising scrum-half coming through at the time called Rob Howley. Some good judges told me to watch Rob because he was going to play for Wales one day and maybe the Lions. They were right.

The Boxing Day match between Bridgend and Maesteg was one everyone looked forward to. There would always be a massive crowd and people would be talking it up for weeks before. But Dad wouldn't get nervous. It certainly wouldn't put him off his Christmas Day dinner. One match that sticks in my mind was the day Maesteg beat Ebbw Vale to gain promotion to division one of what was then the Heineken League. They were awesome that day. Dad was captain and Heineken were the sponsors and so they turned up that day with truckloads of beer. The whole town turned out to watch and then stayed on to make sure the trucks went back empty.

Dad was a prop. He had a lot of natural strength from working on the roofs, but he also had a good technique as a scrummager. But he never wanted me to be a prop or any kind of forward. I started out as a flanker when I was very young, but dad was soon very keen for me to play in the backs. I think he realised that the backs got fewer broken noses, more headlines, and more money – even though the game then was still supposed to be amateur. Dad spent hours helping me practice my rugby on the local pitches. It was never actually stated that rugby was going to be my life, but it was like an unspoken understanding between us. Rugby didn't go professional until I was 13 years old, but even before then it was assumed that it would somehow be the main thing I would concentrate on and it was something that would bring its rewards. But I never felt I was being put under pressure. Those hours spent practising my kicking, and the games on the weekends, were what I wanted to do anyway. I'd have done them on my own because I enjoyed them.

As I grew older we'd spent a lot of time talking about the matches I'd played but in the very early days the thing I really loved doing was practising kicking. We would go to the fields in Pencoed, or down the road in Wick, and he would fetch the balls back after I'd kicked them. If I missed one, then dad would offer some advice and I'd usually end up going nuts at him out of pure frustration. I didn't know it but Jonny Wilkinson, who is three years older than me, may have been standing in a field somewhere else at the very same time, doing the same kind of thing. But the big thing for me, wasn't so much relentless accuracy, but distance. I was obsessed with how far I could boot the thing. I just wanted to kick the ball as far as possible. The pitches may have been a bit shorter than senior ones, but even at the age of 11 or 12 I was kicking goals from around the halfway line. The real buzz for me came in matches for Pencoed junior section when it was a close game. I'd love it if the result came down to a long distance kick and the other team thought I had no chance of landing it. Watching the ball go over from miles out, proving them wrong, that felt great. I loved being known as the kid with the really big kick.

I got into the Bridgend and Districts Under-11s team a year early and managed to do the same with West Wales Under-11s. Between the ages of 12 and 16 at Pencoed, my father was the coach and we hardly lost a game. Richard Mustoe – who went on to play for Bridgend and the Celtic Warriors, and is now with me at the Ospreys – was in the same side. Grant Hall, a scrum-half whose father Wayne went on to become Wales Under-21 team manager, was another very good player. Owain Ford and Gareth David were up there, too. There were no problems with dad being the coach. It never felt odd or uncomfortable. The other players liked his coaching as he always tried to bring in new drills and fresh ideas he had picked up from Maesteg.

When I was about 14, Pencoed were trailing by two points in a match against Caerphilly, who were always our big rivals. The referee was about to blow up when I scored with a drop-goal from near my own 10-metre line. I saw it in my mind's eye before I struck it. When I hit it, it was exactly as I had imagined it. I ran around for about 50 yards, with all my team-mates chasing behind, before they all jumped on me. It was a great feeling to create that kind of reaction. The referee was also the Caerphilly coach and he came up to me afterwards and told me he was just about to put the whistle to his lips for full-time before I kicked it. He looked gutted.

We won a lot of matches and picked up a lot of trophies. I liked the feeling of success and that was the normal outcome, but I wasn't too good at handling failure. We had quite a poor side one year at Bridgend and Districts Under-15s level and I found that hard to cope with. But the most difficult setback to deal with was at Wales Under-16s level. I made the squad of 22, but missed out on the starting position of outside-half and found myself on the bench. Nicky Robinson, who went on to become a Wales team-mate of mine, got picked ahead of me. It was my first real taste of rejection and I was devastated. I had desperately wanted a Wales Under-16 cap. It was always considered the hardest of the age-group caps to get and I didn't know many people who had done it. I had set my sights on it and when I didn't make the line-up I was distraught. I couldn't sleep. I couldn't think of anything else except the rejection.

I missed out against England, but had a reprieve of sorts when I came on as a replacement in the next game against Portugal. I managed to score a try within a few minutes of coming on, but it didn't make up for the original snub.

I didn't know it then but there was a much bigger set-back just around the corner. At 17, I was playing in a sevens tournament for Pencoed Youth when I broke my leg. It was a game against Bridgend – typical. I stepped around one player but got hit by another from the side. There had been a lot of rain and the pitch was very heavy. My left foot got stuck in the mud and as my body went over the bottom half of my shin it was locked into position and the bone fractured. They called it a spiral break. It basically means the bone has twisted before breaking and it's a common break among skiers. I could tell it was broken straight away. For one thing, I'd actually heard it. The pain was horrible and I soon went into shock. For a rugby player a spiral fracture is serious stuff. I thought my world had ended.

At the hospital, they attempted to bend my leg back into place. I was in a ridiculous amount of pain. It was horrific and very upsetting for my parents. I spent two weeks in hospital and it felt like six months.

The problem with this type of break is that it can be very unstable. One option was to have a pin put in, but dad and I decided against that. We wanted to let it heal naturally, hoping that nature would make a firmer fix.

The surgeon was happy to go down that route although he pointed out that there was risk it may not heal and the five months spent in plaster might prove to be a total waste. We decided it was worth the risk and so they put my leg in plaster and after a fortnight I went home. I spent the next 10 weeks laying on the sofa in my parents' living room. I was an invalid. I couldn't even go to the toilet until I learnt to shuffle across the carpet on my backside with my leg sticking out. It wasn't just my leg that suffered, either. I became very miserable and bitter about what had happened. I was a pain to live with for my sister Sarah and my mum and dad and a complete arse to anyone who came round to visit. It didn't matter what they said, I'd end up being short-tempered and nasty. In the end, I think most of them just left me alone.

After five months of sitting around getting on everyone's nerves, it was eventually time for the plaster to be removed. I almost went into shock all over again. My leg had shrunk so much through muscle-wastage it looked like it didn't belong to me. It was like a stick. But what made it worse – and made me feel physically sick – was how hairy the leg had become. Underneath the plaster, with no air to get at them, the hairs on the leg had grown really long. I couldn't look at it. It was repulsive – just skin and bone and long black hair.

There was only one thing for it. I would have to shave. Those hairs would have to go. I took my dad's razor and got to work. It still looked horribly thin, but at least it was no longer like some hairy growth. With one leg shaved, the right one looked a bit odd. So I shaved that one, too. And I've been shaving my legs regularly ever since. Most people assume my shaving routine is down to vanity or some desire to get noticed. But it's not. It started when I was 17, the day they took the plaster off my broken leg.

With the plaster removed I stopped moping around, feeling sorry for myself and concentrated on getting fit. I'd been sure to take in plenty of calcium and was very relieved when the doctors told me the bone had healed correctly. For the next six months I worked really hard. I quickly re-learnt how to walk properly, thanks, to the physios, and then concentrated on single-leg exercises to build up the muscle. My father got me a personal trainer – a guy he knew from Maesteg called Tony Jones. Tony was a runner and he took me down the sand dunes where I'd have intensive sessions in order to build up the strength in my leg. Tony did a great job and I slowly began to see the progress I was making. I went from feeling bitter to realising that some people had gone through much worse. I knew I wasn't the first rugby player to break a leg and that if I was dedicated enough I could come back. It may have been a career-threatening injury, but it was now down to me.

Once I could see the progress I was making, I began to feel a lot more positive. A lot of people helped me, including Bridgend Rugby Club, who let me use their facilities to work on my fitness. It was almost enough for me to start wanting them to win.

Six months after starting the re-habilitation, I was ready to start playing rugby again. I had missed the best part of a year but I was relieved to discover my confidence on the field hadn't really been affected. I was assured the leg was stronger than ever and that's exactly how it felt.

That summer, after a few short months playing again, I went to the trials for the Welsh Schools Under-18s. The confidence had returned. In fact, my ability to come back after the injury made me feel even more confident. I felt invincible – the best player there. Afterwards, I was convinced I would make the squad, but they didn't even invite me back for the second trial. I was told I still wasn't ready and needed more time following the injury. Once again, I was devastated. I had been playing really well, I'd shown up well in the trial. They were just wrong – plain wrong. I carried on playing for my school – Brynteg Comprehensive – where I had always felt at home and continued to perform. I felt gutted inside but I didn't let it affect my game. I never do. I played a game against Neath College, whose No.10 Michael Hook had been selected ahead of me, and scored two tries. Then, Brynteg played against Stradey School, and I was up against another boy who had got in ahead of me, Paul Fisher. My grandfather, Trevor, had died a couple of days before and so my parents weren't watching but

I knew the selectors were there and I wanted to make my point. They were a strong side, but we stuffed them and I scored five tries and ended up scoring 40 points. I thought, 'Now, they'll have to pick me.' But they didn't. Instead, they sent me a two-line letter saying I wasn't ready. I pinned it up on my bedroom wall.

Now I was really desperate. I began to believe they must have something against me, that I'd offended them. I wasn't going to get their side of the story, though, and hear it from their lips. That was a boundary I wasn't prepared to cross. I've always had this feeling that players shouldn't seek out coaches for explanations. You should just take it on the chin and prove them wrong. If I saw a kid talking to a coach I always felt he looked as though he was sucking-up to him. It's an attitude that has probably cost me over the years – with both Wales and the Lions. I let things drag on with Graham Henry, Steve Hansen and Sir Clive Woodward until I was left out of their teams. I never sought a view on how I was doing until the moment I was out in the cold. Sometimes, that's when it's too late. If Welsh Schools didn't want me, then it was their loss.

Luckily, in Wales at that time, there was also an opportunity to play for Wales Youth – a side which often included boys who had left school at 16. I had trials with them and managed to get picked. The Youth side always play against the Schools and I did well enough for the Youth for the Schools to then get back in touch and ask me to join their squad. The Schools team was always considered more prestigious, but I was still bitter over their rejection so I turned them down. They hadn't shown any faith in me, I thought. Wales Youth had. Why should I let them down? My parents supported my decision and I ended up winning the Four Nations championship with Wales Youth. At a tournament in Ireland, we beat the hosts 20–3 and then overcame England 21–14 where I managed to score all the points. We drew our final match 18–18 with Scotland but that was enough to win the tournament and I ended up with 41 points from the three games.

I now had a big decision to make – where to play my senior rugby. Bridgend were offering silly money for an 18-year-old still at school – £10,000-a-year. Llanelli's offer was eight grand and Swansea said they wanted to pay me two-and-a-half. I weighed everything up and talked it over with my old man. In the end, it was an easy decision. I got straight down to St. Helen's and signed for Swansea.

CHAPTER SEVEN

Up On The Roof

Some of my mates thought I was mad. I'd turned down five-figure sums from Bridgend and Llanelli in order to join Swansea. But it wasn't about money. I had trained with the first-team squads at each of the three clubs and the biggest wow factor had come at Swansea. They were a very strong team at that stage with some big-name international players such as Scott Gibbs, Mark Taylor, Colin Charvis, Arwel Thomas, Darren Morris, Garin Jenkins, Ben Evans and Andy Moore. Llanelli could almost match them for names, but I just felt more comfortable at the Swansea training session than I did with the Scarlets. I was just made to feel more at home – as if I really was part of the group.

The Swansea coach at the time was John Plumtree, a New Zealander who had been in charge for three years but still looked young enough to be a player. He had performed at provincial level in both New Zealand and

South Africa and his attitude seemed to reflect the competitive environment in which he'd been raised. He was also lively and likeable. In many ways, 'Plum', as everyone called him, was more like a player than a coach. He got on very well with everyone in the squad – maybe, too well, I'd later come to discover – and the atmosphere was friendly, upbeat and vibrant. The St. Helen's ground may have been dilapidated and in decay, but the squad were very much cutting edge in Welsh terms and it seemed the best choice of where to begin my professional career.

The money wasn't great but the club quickly bumped up the figures by putting me on some sort of government-funded training scheme. On top of that, if I was part of the first-team squad then I was entitled to a further £200 per match. My father also insisted I was registered as part of their squad for the Heineken Cup that coming season, even though few people at Swansea felt I had any chance of being involved and they had laughed when he dug his heels in.

It was the summer of 2000, I was 18, and had recently left Brynteg Comprehensive School. I had sat my GCSEs at 16 in nine subjects and got nine grade Ds. Consistent, if nothing else. One of those Ds was in physical education. It wasn't that I didn't like school. I loved it there. I also found the subjects really interesting. The problem was that once I came out of the building I didn't do a scrap of work. There was simply too much rugby to be involved in and somehow the homework got pushed to the back of the queue. At Brynteg, there was always plenty of rugby to be found if you wanted to look and the school had a rich history of talented players. Six former pupils at the school had gone on to become British and Irish Lions – Dr Jack Matthews, JPR Williams, Gareth Williams, Mike Hall, Dafydd James and Rob Howley. I wanted to be the seventh. I didn't do any revision for the exams and my poor results were no big surprise. But I honestly felt that my GCSEs were my age-group caps.

My younger sister, Sarah, was the brains in the family. As well as doing well at netball and running, she got all her qualifications and now has a good job, working at Cardiff Airport. For me, my parents knew that rugby was my priority. They would probably have liked me to have done more schoolwork but they never really made a big issue of it. If rugby didn't provide a living, then I could always go and work for my father. I considered leaving school at 16 after my exams but the teachers persuaded me not to. My headmaster, Keith Crockett, was keen for me to carry on playing for the rugby team in sixth form. He encouraged me to stay on and they set-up a new course – Leisure and Tourism – at GNVQ Intermediate level which would allow me plenty of time to train and play rugby. I think there were four of us in the class and we had to attend about two or three hours of lectures a week. I actually managed to pass the course, but more importantly for me I was able to spend a lot of time practising kicking or working on building strength at the local gym in Bridgend Recreation Centre. After Leisure and Tourism came Business Studies in the second year but I found that course a bit too intense and never completed it.

Instead, in the months before I started playing for Swansea, I went to work for my father and his flat-roofing business. These are mostly garage roofs or industrial premises. It involves climbing up on the roof and removing the damaged felt cover by hacking it off with a spade. Ripping the stuff off, when it's been stuck down with hot bitumen, is not exactly easy. It's dirty, dusty and physically draining. It's also quite dangerous. You are working high up, and quite often there are hidden wires and cables. My dad has been electrocuted a few times. One time, the current passed straight through him and blew two holes out of his knee-pads. The other danger is a financial one. There have been a few times when companies have asked for a new roof, knowing their business was about to go bankrupt. If they didn't pay up then my old man would have to go around and sort things out. I'd normally wait in the van.

It was tough work, but I enjoyed it. In the summer months it would mean 6am starts because once the bitumen becomes sticky in the mid-day heat then it's impossible to remove. That meant early finishes and time to train or else go down the beach with my mates.

Dad was also a good payer and it meant I had a bit of cash in my pocket. It was good fun and I enjoyed working for him. It helped with my fitness. But one full summer was enough. My dad works extremely hard and only employs one person to help him. There's a fairly rapid turnover as no-one sticks it for long. My cousin is doing it at the moment. We'll see how he goes.

As a kid, a huge hero of mine was Scott Gibbs and he was a big part of the reason I joined Swansea. I had huge respect for him as a player and I liked his honesty. Whenever he was interviewed, he gave it to you straight with none of the usual bullshit. I had followed his career closely as he was from my village of Pencoed. I can remember watching him on TV, making his Wales debut against England along with Neil Jenkins when they were both 19. I was eight-years-old at the time. Scott's first club was Neath and one of my prized possessions as a child was a Neath jersey bought for me by my father. It was special because Scott had signed his name across the white of the emblem of the Maltese Cross. He'd signed it at some function in Pencoed Rugby Club, although it wasn't me who approached him. I think I was too scared to ask, but part of me didn't want to look in awe of him, either. In fact, I was always like that and I don't remember ever asking a single rugby player for his autograph. But dad must have known I would like Scott's signature and he managed to get it.

My other significant childhood memory of Scott was

from 1993. He got nicked by the police for driving away a taxi after he'd had a few beers with his mates. He only moved it a few yards down the road but it became big news in Pencoed, especially when he had to go to court and there was a cloud hanging over his participation for the Lions tour to New Zealand. He eventually went on tour and at 21 he got into the Test side, ahead of Will Carling. When he came home the whole of Pencoed turned out to welcome him. It was a real, massive day in the village.

Scott went on to be a hero in both rugby union and rugby league, and was the man-of-the-series in the 1997 Lions tour to South Africa. By 2000 he was still one of the biggest names in rugby and captain of Swansea, but he was very helpful to me as an 18-year-old because he just treated me as another senior player – someone who deserved to be there. He was a great captain, the best skipper I've ever played under. I loved his attitude and was especially taken by the way he just switched on when training started. We only did very short sessions of an hour, but for those 60 minutes he would insist we went at 100mph and were completely focused. Everything had to be needle sharp. Once we had finished, we'd be off and changed. Methods have altered and nowadays everything is much longer and more drawn out. Everyone stops to have their say these days but I'm not sure it's a big improvement.

Scott's attitude was a big influence on me and it was

a brilliant experience to be around him and the other senior players. There was an air of mystery about him. After matches he would be the first to leave and jump into his car. Once the match was over, he was gone. Sometimes he wouldn't even bother showering. He didn't want to sit around and chit-chat. A few players found his approach unsettling, but I didn't. I admired him for it and could completely understand his desire for a quick getaway. I often feel that way myself.

As I became more established, I became good friends with Scott. He liked to switch off from rugby and as soon as he came off the field, he wanted to do something else entirely. He'd be packing his stuff into his bag as some players were still coming through the dressing room door and he'd lean over to me and whisper, 'Fancy coming out tonight?' and I'd say, 'Aye, alright.' So we'd go off to Cardiff and he'd take me to some little exclusive club where everyone seemed to know him. It was an eye-opener. I enjoyed Scott's company and as he lived not far from me in Wick I would give him lifts to Swansea for training and matches. We had a good rapport.

But Scott wasn't the only strong personality in the Swansea dressing room. Garin Jenkins, Colin Charvis, Mark Taylor, Darren Morris – they all had a positive influence on me when I first arrived at the club. But there was a difficult side to trying to make my way there, too. As an 18-year-old I wanted to do everything by the book in terms of my fitness and preparation. I liked the idea of being a total professional. But there were a group of players that the youngsters did well to stay clear of. The guys that lived in Swansea – Morris, Charvis, Andy Moore and Dean Thomas – were all good characters but they just loved to go out on the piss. They were good fun, socially, but it was easy to get sucked into and professionally not very advisable. When the club went into the dark days of administration, I dealt with it by mixing in the same social circles as those players but that was mainly because the whole rugby side of things was just collapsing around our ears.

Rugby and drinking have always gone together, but I've never found it an easy mix. That summer of 2000 when I joined Swansea, John Plumtree decided we needed a 'bonding session' to pull the whole squad together before the season started. The bonding consisted of a drinking marathon down the sea-front from St. Helen's in Mumbles, a village where the pubs and bars are all within easy staggering distance of each other. Dean Thomas, the Swansea flanker at the time and a hard player, grabbed me and insisted I start off matching him round for round. I was even more of a hopeless drinker then than I am now and it wasn't very long before I was completely leathered. I may have 'bonded' with Dean but I don't remember much about it. Too smashed to go on, I rang my parents and my father drove the 30 miles from Bridgend to come and pick me up. I spewed all the way home but dad didn't seem too shocked. I think he understood.

I may not be much good at drinking, but I think there is definitely a place for it in professional rugby. Every once in a blue moon – as a way of getting every player to feel part of a solid group – it certainly has a value. Some of Plum's team-talks before a game were legendary. 'Right, guys, let's give this lot a fucking spanking and then we're all out tonight to get smashed. Let's go.' That summed up Plum's methods. Short, sharp training sessions in the week. Get out and do the business on the Saturday. Go out and hit the town. It was quite basic stuff, but John was shrewd enough to have others around him with different skills and personalities. Clive Griffiths – a former rugby league coach – came in and organised our defensive systems. Clive was meticulous, organised, and really knew his stuff. He was a good foil to Plum and the pair made an effective coaching team.

At this time, Wales were coached by Graham Henry and the first time I met him I thought he was brilliant. He had an aura about him and he seemed to know exactly the right thing to do, the right thing to say. In the summer of 2000 it was announced that Henry would coach the Lions the following year for their tour of Australia. That's when he started to take his eye off the ball. Certainly, when he came back from the Lions tour he was a different man. Instead of being approachable, he was remote. He also seemed less sure of himself. His ability to get results deserted him and when that goes so does that aura as far as players are concerned. His doubts became their doubts.

My first conversation with Henry came in November of 2000, just a couple of months into my Swansea career. He picked me to play outside-half for a Wales Development XV against the USA at Neath. We won 46–20. Henry seemed very switched on and full of hints. His advice seemed well worth listening to and I made sure I paid full attention.

Later on that season, Henry selected me again for a match between Wales and the Barbarians. It wasn't a full-capped game as Henry, quite rightly, felt that would devalue the honour. So, although I came off the bench to replace Neil Jenkins, it was not my first Welsh cap. That didn't bother me. I knew I wouldn't have to wait long. I had been named by Henry as a member of the Wales squad that was off to tour Japan that summer. What's more, Henry came up to me after the Barbarians match and said: 'Well done. Enjoy the trip. You'll be starting both Tests at No. 10.' I thought, fantastic. I'd have gone through the lot in my first season – Wales Under-19s, Wales Under-21s, Wales A, and finally a full Wales cap. I couldn't wait to get on the plane.

Henry himself, of course, was not going to Japan. He selected the squad and then jetted off to Australia where his Lions lost 2–1 to the Wallabies in a very close series.

I wasn't worried about his absence. I assumed he'd briefed the coaches who were in charge. I thought he would have told them exactly what he wanted. Lynn Howells, who was Henry's forwards coach with Wales, was the senior coach in Japan and his assistants were Geraint John, Leigh Jones and Clive Griffiths.

Our first game was in Tokyo against Suntory, the champion club side, and we were just edged out, 45–41. I played at No. 10, with Stephen Jones at No. 12. I thought I'd played reasonably well but it was difficult. It was the first time Steve and I had played together and because we were both then very much outside-halves we kept getting in each other's way. After the game the coaches mulled things over and decided it wasn't a good idea to go into the Test against Japan with two guys who shared a favourite position. The solution they reached was to pick Steve at No.10 and leave me out. I spent the rest of the tour sitting on the bench.

We struggled past a Japan Select XV but then won the first Test, 64–10. The fourth match brought another defeat as we lost to the Pacific Barbarians, but I stayed on the bench for the second Test line-up, too. I felt miserable and just wanted to go home. I could tell the coaches didn't have any faith in me and that there was nothing I could do to change their minds. It felt like the Wales Schools situation all over again. Rejection . . . devastation . . . misery.

I didn't get on with Lynn at all. I don't really know

why. We just didn't hit it off. I tend to make instant judgements of people and one of the things I decide is whether or not they believe in me. Lynn, it seemed to me, obviously didn't.

The whole experience became soul-destroying. I was really looking forward to starting the Tests as the No.10, calling the shots, as Henry had suggested. Instead, I was sitting on the bench watching others. It felt so bad that I couldn't even celebrate my first cap for Wales. In the final few minutes of the first Test I came on as a replacement full-back for Kevin Morgan. Lynn didn't seem to have any intention of putting me on and I think Kevin did me a favour. He signalled to the bench that he was hurt, knowing that it might be my last chance of the tour to get a cap. As I passed Kevin he looked at me and winked. I came on, but didn't feel proud. I felt nothing. For years, when I'd dreamed of playing my first match for Wales, I'd imagined the Millennium Stadium, a packed crowd, England on the other side, 70,000 Welshmen signing the national anthem. But here I was, running on for the last five minutes in a half-empty stadium in Osaka, thanks to a favour from a mate. It didn't feel good.

We won the match, 64–10, thanks to tries from players who would later go on to become my Wales team-mates. Shane Williams scored four, to equal the Welsh record, Kevin Morgan got two, and Gareth 'Alfie' Thomas scored as well. But those days as a Wales regular were still a long, long way off for me. I was an outsider, and although I'd been capped, I still felt an outsider. Adrian Durston, Andy Lloyd and Gavin Thomas had made their debuts from the start and it was arranged that we'd all go out and celebrate that evening after the game. But I couldn't face it. I went back to my room, instead, and stayed in, sulking.

The last week in Japan felt like a long one. I didn't get on the field for the second Test, so Kevin's hunch proved a good one. Not that my cap made me feel much better. I think Lynn Howells felt I should have been content with being able to sit on the Welsh bench at 19, even though I'd expected more. At any level of rugby, sitting on the replacements' bench is not a pleasant experience. The only time I ever get nervous in rugby is when I'm sitting on the bench. It's that element of uncertainty, the feeling that you could be rushed on at any minute. When you start a match, you have time to prepare for the moment you kick-off. You can count down the minutes and prepare yourself mentally. But from the bench, it's just an anxious wait all the time. You're constantly on edge. And when you do get sent on, you feel unnatural as it takes a while to adjust to the pace of any match. The other thing that strikes me watching from the bench is just how physical the sport really is. You are close to the action. You can hear the hits. You can almost feel them. When you are on the field, you have to concentrate so hard that the brutal nature of what's going on around you doesn't quite sink in. On the bench, it's stripped bare.

Fortunately for me, Graham Henry's faith in my ability didn't seem to have disappeared just because of my problems on the Japan tour. There was an early season international match at home to Romania and although the 10 Welsh Lions had all come back from Australia, Neil Jenkins had been ruled out until Christmas with a knee injury. That provided an opening at outside-half and Henry decided to pick me there, with Stephen Jones at inside centre ahead of Scott Gibbs. Most of the other Lions tourists were back – Colin Charvis, Dafydd James, Rob Howley, Robin McBryde, Dai Young – and I felt incredibly excited. I'd had a false start, but this felt like a proper first cap. Again, though, it was a match that ended in massive anti-climax.

Around 15 minutes into the game, I took a bang on the hip. It didn't feel too bad at the time but because the impact was right on the bone it became sore very quickly. Within a few minutes I couldn't even run. It was just too painful. Mark Davies, the Wales physio, came on to the field and I told him I was struggling. He checked it out, but decided straight away there wasn't much he could do. I'd have to come off.

I felt gutted. Here was the opportunity I'd really wanted and it had backfired. Stephen switched to No.10 and had a really good game against strictly limited opposition. Wales scored 11 tries and won 81–9. Everyone seemed happy – except me. The only way I could get my head around what had happened was to think I'd get another chance fairly soon. Instead, a week or so later I was told Henry wanted to see me in his office in Cardiff. I didn't think things could get worse, but they did.

'Gavin, you need to have a little think about your career,' he said. 'You need to decide what position you are going to play.' I told him I was a No. 10. That was the position I had always played, it was where I enjoyed playing, and I wanted to stay there. 'Well, the thing is Gavin, I've already got two good No. 10s in Neil Jenkins and Stephen Jones. They are my first and second choice. Then it's you.' I was stunned. It wasn't that I expected to be told I was first choice. Neil was a legend and Stephen was a class act. But Henry seemed to have written me off from ever being an international outside-half on the basis of 20 minutes against Romania, most of which I'd spent hobbling around. I couldn't believe it. 'Okay,' I said. 'I'll give it some thought.' I came away feeling very demoralised. I'd never wanted to play in any other position. Henry had appeared to believe in me. Now, it seemed he'd changed his mind after some pretty dubious evidence.

Within a few weeks we were preparing for the November internationals and two new faces were now part of the Wales squad. The first was Iestyn Harris, who had switched codes from rugby league. The deal attracted massive publicity because Iestyn was a major star and for the fact that it had cost the Welsh Rugby Union £1.5 million to get him. The other new bloke was a grim-faced Kiwi who made Graham Henry look like one half of the Chuckle Brothers. His name was Steve Hansen and he had just been hired from the Canterbury Crusaders as Henry's new right-hand man. Pretty soon, though, these two were settled in the squad and it was me who was on the outside looking in. And it was all my own fault.

I was in a squad meeting at the Vale of Glamorgan Hotel. Hansen had just been introduced to everyone and it was the first meeting he had sat in on. Henry was talking and everyone was listening. He went on about the matches against Argentina, Tonga and Australia, about what the game-plan was going to be, about Iestyn, about Stephen, about the squad he would use and the players who would be involved. It was all a bit of a lecture. The old Henry, who was full of quick remarks and sounded really fired-up, had been replaced by someone who seemed strangely distant and a bit unsure. The rapport with the players wasn't there any more. What was certain, though, to me, was that I wasn't going to be required. With Iestyn there, and Neil to come back, I wasn't third choice as Henry had said. I was fourth. Suddenly, I stopped listening. I just didn't want to be there any more. I had to get out. I got up from my seat – I think they thought I was going to the toilet – but I kept on walking straight out of the main door and into the car park. I got in my car and drove home. I didn't know it then, but it would be two years before I pulled on a Wales shirt again, and three years until I started a game.

I still really don't know why I walked out. It was just one of those daft things you do when you're young. It obviously didn't endear me to Graham Henry – who never picked me again – and it wasn't exactly getting off on the right foot with Hanson, either. Rupert Moon, who was some kind of players' adviser employed by Henry, rang me on my mobile as I was driving away. 'What are you playing at?' he said. I told him I'd just had enough and after a while he gave up trying to convince me to come back.

Normally, my parents back my rugby decisions, but this time they weren't happy. They thought I was being ridiculous and that the only person I was really harming was myself. They were probably right, but I couldn't see it like that. I just didn't want to go back. My interest in playing for Wales that season had just all drained away.

Back at club level it was going well for me again, but I had no real hopes of being named in the Six Nations squad for the 2002 tournament. Henry was still in charge and even though he quit after the opening match thrashing against Ireland, my chances of a recall didn't exactly improve when Hansen was named as his successor. I managed to slip straight through the Wales

A squad and found myself back with the Wales Under-21s. In the space of a few short months, I'd climbed right up the ladder and then come all the way back down again. At least nothing could go wrong within the Wales Under-21s squad and I could start re-building my career. Or so I thought.

Things started promisingly. We beat Ireland Under-21s, 38–36, in an incredible match in Dublin where I scored the winning try in injury time. But we lost 30–22 at home to France in our next game and I was dropped to make way for Nicky Robinson. It meant I was now back on the bench, where things had a habit of turning out badly. The match was at home to Italy at The Brewery Field, Bridgend. We were all in the dressing rooms before the game when the kit was handed out. It looked a bit suspect to me, as if it had shrunk in the wash. A few boys managed to stretch themselves into things but when I came to put on my red socks I noticed that one of them was three times shorter than the other. I tried to pull it on, but it was useless. 'I need a different pair of socks,' I said to the team manager, Wayne Hall. Fine, they said, but put this black pair on for the warm-up while we find you a new pair of red ones. I did as they said. I didn't want to cause a fuss. I'd had enough of causing a fuss. We came back in from the warm-up and I put on the new pair that had been found for me. It was the same pair as before. Things were getting a bit ridiculous now because the referee had called the teams to come out and the anthems were about to be played. Just stick it on for now and we'll sort it out later, they said. But I couldn't get it over my foot. I decided to sit it out and wait for the new pair. Eventually, a new pair was found and I ran out to take my place on the bench. By this stage, however, the anthems had long gone and the game was five minutes old.

I dismissed it as irritating, but no big drama. I came on for the last 10 minutes of the match and we ran out comfortable winners, 65–12. A couple of days later, Wayne got in touch with me and said we needed to talk. We met in a Harvester restaurant at Sarn Services on the M4. While the waitresses dashed about, and little kids pushed each other in and out of the ball-pit, Wayne leaned across the table. 'Look, Gav. This is a difficult one for me,' he explained. 'The committee members on the Union. They're not happy about the sock.' It seemed that in the midst of Wales' record defeat to Ireland, Henry's resignation, and all the rest of the chaos, my socks had become a major issue. Another problem was raised. They were unhappy with me for not wearing the proper blazer at the game in Dublin. I had explained to them that I'd never been given the proper blazer – someone had assumed I'd still have one from the previous year – but this didn't seem to have cut any ice. The upshot of all these kit crimes was that people felt my whole attitude was out of control.

I should have just bit my lip and counted to 10. I should have learnt my lesson. But I just couldn't believe how these things could really count against a player involved in international rugby. So I freaked out and withdrew from the squad before the game against England Under-21s.

It wasn't a proper walk-out, like the one before. I had a slight illness, which offered me a way out. I could have played at a pinch and they knew it. But I felt bitter so I used the illness as an excuse to withdraw from the squad. The result was that I was overlooked for the final match of the championship against the Scots. So, now I had nowhere to go – no more bridges left to burn. I'd gone through the lot.

The Wales Under-21s squad were off to South Africa that summer for the Under-21s World Cup. I made myself unavailable. I can't really recall my reasons. That whole period is a bit of a blur. My head was in a bit of a mess. I don't think I really felt that the coaches had faith in me, so I decided not to go through another bad experience. I knew I couldn't cope with another set-back.

After John Plumtree had gone, Swansea appointed John Connolly as coach. John was an Australian and someone I had a lot of time for. He had some great ideas and he was a bloke you wanted to do well for. But before he had time to get his feet under the desk, lots of players left the club for more money on offer elsewhere. He was also badly undermined by some of the senior players who didn't seem to take to him or his methods. We would be in team meetings and John would outline the approach he wanted for a particular game. But as soon as he left the room, senior guys like Darren Morris would say, 'Don't listen to him. That's not going to work. This is the way we're going to play it.' It was a ridiculous situation for any new coach to be in.

Morris summed up a lot of what was wrong at the club. You couldn't argue at his talent. He could have been one of the best props in world rugby. He had all the skills. But he just didn't want to work. His diet and his off-the-field habits meant his fitness was never what it should have been. I also found Charvis a difficult character to work out and never really got on with him. He was captain of Wales at this time and seemed to be on a bit of a power trip. He tried to give me advice about being professional off the pitch, but there was an air of superiority to it. That felt hard to take because although he was a naturally fit guy, he loved to go out on the piss as much as anyone. The drinking culture at the club didn't seem to affect results in my first season. Morris, Charvis, Moore – they'd all be out – but they would do the business on the field on the Saturday and we won the title. Results started to slip in my second season once Plumtree had gone, and Connolly was unable to stabilise things in that third season. Then, the financial problems struck and everything fell to pieces. The club went into administration. It was carnage.

Before that mess erupted, though, there were some other lessons to be learned. On 4 October 2002 we played an away match at Llanelli. These derby matches always got the juices flowing, for both players and fans, and this one proved no exception. The rivalry between the squads had been simmering since Swansea's 'break-away' season three years before and infamous 'men against boys' Welsh Cup Final. Gibbsy had whipped up a storm with that remark and he was at the centre of things again in the build-up to the first clash of this season. BBC Wales were showing the game live on TV on Friday night on their 'Scrum V' programme. Before the game, they always show clips from players being ever-so respectful about the other side. But in the interviews filmed in the build-up to this match, there was plenty of disrespect flowing in both directions. Leigh Davies, the Llanelli captain, said he was expecting plenty of 'cheap shots' from Swansea as he claimed that was always our method. Scott took the bait and said, yeah, his side used cheap shots – and promised there'd be plenty more coming in their direction on Friday.

Of course, it was all over the Welsh papers all week – big headlines. By kick-off time there was a real edge at Stradey Park and the fans were whipping themselves up into a frenzy. It felt great to be in the middle of such passion and excitement. I was playing on the wing and anxious to get involved early on to get settled. As it turned out, the ball just didn't come my way and it was 30 minutes before I had my first touch. By then, our flanker, Dean Thomas, had been sent to the sin bin before Scott and Llanelli's big Tongan, Salesi Finau, were warned for a punch-up. I chased a long kick down field and watched as Garan Evans, their full-back, dived on the ball near the touchline. I didn't want to give a penalty away so I waited until he got up. But he didn't. So I picked him up, while he was holding the ball, and threw him over the touchline. The problem was I had my back to the advertising hoardings, so I had no real idea of how close I was. Garan is quite slight for a rugby player and so he flew a fair way. I was also very frustrated at not having touched the ball, so I put a lot of effort in. Suddenly, there was a big bang as he hit the boards, before falling in a heap on the ground. The next thing I knew, Finau was trying to knock my head off with a punch – and probably would have done if I hadn't ducked – before the whole of the Llanelli side came racing over to join in. 'Oh, shit,' I thought, and started backing away. There were a few more punches thrown by both sides and the crowd started to go nuts before the referee, David McHugh, managed to calm things down. The Scarlets fans had given me a lot of stick that night. They always do. At the time my hair was dyed silver to match my boots – I thought it was a great haircut – but the fans at Stradey probably felt it was a bit flash. 'Oi, Henson! You twat, you're goin' off for that,' someone shouted. 'Look, he's got a chip pan on his head!' 'More like a fuckin' bog brush.' 'Don't worry. Finau's gonna get him.' The abuse went on for ages as McHugh called me over. I don't mind the stick from the Llanelli fans. In fact, I quite enjoy it and I'm sure they do. It reminds me of the stuff that used to make me laugh when I was a kid watching Maesteg. It's part of what Welsh rugby is about and, hopefully, always will be.

McHugh didn't hang about. 'You threw him into the hoardings. That's a straight red.' I just said, okay, and I walked off. It was the first and only time I've ever been sent off. It was a mistake on my part, but I'm not ashamed about it. People have done far worse on a rugby field.

I walked into the dressing room and sat down. I just wanted to get out of there so I tried to phone a taxi. The next minute, there was a massive noise which sounded like someone was trying to kick the door in. For a moment I thought the Llanelli players must have followed me in. But it was Dean Thomas. He'd just been sent off for a high tackle and was taking out his frustrations on the dressing room door until a policeman intervened. He looked at me and tried to say something, but he was so angry he couldn't get any words out. We both just sat there.

Swansea lost that game 62–6, but with just 13 players

on the field it could actually have been a lot worse. I received a four-week ban but Connolly was sympathetic and so it was never a disciplinary issue within the club. Garan didn't make a meal of it, but then he'd have his own back just before the 2003 World Cup. If I didn't know it already, that game showed me just how intense and tribal the rivalry is between Swansea and Llanelli. It's still there, even though it's now in the regional form of the Ospreys against the Scarlets. The towns may only be 15 miles apart but they may as well be at different ends of the universe.

When rugby in Wales went over to a regional structure in order to survive, I joined the Neath-Swansea Ospreys. I was offered a deal by the Newport Gwent Dragons, who were coached by Mike Ruddock at the time. But I'd always had a sneaking regard for Neath and for their coach, Lyn Jones. They took the best players from both Swansea and Neath and added a few more from outside. It proved to be one of my better decisions.

Out of the blue, I had a call from the Wales coach Steve Hansen in February 2003. He said he wanted me to play for the Under-21s but if I turned them down I'd never play for Wales again. It was up to me. We talked it over and he told me a few home truths. He said he respected my talent, but not my attitude. I also chatted with Scott Johnson, an Australian who came over as skills coach under Graham Henry, and is now right-hand man to Mike Ruddock. Johnno has become a huge influence for me and it was that conversation with him two years ago that convinced me I had to get back on the ladder. He said I needed to forget the past and concentrate on the future. It was time to wipe the slate clean and make a fresh start, back with the Under-21 side. He also said he wanted them to play me at inside centre because that was the position in which he saw my international future. I mulled it over and thought he might be right.

CHAPTER EIGHT

You're Not Going

The World Cup was due to kick-off on 10 October 2003 and it was date imprinted on every Welsh player's mind. It was certainly on mine. I was 21 years old and it had been two years since I had played my first game for Wales. There'd been some stumbles along the way, but having regained my place in the senior squad I really imagined I'd found my feet again. All I had to do, I thought, was to stay fit, train hard, play well and keep out of trouble and I'd be off to the biggest rugby tournament of them all.

Like every other country, Wales went into a playing and training frenzy in those few months before the tournament started. The tournament rules did not allow countries to turn up early and acclimatise, so all our work had to be done in Wales. No detail was left to chance. Steve Hansen even had large heaters, powered by generators, installed at our Vale of Glamorgan indoor

In the shadow of the dragon. Everyone who plays for Wales is aware of the symbolism the game represents for a small nation fighting against the odds. I'm no different.

ABOVE: Alive and kicking. I've always loved kicking, whether it's in a Test match or in practice for the Ospreys.

LEFT: Lean on me. Stephen Jones helps takes the strain in Rome before our game against Italy in the Six Nations.

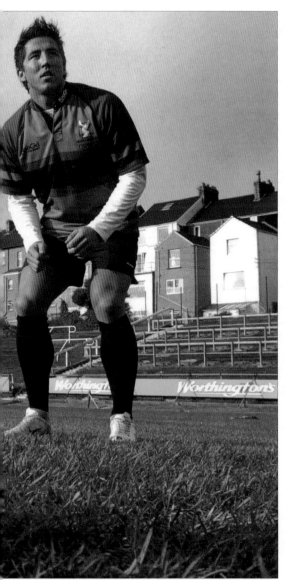

TOP: Royal ascent. Winning the Grand Slam led to a meeting with HRH Prince Charles, the Prince of Wales, at a celebratory function in May.

ABOVE: Out on the town. I still like to socialise now and again when training and playing commitments allow it.

LEFT: Signed and sealed. Hopefully, our Grand Slam success has inspired a whole new generation of Welsh youngsters.

ABOVE: Catch 'em young. I managed to get to grips with teenager Mathew Tait, on his international debut, with two big tackles early on in the match against England.

RIGHT: Getting shirty. Mathew got his revenge later when he pulled off this saving tackle by hanging on to my shirt. Next time, I'll have it tucked in.

RIGHT: Just for kicks. The 50-metre penalty that clinched our victory over England at the Millennium Stadium. As soon as I'd struck it, I knew it was going over.

ABOVE: Flying high. The final whistle goes, we've beaten England, and I already feel as though I'm on cloud nine.

RIGHT: Captain of industry. The joy is evident on the face of our skipper Gareth Thomas – known to everyone in the game as Alfie – as he gives me a winners' hug.

RIGHT: Glory boys. Gareth Thomas and Michael Owen – our two captains during the tournament – lift the RBS Six Nations trophy after we clinched the Grand Slam.

ABOVE: Roman conquest. I manage to hand off an Italian tackler at the Stadio Flaminio in Rome where Wales romped to a 38–8 victory.

RIGHT: Running man. My Wales and Ospreys team-mate Shane Williams was at his brilliant, elusive best in the second-half in Paris. But this time he is pinned by France's Serge Betsen.

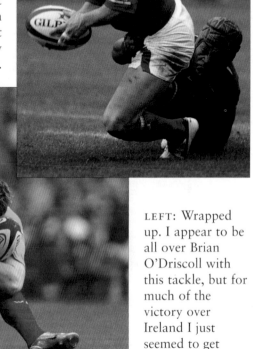

LEFT: Wrapped up. I appear to be all over Brian O'Driscoll with this tackle, but for much of the victory over Ireland I just seemed to get under his skin.

ABOVE: Eyes on the job. Like all goal-kickers I have a set routine before every kick.

BELOW: Pointing to the exit. Former Wales coach Steve Hansen and current team manager Alan Phillips. My international career stalled until Hansen left to go back to New Zealand.

Silver Service. I like wearing silver and gold boots. I've always admired the sight of certain soccer players in silver and gold boots because it emphasised their quick feet.

Tee time. Off to a goal-kicking session in Paris before our Six Nations match against France, with water and kicking tee in hand.

training centre as a way of trying to replicate the heat and humidity we would experience in Australia. There was also a busy schedule of matches to get the squad battle-hardened and to make sure everyone was familiar with our style. We were due to play Ireland, England, Romania and Scotland before the squad of 30 players would be announced in the first week of September.

I was included in the July training squad of 44, which was mainly made up of those who had toured in the summer, plus others who were on their way back from injury, such as Iestyn Harris. Hansen viewed the four matches as nothing more than training exercises on the road to the World Cup and repeatedly told the media that 'results were not important' and that all that mattered were 'performances.' The trouble was that when results had mattered – in the Six Nations – Wales had lost the lot. That meant, added to the defeats the previous autumn, plus the two Test defeats in the summer, the team was on a nine-match losing streak. The performances hadn't been great, either, so it was inevitable that people would start to question the coach's record. In Wales, that level of scrutiny is intense. With rugby being so high profile it's the equivalent of being the manager of the England soccer team or of Manchester United. The pressure was obviously getting to Steve and there was an infamous TV interview before one game where he lost his temper and began 'effing and blinding.

The first of the warm-up games was against Ireland in Dublin. They put out all their big guns – Brian O'Driscoll, Keith Wood, Malcolm O'Kelly and the rest – while Steve picked an experimental-looking side. The experiment didn't seem to reveal much. Wales lost 35–12 and by five tries to two.

I hadn't been involved in that match, but nor had lots of other players considered strong candidates for World Cup selection. I felt more relieved when I was picked on the bench for the England game at the Millennium Stadium on 23 August. This looked a much more familiar squad and this time it was England who experimented. But England's second string completely overran us that afternoon and the result was an absolute hammering, 43–9. Lewis Moody, Dan Luger, Joe Worsley, Stuart Abbott and Dorian West all scored tries against us and yet not one of them was an England regular at that time. All we could manage were three penalties from Stephen Jones. At the final whistle, the Welsh players were booed off the pitch. I didn't get on the field, but once again it might not have been a bad one to miss.

A few days later, we played the Romanians up in Wrexham. Again, Hansen picked a team that was generally viewed as featuring a lot of players who might not get to Australia. The onus was on us to make an impression, both individually and collectively, in order to press our claims. Hansen himself didn't actually coach the side for this match. He handed things over to Mike Ruddock, who was Wales A coach at the time, while Hansen remained in Cardiff with the players who would play against Scotland.

Romania are always the whipping boys – every autumn they turn up to get drubbed – and this was no exception. But you can only try and be as accurate and clinical as possible and I felt we did that. We scored six tries and won 54–8. I kicked 24 points and didn't miss once in 10 attempts. We all knew it was 'only Romania' but Mike was pleased, it broke the 11-match losing streak, and I felt my own performance had gone well.

The pressure on Hansen was now pretty intense with lots of former international players calling for him to resign. His position looked bleak going into the last of the four August games, at home to Scotland. There were claims in the media that he really was in the last chance saloon. But the team responded well to the pressure on him and battled out a 23–9 win, although it was a pretty uninspiring game to watch – which is exactly what I was forced to do. I didn't make the squad of 22 for that game, either, but I still felt I'd go to the World Cup. I had made the 22 for the biggest game, against England. Even if I wasn't in his first choice 15 or 22, I still thought I was in Hansen's favoured next eight players. I had trained with the squad all the way through the summer and felt those sessions had gone well.

In the week of the World Cup announcement, things

seemed to be going well. I had begun the season in good form for the new region, the Neath-Swansea Ospreys, and had been playing regularly at full-back. It was another position I enjoyed and felt comfortable in. I felt it provided another string to my bow as I could cover four positions for the World Cup squad – outside-half, centre, full-back and wing. My team-mates at the Ospreys also kept telling me I was bound to make the squad and I think I believed them.

The night before he revealed his squad, Hansen rang me. 'Gavin, I've got some bad news for you, mate. I haven't picked you.' I was dumbstruck and there was a silence. He said it again. I felt sick, physically sick. My head started throbbing and my stomach was turning over. It felt like being 18 again and left out of the Welsh Schools, or two years before that and the same thing with the Under-16s. The shock, the churning feeling in the pit of my stomach, the anger . . . it all tasted so sour and so horribly familiar. 'What? Are you serious?' I said. I think he seemed a bit taken aback by that. He probably expected me to tell him I was disappointed, but thanks for the call and best of luck for the tournament. Bollocks to that. I was way, way beyond that. It felt like the worst news of my life. I had trained hard, I'd done everything they had asked in terms of switching position and going back to the Under-21 squad. And yet still I was missing out on the tournament I had dreamed about for years. The World Cup meant everything to me and I wasn't going to be involved. He mumbled something about wanting a bit more pace from his full-back. I asked him who he was taking instead of me. 'Garan Evans.' At that point I just laughed. 'Garan Evans? You honestly think Garan Evans is a better choice than me?' Garan was the guy I had thrown into the perimeter fence the previous season, when I was sent off at Llanelli. He was a good full-back and was versatile enough to play on the wing. But he didn't play in any other position. He was also a lot smaller than me and I felt he was physically vulnerable at the very top level. 'Look,' said Hansen. 'I can see you're upset. Come over to my office tomorrow morning and we'll talk things through.'

Yeah, right, I thought. Like that's going to make a big difference. I told him I'd see him there but I didn't sleep much that night and I was still devastated when I got up the next day. I drove straight to the Vale of Glamorgan complex and walked up to Hansen's office. The anger hadn't died down. It was still buzzing around my head and ready to come pouring out of my mouth.

I knocked on his door and went in. He repeated the stuff he'd come out with the previous night but it still made no sense to me. I just sat there, staring at the floor and shaking my head. I told him he'd got it wrong. He'd made a mistake. I was a better option than Garan. I was more physical, more durable, I'd met all the fitness targets I'd been set by the Wales fitness coach, Andrew Hore. I'd been playing well for the Ospreys, plus I offered an extra goal-kicking option as I'd proved against Romania. As for the issue of pace, Garan may well have been quicker than me over a 40-metre sprint, but I'd worked hard on that area of my game and I still felt that overall I should have been in his top 30 players. I felt better having got things off my chest, but he wasn't going to change his mind. We shook hands and I left.

I felt let down and harboured my resentment over the next few weeks. But I refused to let it affect my form for the Ospreys. That's one thing I've never done. I may not be the best at handling rejection, but I never allow my next performance on the field to suffer. When the World Cup started, I watched all the matches on TV as Wales made their way past Canada, Tonga and Italy. They weren't very convincing in any of those pool matches but they did enough to qualify for the quarter-finals before they met New Zealand in their last game of the group stages. It also happened to be Garan Evans' first start of the tournament. After two minutes, Joe Rokocoko scored the All Blacks' opening try and then two minutes later the same player bumped off Garan in the tackle. They brought a stretcher onto the field, scraped up Garan, and carried him off. He was injured and out of the tournament and it wasn't long before he was put on a plane and sent back to Wales. Watching him last only four minutes just brought back all my frustrations. I should have been there. I should have been wearing that shirt against the All Blacks and I knew I would have been physically strong enough to cope.

It's strange how things work out. After Garan went off in that game, Gareth Thomas got switched to full-back and did superbly. He's been in that position for Wales ever since and he went on to sign for Toulouse and become a European champion. But it was only through circumstance that Hansen stumbled across Alfie's suitability as an international full-back. I'll never know what might have happened if I'd gone to the tournament and played at No.15. The other big talking point after that All Blacks match was whether the positive, attack-minded playing style revealed that day was Hansen's idea or the players'. I wasn't there so it's difficult to know the truth of the matter. A lot of Welsh players in that squad had huge respect for Hansen, but sometimes real belief is sparked by those actually out on the field during a game. Wales lost that match to New Zealand, 53–37, but they won a lot of new friends and admirers for the way they played. I was one of them and I was willing them to beat England in the quarter-finals in Brisbane, especially when they were 10–3 ahead at half-time. England sent on Mike Catt and managed to steady the ship and they eventually won 28–17 on their way to winning the tournament. But players such as my two Ospreys colleagues – Shane Williams and Jonathan Thomas – had really come of age at the tournament. I was pleased for them. They're great mates and superb players. But it also highlighted my own situation. While they were appearing on the world stage and letting everyone know who they were, I was back home in Pencoed watching it all on the telly. I don't mind watching rugby if it's a game between two teams that have no relevance to me. But if it's my team, and I'm not playing for some reason, then I hate it. Watching that game against England was a real struggle, emotionally. Part of me wanted to turn it off because it hurt so much not to be out there. Another part of me was cheering on Wales, like three million other Welsh supporters.

While the World Cup was going on, the Celtic League continued – only without all the Welsh, Irish and Scottish current international players who were out in Australia. I had chosen to join the Neath-Swansea Ospreys and rejected a few other offers. There were a couple of English clubs who were keen to sign me, but I wanted to remain in Wales for the time being. The other opportunity came from another of the Welsh regions, the Newport Gwent Dragons. As things had ended sourly with Swansea, I gave the Dragons offer a lot of thought. Mike Ruddock, who was the Dragons coach at the time, came to my house and I was impressed by his positive attitude. Lyn Jones had been appointed to coach the Ospreys and he was someone I didn't know at the time. All I knew of Lyn were the stories you heard from Neath players, most of which painted him as some kind of complete nutter.

I didn't really know what to do. The fact that I ended up at the Ospreys was actually down to Steve Hansen. That summer – before he left me out of his plans for the World Cup – Hansen rang me and asked me what I was intending to do. I was unsure, so he went through a list of questions which appeared to lead me down the road of favouring the Ospreys. Perhaps that was his intention, I don't really know. Either way I decided to go with the Ospreys – probably because I knew more of the players there than I did with the Dragons – and it's a decision I've never regretted. Money was not really a factor. I just wanted to make the right decision for rugby reasons. The Dragons have done quite well to establish themselves, but the Ospreys are generally accepted as having led the other regions both on and off the field. We are the current Celtic League champions and we've got a brilliant new stadium in Swansea that is the envy of the other three regions.

We are only two years into the history of the Ospreys, but already it's hard to believe just how much animosity there was in some quarters to the whole notion of that merger and to regional rugby in general. Swansea and Neath were age-old rivals and lots of people predicted it was never going to work. I never really shared that view. As a Swansea player, I knew that it was far more likely to succeed than the other mooted merger between Swansea and Llanelli. This was the alliance favoured by the WRU, but it would never have worked. Never in a million years. Swansea and Llanelli are very different types of places. It seems to me that Llanelli has always seen itself as the team that represents a region anyway, the whole large area of West Wales. People in Swansea view Llanelli folk as foreigners, even though they're only 15 miles away. It was certainly like that when I was at Swansea. Neath people were considered almost normal, but people from Llanelli were weird. They spoke funny and had a different outlook. As a Swansea player, there was a rivalry with Neath. With Llanelli, it was more of a hatred.

Neath and Swansea came together to form the Neath-Swansea Ospreys in the summer of 2003. The squad mainly consisted of promising young Swansea players, who had stayed around after the club had gone into administration, together with the more experienced quality players at Neath. Although Swansea had been the bigger club, it quickly appeared as though the Neath end of the partnership was where the influence lay. We were the Neath-Swansea Ospreys and not the Swansea-Neath Ospreys. (Thankfully, we are now just known as the Ospreys.) Our new kit, when it was revealed, was all black with a little bit of white trim, rather than equally black and white. Lyn was appointed coach. And although both Roger Blyth and Mike Cuddy were joint chief executives, it was Mike, from Neath, who appeared more hands-on. The only area where Swansea had held sway was in the choice of captain. But then

Scott Gibbs had such a massive standing in the game, and was held in such huge respect, that no-one at Neath was going to argue about that.

We beat Ulster, Munster, the Celtic Warriors and Edinburgh in our first few games with our only defeat coming against the Dragons. It put us top of the Celtic League and no-one could quite believe how quickly the new team seemed to have settled. It didn't last. Towards the end of October, we went to play the Cardiff Blues at Cardiff Arms Park and were thumped, 43–6. It was one of those games when we just didn't turn up and didn't compete, although no-one could put their finger on exactly why. We then lost at home to Connacht and away to the Scottish Borders – the two sides considered the weakest in the new league. It was then that Lyn started to doubt himself. Instead of trying to attack our way out of trouble, we opted for a much more basic game-plan. We became a lot less ambitious as a handling team and much more reliant on a safety-first kicking game. It was a strategy based on fear – fear of making mistakes and fear of losing. The trouble was, we kept on losing and so the fear grew. Lyn became quite with-drawn and wanted an even more basic approach that involved hardly any running rugby at all. I've seen this with a few coaches over the years. They start to lose and they start to doubt their methods. Everything is made to tighten up and the result is that the team gets lower and lower on confidence. In the end, players are almost afraid to pass the ball for fear of making a mistake so they just kick it back to the opposition. I had seen it before with Graham Henry and Wales after he came back from the Lions tour in 2001.

It was true we needed our forwards to dominate teams away from home and maybe keep things a bit tighter. But the change of emphasis was too drastic. We kept losing and actually suffered a 10-match losing sequence, which was just nuts given the start we'd had. Having been left out of the World Cup squad, I didn't really need any more drama in my life, but I was right slap, bang in the middle of another one. What kept us all feeling positive, despite the results, was the knowledge that the Ospreys were a proper, professional rugby operation. True, we were badly misfiring as a team on the field, but off-the-field things looked impressive. In terms of the professionalism of the whole structure, the Ospreys were miles ahead of where Swansea had been the previous season. The training was better, the analysis of our opponents was much sharper and up-to-date, and the feedback to every player was taken seriously. Also, the Ospreys were thinking about the future and about developing new players, but there was virtually no development going on at Swansea.

A few people probably expected me to go off the rails that autumn. My latest setback with Wales, coupled with the Ospreys' slump, was bound to see me screw things up, according to some. But the whole period made me even more determined to succeed with both my region and with Wales. I really knuckled down and decided I was going to get fitter than ever. I was going to use the set-up of the Ospreys to take my personal fitness and conditioning on to a whole new level.

I also wanted to repay the faith that both Lyn and his assistant at the Ospreys, Sean Holley, had shown in me. For the first time in my rugby life I had coaches who really believed in me. They were confident in my ability and that gave me confidence. Lyn more or less told me I was going to get loads of rugby because he viewed me as one of his front-line players. All I had to do was go out and play. I missed a few matches over the Christmas period because of a broken bone in my hand, but other than that I played in almost every game.

That guarantee of regular rugby was a massive weight off my mind. In the past, I'd never had regular selection. It had always been one game here, then three weeks off, then another game. I'm the kind of player who needs to get into a rhythm but at Swansea I was always having to make way for someone else and it became hugely frustrating. All I've ever wanted in senior rugby is the chance to play regularly. When I was a kid playing at school, I used to play two matches a week and that would mean 50 or 60 games a year. I know rugby at the very top level is too physically demanding for that kind of workload, but one match every week is ideal for me. One game a month was never enough and it led to my inconsistencies. I was unable to show my best form with just a few, fragmented opportunities.

When the Ospreys began I hadn't really known what to expect with Lyn. His reputation with Neath was that of a very talented coach, but something of a maverick. He had been briefly involved with the Wales A set-up at one stage, but walked away because he didn't approve of the way certain things were done. He is very much his own man, but he was a big supporter of the regional concept and felt the merging of Neath and Swansea offered the only hope for Welsh sides to compete with the best in Europe. He also enjoys a good laugh with his players and I soon learnt in early Ospreys team meetings that Lyn's humour was a great way of relaxing people and defusing any tension. He can be very sharp and no-one escapes his put-downs and mickey-taking. When it comes to the serious business of coaching and preparation, though, Lyn is extremely switched on and very up-to-date.

Both Lyn and Sean were just what I needed in those first few weeks of life with the Ospreys. They showed me a level of preparation and analysis of my own game that I'd hoped to find with Swansea but never did. They would sit down with me after matches and carefully dissect my performances. We'd decide what was good and what wasn't so good and then work on things in training. Sean is also an excellent young backs coach and someone who'll go far. Like Lyn, he's got a very good understanding of the modern game . . . of players, teams and trends. You always have to be receptive to new ideas and the Ospreys coaches certainly are.

Lyn also admits to his own mistakes and I'm sure he would look back to that 10-match losing streak in our first season and confess to making errors. We all made plenty of those. At the time it was hard to see where the next win was coming from. We were not getting badly beaten – apart from that first defeat to the Cardiff Blues – but we were in a rut of losing matches. It was during this time that Scott Gibbs decided to retire. He was finding it difficult to combine playing rugby with his outside business commitments, but I think he also feared the Ospreys' bad run could develop into another nightmare situation – like the one he'd been in the middle of when captain at Swansea. At nearly 33, and with nothing left to prove to anyone, he decided to get out halfway through that first Ospreys season.

Scott's retirement left us without a real leader on the field until Barry Williams, our hooker, stepped forward to fill the void. Although it was a difficult time, I didn't share Scott's fears. The dark days at Swansea were reflected in real thrashings out on the field, but our Ospreys defeats were narrow ones. In some of those defeats I felt I'd played quite well. But that's the harsh fact about being involved in a team sport like rugby. It often doesn't matter how well an individual plays; if his team are going through a bad patch and losing games, then he tends to get tarred with the same brush. I've always found defeat easier to take if I feel I've played well myself, especially when I've had a while to reflect on it. But that doesn't apply in the immediate aftermath of losing. Then, I'm always feeling very frustrated. Sometimes that will come out with a blunt remark to a team-mate, or to the forwards, and I'll make my feelings known. At other times, I might just bite my lip.

There was a great deal of frustration in that losing run and it boiled over in the dressing room now and again. Fortunately, we managed to stop the rot with a home victory over Leeds on 31 January 2004. Our chances of making it out of our pool in the Heineken Cup had long since gone, but the win couldn't have been more priceless. Andy Williams scored the only try of the game and I converted and added a penalty. It was a very scrappy 10–3 victory, but it ended a nightmare spell for us of almost three months without a win. I felt incredibly relieved – especially for Lyn who looked like the weight of the world was on his shoulders. Whether or not he was under real pressure from the Ospreys directors, I don't know. But no coach can survive if his team stops winning. Steve Hansen had come close to proving that just prior to the World Cup, before turning things around. Now, Lyn was about to enjoy the good times – although he'd have to wait a little longer.

CHAPTER NINE

A Fresh Start

If you are going to attempt to be the best on the field, then you have to prepare like the best and that means attention to detail. So long as players aren't flogged in training, or bored rigid by too many meetings, then the buzz of being a full-time rugby player can be stimulating. It's all about keeping things fresh and enjoyable.

The average week as a member of the Ospreys squad begins on a Monday when we do a video review of the match we have just played that weekend. It can be a light comedy or a slash movie, depending on the result and the way we performed. The day is broken up with weight-training sessions and one rugby session. Tuesday will normally consist of two rugby sessions. On Wednesday, we'll have one more rugby session and more weights. We get Thursday off, Friday is a team run with detail specific to the next day's game, and Saturday is match day. Sunday is for repairing the body with a pool recovery session. This might vary slightly if we're playing on a Friday night instead of a Saturday, but we'll always be working on a six-day week.

It's intense, but well-organised. We've got fantastic new training facilities at Llandarcy, near Neath, and a breathtaking, state-of-the-art new stadium on the out-skirts of Swansea. The only slight worry for me is that some of the medics are concerned that the hard surface of our indoor training facility may have given me the groin problem that troubled me off and on through the 2004–05 season. The Wales team physio, Mark Davies, has tried to keep me off it. He feels the heavy impact from a surface without much 'give' is not doing my groin much good. He may well be right, but it's a difficult issue as this is obviously where the Ospreys want to train and the other players haven't had similar problems.

Training with the Ospreys has always been good fun in a happy environment. There's plenty of banter and humour and no-one is allowed to get ahead of them-selves, whatever they've achieved. My closest mate in the squad was Adrian Durston but at the end of the 2004–05 campaign, Adrian left to go and play in Italy. Richard Mustoe is another good mate. Like Adrian, Richard is someone I've known for years as we grew up playing together in the Bridgend area. Jonathan Thomas, who I played with at Swansea and at Wales Under-21 level, is also a good friend and so was Andy Williams before he moved to Bath.

A Fresh Start

In that first 2003–04 season, I also got to know Shane Williams. I knew of Shane from his Neath days and for the massive impact he made when he first got into the Wales side, but I didn't know him well. Initially, he comes across as quite a shy guy, but once I got to know him I discovered we had a fait bit in common. Like me, he may not seem a confident person socially but he's got huge confidence in his own ability as a rugby player. He wants to take on the world and has a lot of belief in himself. It's not misplaced, either, because he's proved in the last couple of years that he's definitely one of the best wings in the world. Since the World Cup, when he came back into the Welsh side in a blaze of glory, Shane's profile has risen. I think the whole fame thing appeals to him a lot more second time around. He's into looking his best and wearing good clothes and cares about his appearance. During our Grand Slam Six Nations, Shane even started shaving his legs, although I'm not quite sure if he knew what he was doing. He ended up with a terrible rash. He asked me for some advice and I had to point out that he was shaving in the wrong direction.

As a player, though, there's no-one I'd rather have in my side. It's hard to overstate the value of someone like Shane. He's not just a crowd-pleaser. When you are in a tight game – especially if you are playing at No.10 – and the side is struggling to break down the opposition, then you need a player like Shane who can create something out of nothing. So many times for the Ospreys, we've been going nowhere and the game-plan has not been working. We've then managed to get the ball out to Shane and suddenly he's broken the defence and scored a try which has turned the game. He's just awesome.

It's been the same for Wales and Shane was certainly a catalyst for some of our best moments in the Grand Slam campaign. Defences are now so well organised that they can cope with the predictable. But few people can work out what Shane is going to do when he gets the ball, or where he might be when he takes it. He can change direction so quickly and find space where there doesn't appear to be any. Once he gets in behind a defence then even if he is tackled himself, the door has been opened.

When you have team-mates like Shane it makes life easy. It also means training is enjoyable because his professionalism matches his talent. There's always a relaxed atmosphere at an Ospreys session and it's normally Lyn who sets the tone with a joke or a funny line. I take my share of stick but it's usually about something or other I've done on the field rather than the way I look. The other boys can hardly have a go at me for the tanning and the shaved legs as loads of them are now at it themselves. You'd be surprised at just how many of the Ospreys players spend time on the sun-beds, at the hairdressers, or shaving their legs.

A Fresh Start

I trained hard with the Ospreys and gave them all my focus at the start of 2004 as I knew I was very unlikely to be involved with Wales during that year's Six Nations. Steve Hansen had always said he was going to stand down as coach after that tournament in order to return home to New Zealand. He also said he would do everything he could to keep building a squad to take on the best in the future. But deep down I think I realised I was just waiting for Hansen to go. Until he did – and someone else came in – I knew I was likely to remain out of favour and not part of the future as he viewed it. He didn't think I was good enough for his World Cup squad, so there were few grounds to think he'd change his mind about me four months later. My form for the Ospreys had been good but I'd had no contact from Hansen to indicate I was in his plans.

When the squad of 31 players was announced, I was hardly shocked to find I wasn't in it. Garan Evans was there, though, after recovering from his injuries sustained at the World Cup and Jamie Robinson of the Cardiff Blues was also called up as the extra centre to add alongside Tom Shanklin, Sonny Parker, Mark Taylor and Iestyn Harris. Wales beat Scotland 23–10 in their opening game and there was genuine optimism around the country that the progress of the World Cup might be maintained. But they were mugged 36–15 yet again by Ireland in Dublin and then lost at home to France, 29–22, where the Welsh scrum was ruthlessly exposed. England then made it three defeats on the trot by beating Wales, 31–21, at Twickenham. I watched all those games on TV but my clearest memory is of watching the final match against Italy. It wasn't the game that stuck in my mind. Wales put away a routinely poor Italian side, 44–10, but it was the sight of Hansen at the final whistle. He walked onto the field at the Millennium Stadium to take a huge ovation from the crowd. He looked around and waved goodbye. I thought, 'Great. He's going. Now, I might get somewhere.' For whatever reason, and I don't really know why, Steve Hansen just didn't like me. My face didn't fit and the quicker he went back to New Zealand, the sooner I thought I might be able to realise my ambition of getting back in the squad.

I didn't actually follow him to the airport to make sure he got on the plane, but I have to say I wasn't shedding a tear the day Steve Hansen left for New Zealand. Mike Ruddock was appointed as Hansen's successor and one of his first jobs was to select a team to face the Barbarians at Bristol on 26 May 2004. Mike hadn't been the front-runner for the job with the media who were putting their weight behind Gareth Jenkins on the basis of his years of success at the Scarlets. The other name in the frame was the Harlequins coach, Mark Evans. I would have been happy with any of them, but Mike's appointment suited me down to the ground because things had gone well for me the night he coached

A Fresh Start

Wales to that pre-World Cup victory against Romania at Wrexham. By this stage, Iestyn Harris had also decided to go back to rugby league, so it suddenly seemed as if there might be a bit of a shake-up.

When the Wales team to play the Barbarians was named, I would have been extremely happy with a place on the bench. Instead, I was told I was starting at inside centre. I was ecstatic. It felt like a completely fresh start, as though I was making my Wales debut all over again. I had missed the Six Nations and the World Cup, but now it seemed the new coach wanted to make a big statement that he believed in me.

I was a little bit edgy in the build-up to the game. It was a new set-up and no-one was quite sure what to expect. But both Mike and Scott Johnson were so relaxed and straight-forward in their approach that it put everyone at ease. Being in that squad felt very similar to being in a club set-up, which I'd never experienced with any Welsh squads before.

Scott told me that he still saw me as a play-making inside centre, someone who could pass and create but who also offered a kicking option. He wanted me to make things happen. Ceri Sweeney was selected at outside-half, with my Ospreys team-mate, Sonny Parker, at outside centre. We seemed to click straight away and the whole team played some great stuff that night in front of a really enthusiastic crowd. We scored six tries and won 42–0. It may have been an end of season friendly against the Barbarians, but the quality of the rugby we produced was high. The Barbarians had some really good backs from all over the world – the likes of Bruce Reihana, Damien Traille, Nathan Grey, Breyton Paulse and Matt Burke – but we ran through them all night. It was the first time in their history the Barbarians had ever been 'nilled'.

I scored a nice try and passed the ball smoothly, so I was optimistic I'd done enough to make the summer tour to Argentina and South Africa. Things just felt so much more comfortable under Mike and Scott than they had under Hansen. It was the first time I'd really come under Scott's influence as an inside centre. I found him superb and have done ever since. He's got to be the most intelligent rugby coach I've ever come across. He thinks very deeply about the game but has a way of coaching that keeps things extremely simple. Even so, I think some of his ideas are revolutionary. He's always a step ahead. I don't think Scott has got the full credit he deserves for the recent success of the Welsh side. His influence has been massive on the way we play. He's not only encouraged us to attack from anywhere, but he's shown us how to do that properly, how to use support and keep the ball alive. People think he's only been an influence on the backs, but he's been a huge influence on the forwards, too. It's in the very basic but crucial things – like how to time your run in support of the player with the ball.

A Fresh Start

You can tell Scott's a bit of a free thinker just by the way he looks, with his long hair and his arm-waving stuff to the crowd when we're playing. But it's not for show. He really is very imaginative and it's been his thinking that has allowed this Wales team to really express itself. Some teams label us as 'quick' but the truth is that we don't really have that much pace in the team – not compared to some. But our speed is in the way we play. We move the ball around quickly and that was the style that took us to the Grand Slam. It's a different approach to what I'm used to with the Ospreys. The Ospreys have a physically strong pack who can often bully the opposition at Celtic League level. That becomes the focus. But Wales don't really have a pack of forwards who can physically crush the best international teams, so we have to use our strengths which are to keep the ball moving and attack in numbers rather than in ones or twos.

The tour to Argentina and South Africa quickly followed the Bristol match. There was not a great deal of time to prepare for the First Test against Argentina in Tucuman, considering we were quite a changed squad under a new coach. I was really looking forward to the trip and felt I was making real progress as I was selected for the starting line-up once more. The trouble was that the team as a whole was being asked to progress just a little too quickly – especially in defence. Clive Griffiths, our defence coach, was trying to get us to play a new 'blitz' defence. This involves our tacklers getting up in line very quickly with the priority of nailing the opponent and stopping him getting his pass away. When it works, it's great and you're on the front foot. But if a team does get the ball out wide then you're dead and buried.

The Barbarians were a scratch team and didn't really know how to counter our blitz policy. Argentina are a proper Test side and had obviously watched their tapes. They kept getting outside us when we used the blitz and we ended up conceding 50 points. It was a mad game, though, because we also scored 44 ourselves. It was a painful lesson, but we learnt that our blitz defence was one option rather than something to use throughout an entire game.

For me, Argentina was also a struggle because I got ill four days before that First Test and had to stay in bed. I think it was some kind of food poisoning – a dodgy steak, maybe – and I ended up losing half a stone. It left me pretty weak going into that match but Mike Ruddock was keen for me to play. I began at centre, moved to full-back, kicked five conversions and three penalties, but finished on the losing side and feeling very, very drained. We shipped six tries, but could even have won it with the last move of the game if Sonny hadn't dropped the ball.

The Second Test in Buenos Aires was a very different story. We sorted out our defence and dominated them from the start. We were 25–0 up at the break and Shane had scored a dazzling, awesome try where he side-stepped his way through the Pumas' defence. I started at full-back and found it hard to get involved, but my goal-kicking went well and I finished with 15 points. Shane scored a superb hat-trick of tries and underlined what a devastating player he can be. We were comfortable winners in the end, 35–20, which only increased our frustration at not having won the First Test. But it was a good comeback which proved the squad had some resilience.

That should really have been the end of the tour and the end of the season, but we were obliged to get on another plane and cross continents again. We arrived in Pretoria to face South Africa feeling a bit jaded, bruised and battered and it showed. The Springboks hammered us, 53–18. It was a game too far. I had a shocker but I wasn't alone in that. Injuries had meant I was moved to full-back again, but I got injured myself. It was a blow to my hip, similar to the problem that had forced me to go off against Romania in 2001. I signalled to the bench that I was struggling to run, but there were players dropping like flies and they weren't very keen for me to come off. After hobbling through to half-time, Mark Davies came over to me in the dressing room. I assumed I was going to be taken off. Instead, I was given a pain-killing injection in my backside and told to carry on.

The second-half didn't get any better – for me or

for the team. We carried on conceding tries and the Springboks continued to bash us up whenever they had the opportunity. Wherever I looked players in red shirts seemed to be limping. It was all just falling to pieces. Near the end of the game, the effects of my injection began to wear off. Now, the pain was back in my hip and my backside was starting to throb from the needle. At the end I walked off the field in quite a lot of pain. There was the hip pain, the pain in my backside, the pain of fatigue from being half a stone below my proper weight, as well as the pain of defeat.

CHAPTER TEN

Elvis and the Ospreys

At the start of the 2004–05 season, I had three main aims. Firstly, I wanted to be part of an Ospreys squad that would challenge for the Celtic League title, now that we had got a first campaign as a region under our belts. Secondly, I was hopeful we could mount some kind of challenge in Europe that would see us make an impact in the knockout stages of the Heineken Cup. Lastly, I wanted to establish myself in the Wales team under Mike Ruddock and play in my first Six Nations tournament. The season was scheduled to end with a Lions tour to New Zealand, but given the way so many of my previous ambitions had ended in disappointment, I couldn't dare even dream about that one.

The summer tour had been a tough one and I came back from South Africa in need of a break. It's always difficult going to the southern hemisphere countries and not just because the likes of South Africa, New Zealand

149

and Australia always produce quality international teams. The calendar for international rugby means that one side or another is always reaching the point of exhaustion. If you're not physically worn out by June then your mental sharpness is starting to go after playing week-in, week-out from the previous September. By the time any of the European countries go on tour down south in June, then they are generally up against it. The reverse is true for the southern countries when they come up here. The All Blacks, Wallabies and Springbok players who arrive in the UK in November have just come off their own hard season of Super 12 and Tri-Nations games. Just like our players in June, theirs are not at their best and are just hanging on in there. In that sense, what Sir Clive Woodward claimed after the 2005 Lions tour was true. The World Cup is the only real test of where you stand in world rugby because everyone is peaking for the same date at the same time. On the other hand, I can see why making that point to the New Zealanders after the Lions had just lost the Test series 3–0 was considered sour grapes. All these tours, it seems to me, have a familiar story. They start off well for the touring team and they win their first few games. But by the end, injuries start to mount, fatigue sets in and the players end up feeling knackered. Then come the defeats, which is exactly what happened to Wales in South Africa that summer.

I managed to take what rest I could in July but was

soon back in the thick of it with the Ospreys come August. My first game of the season was on 12 August, a friendly against Toulouse in France. It was ridiculous that the Welsh squad players were made to play in that match. We were supposed to have the first month of the season off to make sure we could recover properly and be ready for the season ahead. Instead, there we were, in summer sunshine, playing against the strongest club side in Europe. It made no sense whatsoever. I didn't want to play in that match or the next one, another friendly at home to Bath. But I ended up being picked for both. The Ospreys' argument was that they pay our wages and they wanted us to play whenever we were fit. As they're trying to run a business I could see their point, but there's got to be some common sense.

Andrew Hore, the Wales fitness coach, was alarmed that the Welsh international players were not getting proper rest periods and a number of meetings took place between the four regions and the Welsh management. They eventually agreed upon a 'rugby charter' which would limit the number of matches every international player was supposed to play to 30 per season. It also demanded a 10 to 12-week block in the summer where the Welsh players could rest and recuperate before they started playing again. This was the policy being followed in Ireland where it was noticeable that their international stars would always be missing for the first few games of the season. 'Great,' I thought. 'I'll look forward to my rest in 12 months' time.' In the meantime, after playing against Bath and Toulouse, I had to get ready for our first Celtic League match at home to Munster on 3 September.

I don't know whether it was tiredness or staleness, or what it was, but I dropped the ball a lot that day. Every time I came into the line from full-back I seemed to spill the ball and I was also guilty of not hanging onto it when I was tackled. We won 34–17, but it was quite a scrappy game and we should have been more convincing given the fact that Munster were without all their front-line international players. At our next training session, Lyn asked me why I kept spilling the ball. I told him it was just a one-off, that it wasn't a serious problem and it wouldn't happen again. But he couldn't have been convinced or perhaps he just wanted to make a point to a player who'd just come back to the regional set-up having toured with Wales. He took me out into the middle of the field and got me to practise drills of laying the ball back properly in contact – the kind of drills they use to teach 11-year-olds. I didn't know whether he really felt I lacked this very basic skill or whether he wanted to make a point in front of the other players. That's the thing with Lyn. You never know. He likes to keep you guessing.

September proved a good month for revenge. We beat the Llanelli Scarlets and the following week we were at home to the Cardiff Blues who had melted us the year before, the result which prompted our terrible run of defeats. Now was a chance to get our own back. I was kept at No.10 where I could call the shots and dictate the game and I felt in the mood to do both. Cardiff had a young guy playing at outside-half for them, Lee Thomas. He'd come up through the ranks at Pontypridd and people were already talking him up as the new kid on the block, someone with a big future ahead of him. I felt I just had to put him in his place. There was nothing personal in it. It's the same feeling I get when I come up against lots of youngsters who are earning good head-lines. I want to bring them back down to earth. If I'm honest, I think it's a fear of being overshadowed by someone younger than me. I'm 23 now and no longer considered a youngster making his way in the game. I've got this fear that one day a young kid will come along and run rings round me – make me look and feel like an old man – and that's probably going to be the day I retire. So every time I see off the new prospect I feel as if I'm making sure I live to fight another day. That was how I felt about Lee Thomas before the Blues game. It was exactly the same feeling I had towards Mathew Tait in the build-up to the Six Nations match against England. I had to make a point.

I've got no problem with the media building up young players. It's what makes the game exciting and it's really important to give children young role models they find attractive. I love reading about them myself – in all sports. But it just means that when the competitive instinct kicks in before a game, I'm out to stop them.

We hammered the Blues that day at The Gnoll, 39–3. It was just as one-sided as their victory over us the season before. I scored one of our five tries, kicked four conversions and two penalties. Lee Thomas kicked a penalty for Cardiff but they spent almost the entire match defending. It was our third straight victory out of three and we went to the top of the league.

Our next game looked very tricky. Like the Scarlets, Ulster had a habit of rarely failing at home and I'd certainly never won a game in Belfast, either with the Ospreys or with Swansea. They get big crowds at Ravenhill, it always seems to be cold and windy, and they've generally got a strong pack of forwards. They don't play complicated rugby. They just win the ball and then let David Humphreys kick it where he wants. When he's on form, and his pack is firing, then there aren't many better outside-halves at that kind of game-plan. He's also an excellent goal-kicker.

We were pretty lacklustre in the opening half and allowed them to score two tries through Bryn Cunningham and Kevin Maggs. Humphreys converted both. Trailing 14–0 we knew we hadn't got going and had allowed Ulster to dictate. A few home truths were spelt out in the dressing room about how standards had dropped from the matches against the Blues and the Scarlets. In the second-half we came out and blew them away with 21 unanswered points. We scored four tries and I chipped in by kicking 17 points. We won 37–24.

It was after the match that I learned there had been an interesting spectator sitting in the stands. Clive Woodward had gone along with the main purpose of watching Humphreys. Lyn hadn't told me he was there and neither had anyone else from the Ospreys. I suppose Lyn was concerned that anything like that might prove a distraction and he was probably right. But it was good to know that Woodward was out watching Celtic League matches so early in the season, even if his eyes were mainly on the other guy.

After beating Borders, 23–15, up in Scotland we had one final Celtic League match before the first rounds of the Heineken Cup. Leinster came to St. Helen's for a live TV game on a Friday night and they were at full strength with all their Irish internationals, including Brian O'Driscoll. In a very tight game our pack went well and won plenty of possession and it was all set up for me. All I had to do was land my kicks and we would run out easy winners. As it turned out, I had an absolute nightmare as a goal-kicker and scored with just two kicks out of eight. I don't really know why. I always find it tricky to pinpoint where I'm going wrong, especially if I've been kicking well in training all week. But that night the kicks were just flying everywhere except between the posts and I was furious with myself. Most of them weren't easy but that didn't make it easier to swallow.

My misses meant we were only 6–3 ahead, but we got away with an 11–3 victory thanks to a try from Sonny Parker. Afterwards, the rest of the boys were very upbeat as we'd taken a major scalp and beaten one of our big rivals for the championship. It also stretched our unbeaten start to the season to seven matches. But I didn't feel too positive about things. I just spent the whole night brooding over those missed kicks. If I had played really well then I could have put the kicking to the back of my mind. But if I have an ordinary game then I feel I need to be spot on with my kicking. The reverse applies, too. If I'm having a stinker, but I'm kicking really well then I can handle my own poor performance because I realise I've still made an important contribution to the team. When I went back to training on the Monday morning after that Leinster game I made sure I spent a lot of extra time on my kicking. Of course, by then they were all flying over.

The Leinster victory was not the kind of game you'd want to watch again on video. There had only been one try. But the significance of the result was obvious. We were winning tough games against quality opponents with world class players in their side – and we could even do it when not playing particularly well ourselves.

It was against that background of rising confidence that we entered the first two rounds of the Heineken Cup. We were coming off the back of seven straight victories and were sitting pretty, unbeaten, at the top of the Celtic League. We had looked carefully at the opposition in our European pool and felt encouraged we could translate our Celtic League success into the Heineken Cup. The French club Castres, Munster and Harlequins were the other sides in our group. No-one knew much about Castres, but they didn't have the European pedigree of Toulouse or Stade Francais. Munster had a brilliant record in Europe, but we felt some of their players were now a bit long in the tooth. Harlequins were already struggling in the English Zurich Premiership. It was up to us.

Our first game was a trip to the south of France to meet Castres. We prepared well and I had a good feeling that we could do something special. The record of Welsh sides away in France had been dismal, but here was a chance to make people sit up and take notice. As it turned out, we didn't even get close. Our forwards were never able to match theirs for power and momentum and our kicking game wasn't as precise as theirs. They had a very similar game plan to our own. They used their pack to win ball, kicked for territory, and then tried to score tries once they were close to the line. Their plan completely cancelled out our plan and we couldn't respond with an alternative. We conceded four tries and finished up losing 38–17. It was a horribly disappointing start to the tournament and it made for a long journey back.

Having lost our first away game it was vital we didn't

slip up at home the following week against Munster. We knew they had a serious advantage when it came to experience in this tournament as they had twice been to the final and they'd made the semi-finals on three other occasions, all within the past five years. They had a team studded with Irish international players, but capped off by a couple of top quality imports in Christian Cullen and Jim Williams. For me, it would be another interesting personal battle as I was still playing at outside-half and my opposite number was Ronan O'Gara, a guy I'd get to know well on the Lions tour.

I kicked us into a 9–6 lead, but then missed two kicks and we had to settle for a 12–9 half-time lead. I felt we were in control but a couple of mistakes put us under pressure at the start of the second-half and their scrum-half, Peter Stringer, crossed for a try. We were trailing 20–18 and piling on the pressure in the final 15 minutes. Munster defended brilliantly and didn't give away the penalty that would have cost them the game. Instead, we tried to get into a good enough position for me to drop a goal. It was the crucial moment of the match and the crowd could sense it. But every time I got into position to try a drop, the ball just didn't come my way. It was incredibly frustrating. We finally ran out of time and lost.

After the match some former international players accused me of 'hiding' in those last few minutes. They claimed I'd gone missing in action instead of taking the responsibility of trying to win the game. That annoyed me because it just wasn't the case. I was desperate to try and kick that winning goal. I was in the right position on a few occasions, but I just didn't get the pass. It's amazing – and can be irritating – when people mis-read a game situation and give you stick. But I think I was more irritated by the way we played that day. We had been so calm and confident all season, but in that match all the composure we'd shown went out the window. I kicked six penalties but we didn't manage a single try. We panicked and we lost the game.

There had been one sin-binning for either side but it hadn't been a particularly bad-tempered game. But it didn't take long for things to heat up after the final whistle. Our wing, Richard Mustoe, was cited for stamping on the head of Munster prop Marcus Horan. We also made a complaint to the tournament governing body – European Rugby Cup – that our centre, Elvis Seveali, had been racially abused by Horan. I didn't hear any remark. But there were players on our side who claimed that Horan called Elvis a 'f***ing black c***.' The allegation sent Munster into a fury and they strongly denied it. In the end, our team manager Derwyn Jones and Shane Williams went to Dublin to give evidence but Horan was cleared. The report stated that no remark had been made. Richard wasn't so lucky. He was found guilty of stamping and banned for 12 weeks.

I didn't hear any racist abuse during that match, but

it does go on. You hear it in some games. You even get it during training sessions. I've heard it at the Ospreys. Rugby dressing rooms aren't the most politically correct places and so racist remarks do fly around. But there's a big difference between a situation where everyone takes the mickey out of each other, and feels comfortable with that, and the occasion in a match when it's meant to cause offence. That's just not acceptable.

Verbal intimidation on a rugby field, though, of the non-racist sort, goes on all the time and Munster are particularly keen on it. They're one of the noisiest teams around. O'Gara and Stringer like to dish it out, but they can be funny with it. When we played Munster in a Celtic League match at their place later in the season, Matthew Jones, was our outside-half. 'Rat', as he's known, was giving O'Gara a fair bit of lip for a fresh-faced 20-year-old kid playing away from home at a place like Thomond Park. O'Gara just looked at him and said: 'Who are you? The Under 14s are playing tomorrow.' A few players laughed and poor old Rat didn't know what to say.

I've been on the end of my fair share of 'sledging' over the years, but I can honestly say it doesn't bother me. If I get abused, take a sly punch, or get my hair pulled in a ruck, then my response has always been the same. After the match I'll just ask them, 'What's your problem?' But during the game itself I don't want to feel angry or ruffled because I don't want anyone to think they can control my emotions. I want to be in control of those myself. I might have a word with them after the game, too, because by then everything has died down and people are forced to act normally.

But it wasn't the verbal battle that was bugging me after that Munster match at The Gnoll. It was the fact that we'd lost our two opening matches in Europe. It meant that the only way we could qualify for the knock-out stages was to win all four of our remaining ties. Europe, though, would have to wait for a while. The November internationals were about to start – the opening steps on a season-long march of 10 Tests – and, for me, the beginning of the most amazing journey with Wales.

CHAPTER ELEVEN

Clocking Off

Mike Ruddock is a big, round-shouldered guy, with an easy-going nature and a good sense of humour. He's a passionate Welshman with a sound knowledge of both what makes Welsh players tick and what type of rugby most of them feel comfortable with. He also plays guitar in a pub band called Midlife Crisis which suggests he's a bit more normal and less intense than a lot of rugby coaches.

When Mike took over from Steve Hansen in the spring of 2004, there were a few things wrong with the Wales team, but also quite a lot that was right – or at least things that were heading in the right direction. Mike's quite a shrewd bloke and he realised he didn't need to change what had worked for the players under Hansen, even if they weren't quite his own methods. In terms of our style of play, it was a style that was evolving under Hansen and Scott Johnson. I wasn't really part of it, but the boys who were felt comfortable with the whole approach and Mike has wisely not tried to shake things up too much. He could have easily tried to impose a lot of new ideas, but he was willing to listen and I think that's been a big part of our success. There were changes made, but they weren't dramatic changes.

Mike's background is as a forwards coach and he said when he was appointed that his main priority was to sort out the pack and improve the basics such as the scrum and line-out. All the sides he had coached before – Wales A, Newport Gwent Dragons, Ebbw Vale, Leinster and Swansea – were strong in those areas. Those were the things he worked hard on during his first few months in charge but it would have been difficult to see enormous improvements in time for the tour to Argentina and South Africa in the summer of 2004. The first acid test would be the November internationals of that year when we would be together in camp for a month in Cardiff with matches against South Africa, Romania, New Zealand and Japan.

Going into those autumn Tests, for probably the first time in my Wales career I felt secure about my place in the team. You can usually tell whether or not you're going to be in the starting line-up by the way things shape up in training and I felt as though the No. 12 shirt was going to be mine. Scott Johnson had also been very positive about my role and worth to the side and I was made to feel valued, which is always a good feeling.

Gavin Henson

Once again, we were going to try and employ the blitz defence that Clive Griffiths had introduced, although it was important for us to learn to be more adaptable and only use it on the right occasions. We didn't want another flop like the First Test defeat in Argentina.

Jonathan Thomas had been suspended after being sent off in the last few minutes of the Ospreys' Heineken Cup defeat to Castres, so that meant there was a slot that needed to be filled in the second row for the game against South Africa. Mike could have played safe and gone for someone like Gareth Llewellyn. Instead, he moved Michael Owen into the second row and gave a debut to Ryan Jones, another team-mate and good friend of mine from the Ospreys. Ryan came in at No.8 and his inclusion meant there were seven players from the Ospreys in the starting line-up. The region that so many people had predicted wouldn't work was now supplying half the Welsh team. Besides Ryan and myself, the others picked were Sonny Parker, Shane Williams, Duncan Jones, Adam Jones and Brent Cockbain. Strangely, the *Western Mail* – the national newspaper of Wales – chose to lead its back page on the fact that six players with the surname Jones would be playing, rather than concentrating on the seven Ospreys. Perhaps they thought Jones was an unusual surname in Wales.

As usual, Ryan was a heaving, spewing bag of nerves before the game but once he had got that out of his system he played extremely well. Few people would have

164

predicted he would finish that season playing in three Tests for the Lions, but I've always known he's a class act. I think he'll be a big part of the Wales team for a long time to come.

The Millennium Stadium was packed and there was a real sense of expectancy. Wales had only beaten the Springboks once before – at the same venue in 1999 – but against a team as strong as South Africa it's vital you get away to a good start. We didn't manage it. Once again there were some communication problems with our blitz defence and we handed them two soft tries for Jaco van der Westhuyzen and Joe van Niekerk. Before we really had time to re-gather, we found ourselves 23–6 down. We got a bit of a break when Schalk Burger, the Springbok flanker, was sin-binned and Stephen kicked a couple more goals while they were down to 14 men. It was noticeable that we were growing in confidence as the match went on. Our fitness was impressive, too, and it was South Africa who started to fade. They were very lucky not to go down to 13 men at one point when they cynically killed the ball to prevent a try, but we were building momentum.

This was my eighth cap for Wales and I'd yet to score a try. I wouldn't say it was becoming a major anxiety but I'd be lying if I didn't admit it was nagging away at the back of my mind. I badly wanted to get off the mark and experience the thrill of scoring a try for Wales. Early in that second-half against the Springboks I got my chance. Dafydd Jones did superbly to break through from a maul and knocked Percy Montgomery onto the seat of his pants. Stephen Jones got the ball in his hands and attacked and I ran a hard angle back at the inside shoulder of my opposite number. I got past him and then stepped another defender who'd come across, before reaching out for the line. I heard the roar from the crowd and I suddenly realised that although my first cap for Wales may have come out in Japan, my first try had been scored in Cardiff where I'd always dreamed it would be. With a try to my name I felt like a proper international rugby player.

Steve's conversion took us to within a point of South Africa, but to be fair they responded well. We were still making errors in defence, picking up the wrong runners, and the Springboks managed to hit us with two more tries. It meant there was another mountain to climb, but we didn't drop our heads and Sonny fed me a pass for my second try in the corner. This one was more of a run-in but it was all about the team context. It got us back in the match and the Springboks were rattled. Scoring that one earned me another pat on the back from the rest of the boys and that's a fantastic thing for your own confidence. It makes me feel physically bigger and I just want to keep having the ball to show what I can do.

The South African coach, Jake White, made a few substitutions but it didn't alter the way the match was finishing with us throwing everything at them. Our pack crushed them in a scrum near their line and Dwayne Peel scored a third try which Stephen again converted. It meant the score was now 38–36 to South Africa and if we could kick a drop-goal or a penalty we'd get a win. It didn't happen. Moments later the referee blew his whistle for full-time. We weren't really aware of how much, or how little, time was left and everyone felt so flat and disappointed that the game had ended. Normally, when you look up at the stadium clock it shows the actual number of minutes that have already gone. So if it says 78 minutes, then you'd usually figure there were two minutes left plus injury time which can often be about five or six minutes these days. That would mean playing on until the 86th minute. But the rules over time-keeping had changed at the start of the season and the clock was now being stopped every time there was a break in play for injuries. It meant it wasn't going to go past 80 minutes and when it showed 78 minutes there really were only two minutes left because the injury-time had already been included. We were caught out a little by that and it would again become a talking point after the match against New Zealand two weeks later.

Although we lost the game I felt there were a lot of positives to take out of it. We had taken one of the big southern hemisphere teams right to the wire and only lost through a few of our own mistakes. It was not as though we had in any way been outclassed. We felt as good as them and certainly as fit and physically strong. Fitness and strength had been the areas where Wales had seemed to lag behind in previous years but our work under the supervision of Andrew Hore was really starting to pay rewards. I also felt I was starting to properly get to grips with the inside centre role. The more I played there, the easier it became and I was starting to develop a good understanding with Sonny. He'd been a team-mate at the Ospreys for a couple of seasons but I'd been playing at full-back or outside-half so we'd never developed an understanding as a centre pairing. Now it was starting to come.

Sonny is a quiet guy on the field, but he's one of the strongest players I've ever come across. He uses that strength well and he must be a nightmare to play against because he just keeps running hard all day. He's an awesome athlete and he's also got all the skills, but he's had more than his fair share of injury problems. Unfortunately, he got injured after our autumn campaign and missed the whole of the Six Nations which robbed him of being part of a Grand Slam. My centre partner throughout the Six Nations was Tom Shanklin and both Tom and I finished the season by getting selected for the Lions tour. So Sonny missed out there, too. It would have been interesting to have seen Sonny on the Lions tour in New Zealand because that's where he was born and where he lived and played his rugby until he was 21. He then went to Italy for a little while before ending up in Wales. I wonder what the New Zealanders would have made of that if he'd gone back there in a Lions jersey.

Sonny qualified for Wales through residency after living over here for the required three years. It's the same with two other guys in our squad – Brent Cockbain, who's an Aussie, and Hal Luscombe, who came over from South Africa. All three are excellent players and really good guys, but I have to be honest and say I'm not sure I agree with that rule which allows them to pull on a Welsh shirt. Don't get me wrong, here. I love playing alongside these blokes and they've all proved massively important for the team. It's the rule I'm talking about. It's not something that's discussed often among the players but I know of people who feel frustrated when they find their way blocked by these guys and I can understand their feelings. It's a difficult one, because the three of them are mates of mine. But I honestly feel that three years of living in Wales does not make you Welsh. Neither does having a Welsh grandfather if you were born and raised overseas. The regulations should mean you either have to be born in a country, have parents from that country, or if we're going to have a residency rule then it should be more like five years than three. Sonny, Brent and Hal have put their heart and soul into playing for Wales and I love playing alongside them. It would also be ridiculous for Wales not to select players on residency, or the grandparent rule, when the rest of the world takes advantage of it. England have got Matt Stevens – someone I got to know on the Lions tour – who is a South African; Ireland and Scotland have done it, and France have picked both South Africans and New Zealanders. New Zealand themselves have been taking players from the Pacific Islands for years. Sitiveni Sivivatu was sensational for the All Blacks against the Lions, but it wouldn't have happened if he hadn't been spotted as a teenager in Fiji and encouraged to move to New Zealand.

Maybe the rules need to be looked at again or perhaps it's just me. If my father had moved to England when I was 15 and I'd gone to school in England, then I wouldn't have stopped feeling Welsh or wanting to play rugby for Wales. I just can't see how I'd suddenly want to play for England.

One thing that Sonny, Brent and Hal have brought to the team – apart from their skills – is a winning mentality. The countries they're from are winning rugby countries. After running South Africa so close, everyone in the squad felt that we shouldn't fear those teams. We could have beaten them. We weren't used to winning against the big sides and that had probably cost us. But it wasn't a repeat of the game in June when they had hammered us in Pretoria. Our belief was now much stronger. The only difference between the teams was that they were used to winning and we weren't.

Over the next few days we watched the tapes back and it gave everyone a real lift. We had scored tries against them, we'd come back after conceding soft tries, and at the end of the match the Springboks were out on their feet. We made too many mistakes and I was one of the guilty men. I made two errors coming out of our defensive line and it cost us two tries. We still had matches left against Romania, New Zealand and Japan and they would provide opportunities to get things right. We needed to work on our combinations and getting things right defensively. But deep down, though, I think we all knew that the goal was the Six Nations. That was the tournament on which Mike and all the players would be judged.

Six days after the defeat to South Africa, we played Romania on a Friday night under the Millennium Stadium lights. This was to be my ninth cap for Wales. Strangely, a third of that total was made up of games against Romania. I had nothing against them but they're not the really the type of fixture that live in the memory. I was anxious to get this game out of the way so we could concentrate on the All Blacks.

The team was now starting to become popular as people realised we were an exciting unit to watch and a crowd of 35,000 turned up. It was a useful run-out – a chance to run through our attacking plans as well as get our defence sorted – and we eventually won, 66–7. Tom Shanklin, who was playing on the right wing, scored four of our 10 tries to equal the individual record for a player in a Welsh international. I scored one as well to make it three in two games. Luke Charteris, a 6ft 9 inch Wales Under-21 player, made his debut in the second row, but most of the focus afterwards appeared to be on Tom and the fact that he'd made such a convincing case to start on the wing against the All Blacks.

After the match, the Romanian players were in our dressing room within a couple of minutes, on the search for pieces of Welsh kit. This is normally a tradition after a Test game but the Romanians are super keen. You can understand why. It's a struggle for the Romanians to fund their team, never mind lavish the players with loads of expensive items of kit. I had spoken before to their outside-half, Ionut Tofan, the Jonny Wilkinson of Romanian rugby, so I know what difficulties they have to overcome because of their financial problems. Having played twice before against them, I already possessed enough items of Romanian rugby memorabilia for one man, but it's hard to refuse swapping. At least Luke could claim it was his Wales debut and he wanted to keep his first jersey. There's obviously a pecking order to the collecting of jerseys, shorts and socks, which reflects the standing of the teams. In a week's time I would be walking into the All Blacks' dressing room in order to persuade Aaron Mauger to exchange his shirt for mine.

New Zealand had already beaten Italy in Rome but the return to Cardiff for Steve Hansen and Graham Henry – who were now in charge of the All Blacks together – was viewed as the ideal stepping stone before they met France in Paris. We had our own ideas. From a personal point of view I was keen to perform well in front of both of them. Given what had happened to me with both coaches in the past, I wanted to make my point. It wasn't a case of proving them wrong. They were national coaches with Wales and they obviously picked the best players they considered for the job. But at the back of my mind going into that game I wanted to show both of them that I was a good player, a player capable of playing international rugby and being a valuable part of the Welsh side. I knew I was good enough. I wanted them to know it, too.

During the week of the game there was a big dinner in Cardiff and both sets of players had to attend. It was the first time I'd spoken to Hansen since he left me out of his squad. 'Alright, Gav,' he said and we shook hands. 'Aye, alright, Steve.' That was it. There was no more conversation.

I'd always wanted to play against New Zealand in a proper situation, not like the two minutes I'd had against them on tour in 2003. This was my opportunity and I was looking forward to it. As I kid, the first international match I was taken to by my father was Wales against New Zealand in 1989. I was seven years old and don't remember much about the match. What stuck in my mind, though, was the air of mystery and menace that surrounded the All Blacks, especially when they did the haka; that and the strange New Zealand coin given to me by a Kiwi bloke standing next to us. Now I was going to come face-to-face with them.

It was an incredible match. It seemed to run at 100mph and I spent most of the game hitting rucks and clearing out. That was where the real battle was happening, on the ground in the scrap for the ball. New Zealand had Richie McCaw, who was generally viewed as the best back row forward in the world and without a rival when it came to that breakdown area. His ability to re-cycle ball was what usually gave his side such momentum and enabled their dangerous runners in the back line to do their stuff. But that day, our own back row of Michael Owen, Colin Charvis and Dafydd Jones were inspired and there was nothing between the teams. Daniel Carter was playing at No.10 for the All Blacks and it was the first time I'd seen him at close quarters. Later on in the season I'd get more evidence of his ability when I was on the receiving end with the Lions. With most players you look at videos and analyse their weaknesses so you can expose them. But Carter doesn't really have any. He's got all the skills and seems to have a fantastic big game temperament to go with it.

We had a great start. We put them under real pressure

early on and managed to score the first try. Stephen Jones chipped the ball over the All Blacks' defence and Tom judged the bounce perfectly. We were in charge after Steve kicked a penalty to make it 11–3 but we let them back into it and again it was our own defensive mistake. We were on a drift defence but Sonny went up on a blitz policy and got caught out. Joe Rokocoko strolled in for the try. Once again, the high risk defence had taken its toll. It's the responsibility of the guys defending out wide to call the type of defence. They can see whether we should drift across because we have too few markers to deal with their attackers, or if we need to blitz because we outnumber them. If you are always on the drift defence, though, then you tend to concede territory because it's soak-up defending. The blitz is much more aggressive and gives you the gain of putting the opposition on the back foot. Often, they end up losing possession or kicking it away. But the blitz is risky and during those November games it was killing us in terms of giving away soft tries. There were serious doubts about it expressed by some players, but we persevered and finally got it right for the Six Nations.

Our team needs to defend aggressively because we don't really have a big, domineering pack. We just don't seem to breed those type of forwards as England do. So we need to get forward momentum from our defensive game and then switch quickly to counter-attack when we turn over possession.

We were leading 14–13 at half-time and relatively pleased. We knew it was vital to score first in the second-half and we managed it. It was not the kind of try Wales have managed against teams like New Zealand very often. It was a forwards' try. We drove a line-out close to their line, the pack stayed patient and in control, and Mefin Davies, our hooker, wheeled off a maul to claim the score. At least, that's how it looked to me. I'll confess I don't really know what the forwards are doing in those tight areas, like a driving line-out. They're in their own little world in training sessions and it isn't one I'm very familiar with. I just like it when they're going forwards rather than backwards. But the try was exactly the kind of controlled, well-drilled forward work that Mike had wanted to deliver when he came in as coach.

We were 19–13 up but we only held that lead for two or three minutes. The All Blacks have this thing that whenever they concede a try they always raise their game a notch straight away. It's part of their psyche. You know it's coming. You can feel the extra edge in their tackles and their running. They started attacking in waves and Mils Muliaina scored their second try. But it was annoying because we handed them possession by failing to secure the ball at the re-start after our own try. We were back to holding a one-point lead but had a chance to extend it with a long-distance penalty. Steve had started to complain of some stiffness in his back so he asked me to have a go instead. It was a similar kick to the one I'd land against England three months later but this time, although I struck it well, it just drifted a little and hit the inside of the post. It was typical of our luck at that stage. I didn't dwell on it too much at the time, but later that night it would go through my mind a few times.

The game was anybody's and becoming loose – just right for someone like Rokocoko. Sure enough, he picked up a stray ball in his own half and burst into life. He threw the ball up as if he was going to kick it, but caught it again and turned Tom inside out. Tom's no slouch and a very good defender but Rokocoko made him look silly. He was gone in a flash and under the posts. In the summer, Rokocoko would lose his form and confidence and get left out against the Lions. But back on that November afternoon I felt he was the only difference between the sides. He's a special player.

Ma'a Nonu then hit me late after the ball had gone and we won another penalty. Of course, I milked it. But then it was definitely a penalty and I only milked it to make sure we got the decision. You have to do that sometimes – fall on the floor and make the most of it just to remind the referee to blow. It's not cynical, like the way soccer players dive for penalties when they haven't been touched. It's more about emphasising that a late tackle has occurred – giving the ref a little helping hand.

I got up and kicked the penalty to make it 23–22 to

them. Carter then kicked one for New Zealand before I struck another one with four minutes to go. We could sense the game was still there for the taking. We were on top and they were struggling to keep us out, but the seconds were ticking away. We were in our own half, waiting for a line-out. Steve, Alfie and I had a quick chat and it was decided we needed to win the ball and kick for the corner in order to put real pressure on the All Blacks for one final assault. If we could get up there and win a penalty, or work a drop-goal, then we'd win the match. We won the ball, put it in the corner and were just about to give it a big final blast when Tony Spreadbury ended the game. Just as in the match against South Africa we'd been caught out by the clock again, believing there were a few minutes or seconds left when there weren't. Had we realised the ref was about to end the match then we'd have tried to score from that play in our own half, even if it had meant trying a drop goal from a long way out.

It had finished, Wales 25, New Zealand 26. We all felt devastated at the final whistle. This would have been history. Wales had not beaten New Zealand since 1953, which is a ridiculously long time ago. Here was our big chance and it had slipped through our fingers. I hadn't wanted the match to end. Once it had ended I felt as though I just wanted to start the whole thing all over again. I knew it might be a long time until Wales had as good a chance to beat the All Blacks. Once again, I think the result had come down to sheer faith. Like the South African match, we just lacked that little edge in terms of self-belief. We wanted to win, desperately, and we hoped we'd win. But we didn't have that inner core of steel that comes from *knowing* we were going to win. That only exists when a team is completely confident and has no hang-ups or doubts whatsoever. You only possess that complete mental toughness from winning matches against good teams. But I felt – and all the other boys felt – that we were so close. We almost had it but not quite. We matched New Zealand for skills, for fitness, for tactical appreciation and every other aspect. But we were just one per cent short. We just needed a little break to go our way in a big game against a major side and we would gain that missing ingredient – the confidence that comes from winning. I felt so certain about it I even made a prediction in my post-match interviews. Once we got that one big scalp, I said, we would go on a run of victories that would really propel us into the leading group of teams in the world.

As we sat in our dressing room, however, the testing of my claims was a long way off. I swapped my shirt with the All Blacks' No.12, Aaron Mauger, and this time, unlike with my friend Ionut, it was me who had to go looking for him. Not much was said in our dressing room. Nothing needed to be said. We all knew how close we'd come. In the days afterwards we examined the tapes and saw the little errors that had added up to that one-point losing margin. It was a fine line, but we'd just fallen the wrong side.

Six days later we played our fourth and final match of the autumn series, against Japan. The preparation was difficult. A Test against the All Blacks takes a huge toll physically and it's several days before you feel back in shape. We were also starting to feel the affects of three Test matches in three weeks, plus all the intensive training. Scott Johnson put things in perspective, though, when he reminded the players that New Zealand were off to Paris to play against France. Imagine how they felt, he said. At least we only had to play Japan. A few days later when I watched a tape of that France v New Zealand game, I was blown away. The All Blacks did much more than just give France a hard game. They wiped the floor with them and played rugby of unbelievable quality to win 45–6. Whatever tiredness they must have felt after their own long season, and after that game against us, they kept it well hidden.

CHAPTER TWELVE

Chip Alley

Scott Johnson was right. It *was* only Japan. But we were determined to finish on a high, both for ourselves and for the fans who had supported us in fantastic numbers for all four matches at the Millennium Stadium. We beat them 98–0 and although they weren't the strongest international opposition in the world, we did a clinical, professional job on them. It was also a night I'll remember for a number of reasons, starting with the fact that I managed to convert all 14 tries. I had enjoyed perfect kicking days before when I hadn't missed a single shot at goal, but 14 out of 14 was a new personal milestone.

I had worked really hard on my goal-kicking in training throughout that November and felt I was kicking well. It's difficult when Stephen is the recognised first choice kicker, but I like to think that when we're in camp together we push each other to attain higher standards. Some of the kicks that night against the Japanese were easy ones from in front of the posts, but there were others that were 10 or 15 yards in from either touchline. Those can become tough in a game when you are doing a lot of kicking because sometimes tiredness sets in or a lack of concentration.

Steve didn't play in this match because he'd been called back to France by his club, Clermont Auvergne. That was the deal that had been struck with the clubs of all the French-based boys. Their clubs had released them for the matches against South Africa and New Zealand, but they wanted them to skip the Japanese and return to France for training. It meant I was given the goal-kicking duties and I was very keen to make an impression. I didn't tell anyone, but I wanted to be given the role of first choice goal-kicker for the Six Nations.

Colin Charvis scored four tries to match Tom Shanklin's efforts against Romania, and become another joint-holder of the Welsh try-scoring record, and the others were shared between Shanks, Rhys Williams, Mefin Davies, Gethin Jenkins, Gareth Cooper and Shane Williams. The final try of those 14 was scored by Rhys and as I'd succeeded with all 13 of the previous conversions, I was pretty keen to see where he'd touch down. Rhys fancies himself as a bit of a showman and likes to do this spectacular dive whenever he scores a try. He normally takes a bit of stick from the boys for it, too, but that didn't stop him doing his swallow act in the corner when I felt he could have got in a bit nearer the posts to make my kick simpler. 'Cheers, Rhys,' I said and gave him a sarcastic smile as he threw me the ball. He'd grounded it right in the corner which meant my kick would have to be taken from almost on the touch-line. The score at that stage was 96–0 and the referee was about to blow for the end after my conversion. Most people in the stadium probably looked at the scoreboard and thought this kick was no big deal to me. In fact, it was a massive deal. I'd kicked 13 out of 13 and this was either going to give me 14 from 14 or it was going to ruin my perfect night. If I missed it I knew I'd feel gutted all evening and in no mood whatsoever to celebrate.

I was feeling confident, though, and had been striking the ball well throughout the game. I went through my normal preparation and routine and tried to block every-thing else out. I was more careful and thorough for that kick than for any of the other 13. I even tried to imagine the scores were level and this was a match-winning kick. Then, I suddenly realised I'd been in this situation loads of times on the training field. On so many occasions I've been practising my kicking and then realised I've just scored with the last 15 or so. That's when I get a bit nervous. I want to finish the session and get off, but I don't want to end with a miss. If I miss, I know I'll have to score another 15 in a row before I leave. Otherwise, I just won't feel happy at all. It was the same feeling standing over that last kick against Japan. The

183

big difference was that if I missed I couldn't just start all over again.

As soon as I kicked it, I knew it was going over. It's strange to say it but that kick meant almost as much to me as the one I was to score against England in the Six Nations. A lot of people would find that hard to believe, but I think other goal-kickers would completely understand. I didn't know it until after the match, but I'd set a new record for successful kicks in a Test match by a Welsh international player. The previous record was 11 by Neil Jenkins in the 102–11 victory over Portugal in 1995.

It was the end of the November international programme and time to let off a bit of steam. It was late on Friday night and a group of us headed into the centre of Cardiff to enjoy a few beers. I was standing in a bar called Life chatting to Hal Luscombe when a girl approached me and said: 'Hello, Gavin. I'm Charlotte. Well done in the match tonight, it was fantastic to watch.' I recognised her straight away and was flattered she'd come over to speak to me. I thanked her for the compliment and we started chatting about rugby. She seemed to know her stuff and said she'd really enjoyed the games against South Africa and New Zealand. She wished me luck for the Six Nations and then kissed me on the cheek before leaving with her friends. All I could think was, 'What a great night. I've kicked 14 out of 14 for Wales at the Millennium Stadium and I've met Charlotte Church.' She seemed a really nice girl but I didn't think much more of it and went back to celebrating our freedom from camp with the rest of the boys.

Some hours and a good few beers later, I was still out with the younger boys in the squad – Hal, Jonathan Thomas and Ceri Sweeney. It was about 3.30am and we found ourselves looking for a taxi near the top end of Caroline Street in the centre of the city. For those yet to discover the delights of Caroline Street, it's known as Chip Alley. If you've had a drink and you need some stodge before you wander off into the night, then Caroline Street and it's fabulous selection of chip shops and kebab joints is the only place to be. I never eat chips as a rule. In fact, I can go for months without a single chip passing my lips, or any other form of fast food, come to that. But as I say, that's as a rule. When you've had a few too many beers then rules like that are just there to be broken.

I swayed into the best smelling chip shop I could find and then swayed out again, complete with my little plastic tray of chips and wooden fork. I reached the end of the road and suddenly saw Charlotte striding across the junction ahead of me. It must have taken a few seconds for the brain cells to register because she had walked on for a further 30 yards before I yelled out: 'Oi, Charlotte! Charlotte! Wait a minute!' Classy or what? Rather unsurprisingly, she ignored the drunk shouting at her while spilling his chips in the street, and carried on walking with her eyes fixed ahead of her. 'It's me. Gavin . . . we met earlier on . . . Charlotte!' I wasn't giving up. She then turned around to check out this annoying bloke who kept yelling at her. Luckily, she recognised me and smiled. She walked over and we started chatting where we had left off some hours before. I did my best impression of a sober international rugby player, but I could see that she was a little bit tipsy herself. Then the conversation became really bizarre. 'Listen,' she said. 'Why don't you come with me and meet my mother and my singing teacher?' It seemed they were both in a restaurant around the corner, Charleston's, and she was on her way to join them. I assumed the other boys would have given up on me now and found their cab, so we walked together to the restaurant. Just before we went in, I remembered to throw my chips into the bin on the pavement.

I was introduced to Charlotte's mother, Maria, the singing teacher, plus a few other friends that were at the table. We sat down to join them, drank some wine and chatted. At some stage, Maria leaned over to me and said: 'Right, Gavin. What Charlotte needs is a tidy boyfriend.' By this stage, I was in no real fit state to disagree with any suggestion. 'Yeah, fine . . . whatever. No problem.' We carried on getting through some more bottles of wine, I chatted with Maria about rugby, and it was soon six o'clock in the morning. Before we all got up to leave – out of earshot of Charlotte – Maria asked me for my phone number. Charlotte, it seemed, already had a boyfriend but things sounded as if they might be coming to an end. I just about managed to remember my number and write it down, but didn't really think much more of it. I was still chuffed to have spent a few hours drinking wine with Charlotte Church.

We all shared a cab, everyone was dropped off at their own house, and I gave Charlotte a kiss on the cheek before slumping back in the car seat and heading for the team hotel. There's something to tell the boys over breakfast, I thought. And that was it – I didn't see or hear from Charlotte again for three months.

I was right about one thing. My story proved a good source of entertainment for the boys the following morning. But I set myself up for a fall. I got excited when I had a text on my phone from a number I didn't recognise. It said: 'Thanks for a really lovely evening. Can't wait to see you again – Charlotte xxx.' I made the fatal error of showing this to a couple of players, only to discover soon enough it had not been sent by Charlotte, but was a product of the twisted mind of Tom Shanklin. Fair play to him. Shanklin 1, Henson 0. Own goal.

The real Charlotte didn't get back in touch until after the England game after explaining that her mother had lost my phone number. I think she also had some things to sort out with her previous boyfriend. The truth was, though, that I wished I'd run into her in-between times.

187

We had got on really well. I hadn't really had a proper girlfriend for years, not since I'd left school. Rugby had always taken up too much of my time and the social time I had left over was taken up with my mates. As far as I'd been concerned, girls came down the pecking order. I suppose that shows a selfish side of me that I'd have to own up to. But I was always honest. I always told them that rugby came first. In the early days I even said similar things to Charlotte. She understands that my career is very important to me – just as hers is to her – but we're managing to juggle everything at the moment.

I'd spent the whole of November with Wales and we had played four games. Romania and Japan had been thrashed, but we'd lost to South Africa and New Zealand. The margins of defeats had been two points and one point. Apart from drawing, we simply couldn't get any closer and at the end of that month we all felt we were within touching distance of turning a major corner. In the meantime, the Ospreys had stumbled in the Celtic League. The two defeats in the Heineken Cup had undermined confidence and my team-mates had lost away at the Newport Gwent Dragons and then at home to Connacht. In between times, they'd beaten Edinburgh in Scotland. Despite the slips, the Celtic League title was still a target, as was going as far as we could in Europe. Now it was time for me to re-join the squad and get on with the day job.

Chip Alley

Our next two games were back-to-back fixtures against Harlequins in rounds three and four of the Heineken Cup pools. Having lost to Munster and Castres, we had to beat Quins in both matches to have any hope whatsoever of making the knockout stages. The first of the two games was at Swansea's St. Helen's on a Sunday afternoon. It was a strange game. We didn't play particularly well and didn't even manage to score a try in the whole 80 minutes. But Harlequins were quite negative themselves and although they scored a try early on through Tom Williams, they never appeared confident enough to try and build on it. They had been struggling in the Zurich Premiership and their lack of self-belief was evident in their approach, which appeared to be simply to try and stop us scoring tries. It didn't seem to concern them that they were giving away loads of penalties. My kicking form had been in good nick in the game against Japan and I carried that form with me into this first match back for the Ospreys. We eventually won quite comfortably, by 24–7, and I kicked eight penalties out of eight. Together with the previous 14 out of 14, it meant I'd succeeded with 22 consecutive kicks at goal. I felt I couldn't miss.

But I was irritated after the game because it had been my mistake that had presented Harlequins with their try. I was tackled, tried to flick the pass away, only to lose the ball which enabled them to break away and score. Things like that always play on my mind after matches. If I'm honest I'm looking for the perfect game; I want to come off the field one day and remember dozens of things I did well and not a single thing that went badly. I haven't got to that stage yet, but that's still the aim. I've sometimes had games where I haven't made a mistake, but they've been games where I haven't done enough of the good things, either. I've allowed myself to drift through things a bit. I want a game where I demand the ball all day, do everything right, and don't make any mistakes, either.

In the post-match interviews I was asked what I'd thought of Quins. 'Not a lot,' I'd replied and I explained why I felt they'd never threatened us and why we had nothing to fear in the return match at their place. It wasn't meant to be provocative. It's just another of my pet hates. I just can't stand all that false modesty stuff. If I'm watching an interview with a player – rugby player, footballer, or anything – and he starts going on about there being no easy matches, how the opposition are incredibly dangerous, and he wouldn't dare predict the outcome, then I just have to switch it off. I can't be doing with it. It would be the same in the build-up to the England match a few weeks on from the Harlequins game. I was asked direct questions and I gave direct answers. I can't be bothered to play the 'let's not offend anyone' game. Sport is about being competitive. You turn up to play because you think you're better than them and you can win. What's the point of pretending?

Chip Alley

My other reason for always saying I'm not worried by opponents is to put pressure on myself. Sometimes, I can feel as though I've been going through the motions in the build-up to a game. I don't feel anxious or on edge enough so I deliberately make a very self-confident claim in order to wake myself up. It's like I've backed myself into a corner by talking myself up and then I feel under pressure to respond. Some players don't want to feel like that at all. They'd hate it. But for me, I find it normally works. I can feel the prickly heat on my neck when I think about the expectations and pressures I've built up and that's when I feel I really come alive.

Some players take exception to those remarks and let me know about it. The confrontation with Brian O'Driscoll during the Grand Slam clincher against Ireland was an obvious example, but there have been others. I got on really well with Brian on the Lions tour, but he's a very different character to me on the field. He remembers supposed slurs and put-downs. He uses them to wind himself up and he'll get into a real rage with an opponent. Then, when the game is over, he'll normally shake hands with everyone and it's all forgotten. I should be used to that kind of attitude. It's the attitude of most rugby players at all levels. It's what my father used to be all about. Maesteg would stand toe-to-toe and fight with anyone, but they'd all be best mates in the bar afterwards. It's the classic rugby ideal, but I've never really been able to get my head around it. I'm still shocked by someone who wants to rip my head off, call me every name under the sun in a blind rage for 80 minutes, and then buy me a drink afterwards. In Wales, Matthew Watkins is from the O'Driscoll mould. Matthew is a very funny guy and good company off the field. We get on well. But on the pitch he's unrecognisable. Whenever we play against the Scarlets, and I come against Matthew, then I just feel these waves of hatred coming off him. It's as if our friendship off the field just doesn't exist. I'm the complete opposite. When I'm playing and we're at the bottom of a ruck or there's a break in play, I like to chat to my opponent. I try and chill out. 'Alright, mate? How's it going?' Sometimes you'll find someone who shares your attitude. 'Okay, aye. But it's a shit game, this one isn't it?' 'Yeah, ref's havin' a mare.'

One of those players I can't work out is Dafydd James, who was playing in both of those matches against the Ospreys for Harlequins. In the return match at The Stoop, I ran a dummy line which Dafydd bought and he hit me with a tackle. Not only that, but he tried to dump me into the turf. As I was laying on the ground he was pushing his fist into my face with my head pressed against the grass. It's actually one of his favourites. He's renowned for it. I didn't want to react so I just held onto him and then pushed him backwards before I jumped up. It meant I was a couple of yards ahead of him as we ran back to join play. I could hear him breathing hard behind me as we ran but I had that vital couple of yards. Suddenly, I could see that play was opening up ahead of us and that if I carried on running I'd hit our attacking line at the perfect moment to take the pass. I shouted to Matthew Jones to give me the ball and then burst through to score a try. My whole momentum had been created by running late into the line after Dafydd had held me down.

'Thanks, Daf,' I said and held my hand out for him to shake as I walked back. He ignored it and muttered something before walking off back to his posts. I enjoyed that moment because I love the idea of getting even with someone through scoring a try or making them look silly. In the long run, it causes more pain than punching them. We made it a pretty painful day for Quins that afternoon in early December. We were really fired up for the match from the very beginning. You don't get many chances for a night out when you're a professional rugby player, but we'd done some forward planning before that game. A few of us had arranged to go out in London after the match and stay the night in a good hotel. As we boarded the coach on Saturday morning, we were buzzing. We were looking forward to the night out almost as much as the match itself. It reminded me of the old days at Swansea when we'd plan to murder the opposition and then go out and get wrecked.

It turned out to be one of our best performances of the season. I put in a nice cross-field kick for our South

African wing, Stefan Terblanche, to score the first try. Then came my own first try after that spat with Dafydd. We were in control up front and cutting them to pieces behind. I didn't have a particularly good day with my kicking and missed a few, but the team performance was so strong it didn't matter. Will Greenwood got a try back for Harlequins but we let it rip after half-time. Ryan Jones scored our third try, I got my second, before Shane Williams and Matthew Jones finished things off. We finished up winning, 46–19 and embarrassed them in front of their own fans. I scored 26 of our points from two tries, five conversions, and two penalties. Sometimes you get days when you just feel untouchable and that was one of them. I wanted the ball all the time because I knew I could do some damage. I felt physically strong and I felt quick. My second try involved taking the ball on the run and getting on the outside shoulder of Will Greenwood. He tried to tackle me but I stepped inside and brushed him off and carried on all the way to the line. I took Greenwood on a few times during that match and came out on top. It felt good because this was a guy who was a very experienced England international as well as a double Lions tourist. Here I was, on his patch, running through him all day. If a younger player did that to me I think I'd have to consider retiring. Will went on to make a third Lions tour later in the season and I got to know him well in New Zealand. He's a fantastic guy to have in any squad – professional, thoroughly decent, and a really good laugh. He was one of my rivals for a slot in the Test team, but he still put notes under my bedroom door on the eve of the big matches, wishing me all the best. You can't fault him. He also got his own back by getting into the Lions squad ahead of me for the First Test.

One of the other pleasing aspects of that victory over Quins was the confidence shown by the whole team in attack. Prior to that match, we'd got a little bogged down in a kicking strategy that was too negative. Instead of attacking from anywhere when it was on, we'd always try and kick for territory as the first option. At The Stoop, we had such self-belief that we ran at them from very deep positions and it paid off.

The victory meant we had won two out of four in our European pool and if we could beat Munster in Ireland and then Castres at home, we could still make the quarter-finals.

We lost 13–9 out in Munster in the Celtic League the following week, but it was very tight and it certainly didn't dent our self-belief. We still felt we could stay top of the League come the end of the season. We also felt we could go back to Ireland and beat them in our crunch European tie. On Boxing Day we got things back on track with a convincing 28–7 Celtic League victory over the Scarlets before a huge crowd at The Gnoll. Our next trip was to Cardiff to meet the Blues, who had done a real number on us at the Arms Park the season before.

It was New Year's Day and the weather was awful – driving rain and a howling gale. Cardiff were struggling and it already seemed likely they would finish in the lowest position of the four Welsh regions. The Ospreys were going well, the Scarlets and the Dragons weren't too far behind, but the Blues were down the wrong end of the table. It meant there was a lot of pressure on them to win, especially at home. Some of the players were starting to feel that pressure and it was affecting them in strange ways.

Martyn Williams is one of the nicest guys in rugby you could ever wish to beat – modest, generous and a real team man. He's one of the most respected players in the Welsh squad. But he seemed to be in a daze for the Blues that afternoon, as if he'd gone into his own little world. I put a big tackle in on the Cardiff scrum-half, Ryan Powell. At the next ruck, I cleared out a couple of players and fell to the ground. All of a sudden, Martyn came flying in on top of me and started throwing punches. He was screaming, too. 'You don't like it in the face, do you, pretty boy! You can't handle it.' I managed to grab him and turn him onto his back and then some other players came in to break us apart. 'What's your problem?' I said to him but his eyes had glazed over. The referee came across and started talking to us, but I'm not sure Martyn heard anything. Mentally, he was somewhere else. 'Are you okay, or what? What's going on? Are you serious?' But he didn't answer me.

He was just staring into space. I wasn't getting any sense out of him. He just had this fixed expression on his face. The other players were standing around with their hands on their hips, watching. I shouted over to Tom Shanklin, who was also in the Blues' line-up. 'Is he serious or what?' Shanks just smiled and shook his head.

After the match, Martyn came over to me in the players' dining room and said: 'Sorry about that. I was just a bit frustrated.' 'Fair enough,' I said and that was it. He didn't expand on it, but I think the pressure of Cardiff's situation had got to him. He was captain and they were going through a difficult time. Things had rumbled up inside him and then just boiled over. I just happened to be on the wrong end of it. Thankfully, none of his punches really connected and I've been quite luckly in that sense. I've always managed to duck, dodge, or slide out of most of the punches that are thrown my way. We managed to avoid any of Cardiff's counter-punches in the game itself on that New Year's Day and came out 15–9 winners thanks to tries from Richie Pugh and Jason Spice.

The following week was the make-or-break match in Europe, away to Munster. I'd never played at Thomond Park before as the Celtic League match had taken place at their other ground, Musgrave Park in Cork. Thomond Park is in Limerick and is renowned as one of the most hostile grounds in Europe. When 14,000 of their very noisy fans are packed in there, it produces a very intimidating atmosphere. Their record there is incredible – they've never lost there in the Heineken Cup – and all through the week we seemed to read about nothing else in the newspapers. But we felt very confident we could beat them. We'd done it at Swansea in the Celtic League in September and we'd run them very close in Cork just before Christmas. The ground record just wasn't an issue for us as we all felt they were long overdue a defeat and hostile venues were not something we were uncomfortable with. But we got caught in the trap of getting dragged into their type of game instead of imposing our own. The game-plan had been to keep things fast and fluid and run them around a bit. We felt some of their older forwards might tire. Instead, we got bogged down in the kind of tight, close-contact, physical rugby they specialise in. It's going to take a very special team to beat Munster that way on their own patch and we couldn't quite do it. In the last 20 minutes we played some much more intelligent rugby and stretched them, but we just couldn't find the final pass. We eventually lost, 20–10.

We were out of Europe and it felt a massive dis-appointment. Munster are one of the most successful teams in the history of the tournament, but we felt we were a better all-round side. We just hadn't proved it on the day because we'd got our approach wrong. We'd lost to them twice and after both games there was a feeling that we'd contributed too much to our own downfall. It was a bitter pill to swallow. I felt absolutely gutted because I really wanted the Ospreys to be up there among the best teams in Europe, but to prove that you need to be in the knockout stages of the Heineken Cup. The only consolation I could find was that we were a young side and we'd be a stronger and more experienced one next season. It soothed the pain, but only slightly.

Those involved in Welsh rugby may argue that the Celtic League is now a tough competition, but we'll never gain the proper respect of English and French teams until we regularly see Welsh regions in the knock-out stages of the Heineken Cup. Munster are not respected for what they've done in the Celtic League; it's for what they've achieved in Europe.

I had one final match for the Ospreys before it would be time to link up again with Wales for the Six Nations. It was a home game against Ulster at St. Helen's. My groin injury had been niggling me for a few weeks and I was a bit concerned about making it worse before the game against England. I got through the Ulster game and managed to score all our points as we won, 22–21. It certainly wasn't one of the Ospreys' best performances and we were a bit fortunate. But we did enough and we stayed top of the table. That's exactly how I felt about my won game – that I'd done enough. I kicked five penalties and converted my own try which came when I took a high ball in front of me and just kept running straight through the Ulster defence. Even when running in for that try in the first-half, I was only going three-quarter pace. I didn't want to risk stretching and damaging the groin. At half-time, we were sitting in the tiny St. Helen's dressing room and Lyn went beserk. He accused us of not trying and of merely going through the motions. I sat with my head down, looking at the floor. I knew I'd been half-hearted and I was waiting for Lyn to tear into me. Instead, he pointed at me and said to the others that I was the only player who was really trying. Maybe I'd misjudged my own performance, or perhaps I was better at faking it than some of the others. Either way, the praise made me feel much better about things and we went out and got the victory. I had a bit of stick from the boys afterwards, for being singled out, but I felt perfectly able to give plenty back.

The groin injury was still playing on my mind, though. It had been there since November and the game against South Africa when I was hit from the side. I felt the impact all the way down my pelvis and from then on I started to get pains down my backside and in my groin. Playing each week wasn't doing it any good at all. Some mornings it hurt just getting out of bed and if I tried to stand on one leg it felt very unstable. Training was also becoming a bit of a struggle. The doctors and physios made me cut down my training to one session a day and stay off the hard surface at Llandarcy. I was also given a programme of rehabilitation exercises to try and

Back-breaking stuff. If we make a mistake in training then we
are forced to stand with our hands on our heads. Sure.

LEFT: Under surveillance. Heading for the flight to New Zealand at Heathrow Airport – and into the frustrations of the Lions tour.

RIGHT: Hitting the ground running. On my first appearance for the Lions, our 34–20 victory over Bay of Plenty in Rotorua.

BELOW: Easing the strain. My groin injury was always at the back of my mind on the tour and I eventually needed an operation when I returned home.

RIGHT: Facing the future. I scored two tries in the midweek victory over Southland in Invercargill, but in the press conference it was still hard to disguise my disappointment at missing out on selection for the First Test.

ABOVE: Fitting like a glove. I learnt a lot from Ian McGeechan and felt very comfortable with his style and approach to coaching.

ABOVE: Walk this way. The infamous picture of me in conversation with Sir Clive Woodward. I had absolutely no idea that we were walking towards a photographer who had been positioned by Alistair Campbell.

ABOVE: Short changed. I was desperate to make a big impression against Wellington but found myself substituted just as the match was opening up.

ABOVE: Try time. My two tries against Southland gave me a route into the Test team for the second match against the All Blacks.

LEFT: Tape conversation. Training with the Lions was not what I had expected. Sir Clive Woodward took a very detached role.

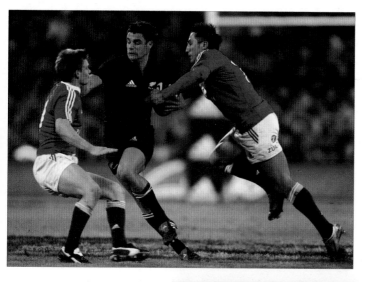

LEFT: Get Carter. Dwayne Peel and I try to get to grips with New Zealand's Dan Carter but it proved a difficult job to stop him in the Second Test in Wellington where he scored 33 points.

RIGHT: Chat room. In conversation with Jonny Wilkinson during the Second Test. Like so much of that Lions line-up, our playing partnership felt very under-developed.

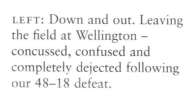

LEFT: Down and out. Leaving the field at Wellington – concussed, confused and completely dejected following our 48–18 defeat.

FAR LEFT: Tana Umaga, the All Blacks skipper, scores in the Third Test at Auckland, despite the attention of my Wales team-mate Ryan Jones.

LEFT: No direction home. Nowhere to turn as the All Blacks convert another try in Wellington.

MAIN PICTURE: Beaten and bowed. Ryan Jones is hit by the devastation of our Second Test defeat. But after coming out late to New Zealand, Ryan proved one of the real stars of the tour.

ABOVE RIGHT: Chick flick. Caught on camera with Charlotte at a gala dinner in London. Rumours that we argue a lot are well wide of the mark.

RIGHT: Stepping out. With Charlotte at the All Star Cup Celebrity Golf tournament at the Celtic Manor Resort where Europe beat the USA.

BELOW: Church recital. Charlotte yells her support for the Lions in Wellington after flying out for a brief few days during the tour.

Fame game. If I'm honest, I enjoy being the focus of attention, on and off the field. Being at the centre of things is stimulating.

strengthen the muscles in the groin area. From the turn of the year, I was put on a course of anti-inflammatory pills.

It helped going into the Wales environment. If anything, they were even more anxious about the injury than I was and every possible precaution was taken to make sure I didn't do it any more damage. They nursed me through it all the way and it involved making some changes in the tournament preparations. After taking some medical advice, the Welsh team management decided to alter training plans in order to protect my injury, which didn't make me too popular with the rest of the boys. Instead of going through routines indoors at The Barn, our facility at the Vale of Glamorgan complex, we trained outdoors at Pontyclun, even in the rain. The whole idea, again, was to keep me off a hard, unforgiving surface which could cause further damage to my groin.

We had 14 days between that match against Ulster and the Six Nations opener for Wales against England. In between times, the Ospreys flew up to Glasgow – minus all our current international players – and drew 27–27 at Hughenden. Those of us with Wales spent that weekend on the training field, fine-tuning our game-plan for the visit of Andy Robinson's England. I felt confident about beating them, although the idea that we would enjoy a triumphant tournament seemed ridiculous to most of the people filling the sports columns in the newspapers. We were quoted by the bookies at 40–1 to win the Grand Slam and when *The Sunday Times* got a load of ex-internationals together to pick their predicted Lions team for the summer, they didn't include a single Welsh player. I didn't read the article but I did notice the selected team because someone pinned it on our notice board at the Vale of Glamorgan.

Mike Ruddock picked a team to play England that was similar to the Wales side that got within a point of the All Blacks, but not identical. Gareth Thomas was still at full-back, where he had looked so solid, but Sonny Parker had been ruled out through injury so my centre partner was Tom Shanklin. Replacing Tom on the right wing was Hal Luscombe. In the pack, Robert Sidoli had come back to form with the Cardiff Blues and had replaced Gareth Llewellyn in the second row. Shortly after that Gareth announced his international retirement. The only other change was in the back row where Colin Charvis was replaced by Martyn Williams at openside flanker. Colin had got himself injured a couple of weeks before while playing for his club, Newcastle. Colin had been the man-of-the-match against New Zealand, while Martyn had been only able to get on the bench. But it was a measure of our depth that Martyn went on to be voted Six Nations Player of the Tournament.

England had their injury problems but the inclusion of Mathew Tait at centre was still something of a surprise. He was not a player we knew much about, but I swatted up on him pretty quickly. After all, he was only 18 – the new kid ready to shoot down the old guard. That focused my mind. I didn't want to feel like Will Greenwood must have felt after playing against me at The Stoop.

We played quite well that day, but not as well as we had played against New Zealand a few weeks before. The big difference, of course, was that we won by two points instead of losing by one. It's hard to overstate the value of self-belief and confidence in professional sport. It's the difference between thinking you *can* do something and thinking you *will* do something. I think the reason we won was not because of my kick, or because of Shane's try. It was because we had 22 players who, deep down, believed that they *would* win. The result, and the manner of it, was to change my life. I've seen it hundreds of times on TV replays and even more framed in my own imagination.

Four minutes left . . . deep breath . . . concentrate . . . believe in your technique . . . don't hit it too hard . . . you've got the legs . . . keep your head down . . . stay nice and light on the left foot . . . be flexible . . . strike it down the middle.

Thanks for coming.

CHAPTER THIRTEEN

Routine Entertainment

On Sunday morning, 6 February, I went down to have breakfast in the team hotel and was told by Simon Rimmer, our Wales team press officer, that I was required to do some media interviews. There was a function room where a TV camera had been set-up by the BBC. There was one chair in front of the camera, another behind it, and then behind that about 40 chairs set out in neat rows, each one occupied by a journalist. I did the television interview and then took loads of questions from the others in the room. They all wanted to know everything about the kick – how it felt, what I was thinking, whether I'd demanded to take it or had been asked, did I feel the pressure, and so on.

The truth was that I just put the ball down on the ground and tried to kick it between the posts. It's what I've been doing since I was five years old. The technique and the preparation may have evolved a little, but it's pretty much the same. When I was a kid, the one thing I wanted to do was see how far back from the posts I could go and still score. I'm still the same now. My whole approach to kicking hasn't really changed much over the years. No-one ever taught me to kick a rugby ball. I worked out my own technique and I've stuck with it. There have been some bits of advice taken on board along the way and Dave Alred, the Lions kicking coach, was useful to listen to, but mostly I rely on my own judgement. We don't have a kicking coach with the Ospreys or with Wales, although it seems that Neil Jenkins is now going to be involved as some kind of kicking advisor for the regional academies. But I don't think a kicking coach is an essential for international players. You should know what the correct technique is by that stage. If Wales ever feel the need to employ someone, then they'd be better off hiring an official ball boy to save me a lot of walking.

I have a few guidelines on my own personal little tick list which I follow when I line-up a kick at goal. I don't want to give away too many of my own secrets but the general principles are probably the same as those of every other kicker. I line up the ball on the tee, aiming it towards the middle of the posts or slightly off-centre if there's a wind. I take my five steps back and then I'm ready. I like to come in at the ball at something like a 45 degree angle. Stephen Jones approaches it almost straight on, while Jonny Wilkinson comes right around, almost from a side-on position. I can't quite work out how he manages to do that, but it works for him. Every goal-kicker has his own little trademarks. Jonny has the clasped hands. Neil Jenkins used to swing his arm before running up. Mine is an exaggerated step with my right leg, where my knee comes high up. Someone once called it a chicken step. It's always been there, ever since I started kicking. It feels natural because it gives me the momentum and gets me into my run up to the ball. It's from the run up that I get the full force into the kick. I like to crouch quite low, too. I want to feel solid and balanced. I want to feel that if you pushed me I wouldn't topple over.

I concentrate on the spot on the ball I want to hit and my peripheral vision takes in the area between the posts. I remind myself to stay light on my non-kicking foot, my left, and then concentrate on getting my weight through the ball. Like a golf shot, the ball generally travels in the direction your body is pointing. I don't go in for a lot of the complicated mental routines that some kickers have. All I like to imagine is that I'm on the practice field and it's just another training session. I focus on where I think the sweet spot is on the ball and imagine how good it's going to feel when I hit it. Like most things in sport, you can get too hung up on theories and stuff for what's basically quite simple.

Before I take them, I really believe that every kick I attempt is going over. You have to be like that. You can't have self-doubts. But, of course, not all of them do. That's just the way it is. There are things that sometimes go wrong; the wind might gust or sometimes the pressure of the ball is not quite right. It can be too high or too low. If the ball is soft you need to make sure you hit it sweetly and not too hard. With a hard ball, kicking it hard tends not to make much difference. You find that the air pressure of a ball can vary between venues. But they'll also throw on five or six different balls in a game, so thinking too much about the air pressure can actually mess your head up. As I say, the best advice I can give a young kicker is find a solid technique and keep your thoughts clear and simple.

The crowd never bothers me. At some grounds in England or Scotland you'll hear an announcer ask the crowd for silence for the goal-kicker, like he was performing brain surgery or something. Silence is somehow considered respectful. I don't get that. If people want to boo and hiss or whistle while I'm kicking, then that's fine by me. It means they think I'm worth trying to disturb, which is pretty respectful in itself. In fact, I find concentrating through booing or whistling – as regularly happens in France – is actually easier than dealing with silence.

Practice makes perfect. Also useful is having an enthusiastic helper. My father used to join me when I was young and was very enthusiastic. In fact, he didn't like me kicking a soccer ball about because he was convinced it was bad for my rugby goal-kicking. When my mates came around the house to ask me if I wanted a kickabout over at the park, I had to tell them that Dad wouldn't like it. Sometimes, I'd sneak out without him noticing but on those occasions I'd be guaranteed to miss a couple of kicks in my match at the weekend. Then Dad would say: 'I've told you. It's because you've been out there kicking a soccer ball.' He may have had a point, but I'm still not quite convinced. But now it's become like a superstition. If the Ospreys are warming up with a soccer ball, then I stay out of the way.

I enjoy goal-kicking because of the individual aspect of it. It's the one time in a rugby match where time stands still and the whole crowd, and the TV cameras, focuses on one player. He's the only one in the spotlight for 90 seconds or so. I enjoy that feeling. It can be a lot of pressure, like that kick against England. But it also gives me an awesome buzz.

That kick also seemed to get lots of other people excited. Suddenly, I was getting far more media interest than I'd ever had before. I did interviews for national newspapers, photo-shoots for men's magazines including fashion and motoring items, a restaurant review for the *Observer Food Monthly*, and got invited on TV programmes like the BBC's 'A Question of Sport' and Sky's 'Soccer AM'. I agreed to some promotional and advertising work for Gillette, EA Games and Nike. I was gaining a much higher profile and I've got to admit it felt good. It was my first taste of real fame and I enjoyed the attention and the pampering. The press soon caught on to my relationship with Charlotte and pictures of the two of us together began to appear in the newspapers. I suppose that increased my own profile further. Peter Underhill, my agent, hired SFX, one of the leading sports agencies, to represent me on a wider basis. It all became very hectic and just snowballed as the weeks went on.

For me, the kick that settled the match against England was reward for practice and a solid routine. I'm a big one for routines and preparation. When I'm preparing for a match I have a set routine and part of that is to spend time on my appearance. It's always been important to me. I've always felt that if I look the part, then I'll play the part. Spending time and effort on the way I look wasn't really commented upon before that kick, but afterwards it seemed as if every other journalist wanted to ask me about how often I shave my legs or what was the best brand of fake tan. I started using tan and going on sunbeds when I was 18. I'd always tanned pretty easily in the summer and liked the look it gave me. So I began topping up the tan in the winter months and realised it made me feel more confident. It makes the muscles look more toned and defined. Nowadays, I try and keep the tan topped up once every two weeks. It makes me look healthier and then I feel fit and healthy. It's all part of my routine.

My match day starts the same as every other day. I

wake up at 7.30am, regardless of what time I've gone to bed. I try to get my head down before 11pm to make sure I get at least eight hours sleep. But even if I've stayed up later than that, the built-in alarm in my brain always goes off at half-past seven. I can't remember my last lie-in.

I always have a proper breakfast and it's the first of at least five meals I'll eat during the day. If I'm feeling a little low on energy, I'll have seven. They won't all be huge meals, but the idea is to eat every three hours to keep my metabolism ticking over. It's not as though any dietician has ever told me to eat five meals a day. It's just something I've learnt that suits me and my body. If I can break down my intake into five portions a day, then I know exactly how much protein and carbohydrates I'll need to eat at each sitting. My breakfast is always the same – six poached egg-whites on toasted brown bread, followed by a big bowl of porridge with soya milk and a cup of peppermint tea. I never touch dairy products as they're hard to digest and make me feel slow on the training field. Egg whites are fine, but the yolks are fattening and full of cholesterol. If I'm still hungry after the porridge, I'll have some fruit. I've been off the dairy products for a couple of years now. I used to have a very sweet tooth and loved my desserts, especially the ones my mother used to make. But after a while I found I stopped craving custard slices and craved the healthy stuff instead.

Routine Entertainment

One of the things I've really got into over the past couple of years is sushi. I can't get enough of it. Strangely, when I toured Japan with Wales as a 19-year-old I didn't fancy it at all. I thought it looked disgusting so I turned down all offers to try some. I ended up eating lots of non-Japanese food there which wasn't particularly good. It's only after I came back home that I started trying it and found I really liked it. There's a restaurant in Cardiff, Zushi, where I like to go and if I'm running late for somewhere they'll often fix me a takeaway I can pick up on the way. I tend to eat a lot of fish because it's got so many good things in it and nowadays if I snack it'll be Ryvita with mackerel.

On the day of a game, I'll finish breakfast about 8.30am and go back to my room. I'll watch TV for a couple of hours and then think about some of the moves we've planned for the match. If it's an evening game I'll have brunch at 11.30 – normally a bit of chicken and brown rice, no sauce, but I'll squeeze a lemon or lime over it and have some plain vegetables. Then, it's back to my room to get ready. I'll have a bath and shave my legs. I don't bother rinsing the razor in a cup on the edge of the bath. I rinse in the bath and if there are loose hairs on me when I come out then I'll take a shower. I shave my face and do my hair, using Dax wax. When it's quite long – and it's about two-and-half inches at the moment – then it can take a fair bit of time to spike it all up, nice and neat.

Normally, my room-mate has started banging on the bathroom door by now. So, I'll have a quick rest on the bed and then afterwards I'll go and check my weight. I like to be exactly 96kg. If I'm a little bit lighter then I'll usually feel quicker on my feet, but not quite as strong in the contact area. If I'm more than 96kg, then I feel a bit sluggish, even though I'm strong. That's why I like to be bang on 96 and I'll work towards that mark all through the week.

My pre-match meal for an evening game would be taken at about 3.30pm. I'll have more chicken or fish, plenty of bread and energy drinks. With Wales and the Ospreys, there's normally a team meeting before we leave for the stadium. I realise these are necessary, but I can't say I enjoy them. I don't mind listening to others, but I'm not a great talker in front of groups of people. It reminds me of being in school and I'd just prefer not to be there. If it was a one-to-one conversation then it would be fine, but being asked my views in front of 30 people makes me feel uncomfortable. The sooner I can get out on the pitch, the better.

In the dressing room, I like to make sure all my kit is the way I like it. The most important piece of equipment is my gum shield. It helps absorb all the hits to the face and ensures you don't end the game minus your teeth. I'd never step onto a pitch without it. When I used to play all my rugby at outside-half I didn't wear padding on my shoulders. But since switching to centre, I now

wear pads because I take a lot more physical punish-
ment. Without them, bruises can take longer to heal.
My pads are ones I've cut out and had sewn into my
tight, long-sleeve top which I like to wear under my
team shirt. I've always had this thing about wanting
my arms covered over. It makes me feel more solid and
compact. These days, almost all the jerseys are short-
sleeved but I don't like the feeling of catching a ball
without clothing over my arms. It can get hot, though,
when the weather's warm so I may need a re-think on
that one.

The silver boots started in the summer of 2003. I was
hoping to wear them at the World Cup, but then I wasn't
picked and so it didn't happen. Shane Williams started
wearing them and beat me to it for Wales as he wore
them in that tournament. I'd wanted to wear them since
seeing lots of Premiership soccer players with them. I
thought they looked great. Football has always been a
big influence on me. I love the way some of the players
look and move, especially the ones with quick feet.
There's nothing better than watching Cristiano Ronaldo
run down the wing, boots flashing as he goes around
defenders. I've always enjoyed watching Manchester
United. Eric Cantona was a real hero of mine. I loved
the way he played, but more than that I loved the way
he strutted about as if he owned the place. There was
something about the way he looked, his mannerisms,
everything. David Beckham was an obvious player to

admire for the way he played, and the way he looked, and I also liked David Ginola when he was at Spurs.

On days when I don't have a game, I'll stick to the same kind of routines for diet and resting. Generally, alcohol is out of the question – except when a team is celebrating winning a trophy or out on a 'bonding' session. But every now and again – I'd say about once a month – I'll go out and have a good few beers with my mates in Bridgend. It's more of a mental thing, to let go from all the rules for a night, and then it's back into the regime the very next morning. I can normally guarantee I'll train twice as hard the following week because I don't want to let my standards slip. A good session on the beer can freshen you up mentally. There are some players, like Jonny Wilkinson, who hardly every touch a drop from one year to the next. If it works for them – and it obviously works for Jonny – then great. But I think I'd go a bit mad if I wasn't able to let my hair down every now and again.

When you're training hard and playing a very physically demanding sport, then getting enough rest in is an absolute priority. I live on my own in a house in Pencoed, which is ideal for relaxing in and I'm perfectly happy with my own company. My mum pops round once a week to do a bit of cleaning, but generally I manage to keep the place reasonably tidy and make my own meals. Mum also does my shopping trips which is a big help as it can take me a couple of hours just to fill one little basket. In Wales, everyone wants to stop and talk about rugby and ask how things are going. It's fantastic to see so much interest, but it does tend to hold you up if you're in a hurry. The local kids near my house are also keen to talk all the time. They'll knock on my door and say, 'Are you Gavin Henson?' If I say yes, they'll go, 'No way! Seriously, are you?' 'Yeah, I am.' 'Really? Wow, cool! What's it like?'

CHAPTER FOURTEEN

Celtic Kings

It felt strange going back to play for the Ospreys again after Wales had won the Grand Slam. Although, myself, Shane Williams, Adam Jones, Brent Cockbain, Ryan Jones and Jonathan Thomas had only missed four Celtic League matches, it seemed as though we had been away for months. Odd things happened at training. We'd call a move and then realise nobody knew what we were talking about because it was a Wales move rather than an Ospreys one. We'd forgotten some of the Ospreys' calls and the difference in tactical approach between the two teams took some re-adjustment. We'd grown used to a running and handling game, but the Ospreys like to use their pack a bit more because it's powerful and can dominate the opposition. For me, there was the switch back to more of a kicking strategy, to get into deeper areas of the opposition territory. With Wales, we had become used to attacking from almost anywhere.

But maybe the most difficult change was simply coming down to earth again after the massive high of winning the Grand Slam. After we had beaten Ireland, we celebrated in style on the Saturday night and then had the 'all-dayer' at the Brains-sponsored bash on the Sunday. It meant I was still feeling pretty bashed myself come the Tuesday when I reported for training with the Ospreys. Of course, if we had merely been cruising along in the middle of the table then it wouldn't really have mattered. We may not even have played for a while. But the Ospreys had remained top of the table while we'd all been away and they still needed one more victory to clinch the Celtic League title. After the Welsh squad boys had left following the victory over Ulster, the rest of the Ospreys squad had consolidated the position by drawing away at Glasgow, 27–27, beating the Borders at home, 34–10, and then winning very impressively away to Leinster, 16–12. The night before we beat Ireland, the Ospreys had also hammered the Newport Gwent Dragons, 30–0 at St. Helen's. But with Munster having rallied well in the second half of the season, the Ospreys still needed to win at least one of our last two remaining league fixtures to secure the championship title. The second of those games was away to Connacht, our bogey team. In our previous three Celtic League fixtures against them, we'd lost every time. It meant we had to beat Edinburgh at The Gnoll on Saturday evening, otherwise we'd face a very tricky visit to Connacht a week later with the title on the line. Far better, we realised, to pull out all the stops and wrap things up in front of our own fans.

After our weekend of Grand Slam celebrations, I was still feeling pretty rough on the Monday and not much better the following day when I turned up for training at Llandarcy. But far worse than the hangover was my sense of regret at how things had turned out on that drunken Sunday night at The Yard. After staggering out of the players' party, and the realisation of the damage I'd caused, I'd spent a pretty uncomfortable Monday. Firstly, I'd been called in to see Mike Ruddock and Alan Phillips for a dressing down over my behaviour. Then, I'd gone to apologise to the directors at Brains. Finally, Alan had arranged a meeting with a South Wales Police superintendent who'd laid it on the line how his officers had been incredibly lenient towards me. I was extremely lucky, he pointed out, that I wasn't arrested for being drunk and disorderly with a likely court summons slap bang in the middle of the Lions tour.

So, all in all, I wasn't really able to get my head around playing for the Ospreys in a championship decider in four days' time. In fact, I told Lyn Jones I was in no fit state to play. He said we'd sort things out later in the week after we'd all prepared for the game. On the day before the match I still felt unable to concentrate, so I repeated my feeling that it would be in the best interests of the team if someone else played instead of me. The last thing I wanted was to go out and have a stinker which might cost us the championship title. I felt I was being honest, because in normal circumstances these are the games I live for – a big crowd, live TV, and a massive prize at stake for the team I'd been part of for two seasons. 'See how you feel in the morning,' said Lyn.

Saturday morning arrived and I rang Lyn to say I was really looking forward to us clinching the championship that night, that I'd be there with all the boys, but I still didn't feel in the right frame of mind to play. 'Fair enough,' he said. 'See you later.' A few hours later, Mike Cuddy rang. Mike is joint chief executive of the Ospreys and one of the real driving forces behind the region. He's a successful businessman in the demolition industry and someone used to getting his own way, even if it sometimes takes a little bit of gentle persuasion. 'Gavin, can I come round to see you?' he said and he was at my house within a few minutes.

Mike is a big guy and he seemed to take up most of my kitchen as we sat around the table. I was adamant I shouldn't play. He was insistent I should. He was also hacked off with the WRU for hauling me over the coals just a few days before the Ospreys' biggest match of the season. Fair enough, he felt, for them to feel the need to come down hard on me. That was up to them. But he was bemused with their timing and felt they should have waited until after the title had been decided. If the Ospreys had hammered a Wales player for his behaviour in the week leading up to the match against Ireland, then there would have been uproar.

Mike left thinking he had persuaded me to play, but to be fair I'd given him no promises. Derwyn Jones, the Ospreys team manager, then called me and pointed out all the reasons why I should play. Finally, Lyn called and said: 'You need to play this game.' I eventually agreed and, far more nervous than I am before most games, I jumped in my car and drove to the ground. I didn't really speak to many of the other players before that game. I needed to concentrate hard on what I had to do. But it all went better than anyone could have thought, especially me, and we beat Edinburgh, 29–12. They actually played some very good stuff that night and we were obliged to pull out all the stops. But there was just no way we were going to be denied. Just like Wales the week before, we'd all come too far to let things slip. Jason Spice scored one try, I got the other, and I also kicked two conversions and five penalties. I won the man-of-the-match award but in my TV interview after the game I said it had been a really difficult week. A handful of people in the country would have known what I was talking about, but most of the viewers must have thought, 'Difficult week? What's he going on about now? He's just won the Grand Slam and the Celtic League!'

Of course, after the match I realised that if I hadn't played I'd have regretted it for the rest of my life. It was a fantastic experience to win the title in front of our own supporters and the atmosphere at the end, when Barry Williams lifted the trophy, was incredible. For the second time in a week I was privileged to be around people who had worked so hard for success, backed by supporters who had shown so much faith and trust to get behind a brand new venture. Neath and Swansea had been around for a hundred years and we had asked a lot of people to set aside those traditions and rivalries. Thankfully, we had managed to offer them something to celebrate in only our second year in existence as well as providing a glimpse of what could become an awesome future. It was a special night.

Barry deserved his moment of glory because he's been a superb skipper for the region since taking over from Scott Gibbs. He's a very funny bloke off the field and sometimes it's hard to imagine that kind of character being a seriously good captain. But Barry's proved himself very knowledgeable and a shrewd decision-maker when you're in a tight game. There was a bit of criticism from some quarters when he announced he was giving up international rugby. Not many players turn down the chance to play for Wales if they're still at the top of their game. But I think Barry did the right thing in concentrating on captaining the Ospreys because he's been able to give the job his full attention. He leads by example on the field and really gets the forwards going well. When he's not there, you're very aware of his absence. I'm sure he could have won a lot more caps at hooker for Wales, but their loss has definitely been the Ospreys' gain.

Having suffered with two hangovers already from the previous weekend, I think I would have settled for a quiet night in with my Celtic League winners' medal. But that was never really a possibility, once the champagne had started to flow. There were too many excited team-mates who were determined everyone in the squad was going to party. We began with a few drinks in Neath and then went on to Swansea, an appropriate enough way for the Neath-Swansea Ospreys to celebrate their success. Lyn, Sean Holley, and Derwyn were all out with the players which summed up the togetherness of the whole group. As we still had a few more games left until the end of the season, the management hadn't laid on any special function for us. I think they didn't want to be encouraging too many wrecked heads and bodies before we'd completed all our games. So we just piled into a few bars and it meant there were loads of fans celebrating right alongside us.

The encouraging thing to me about that night was the attitude of all the players towards success. There was no feeling whatsoever of this being the pinnacle. For everyone involved it was just the start, just a taster of the things we all felt possible. I believe we can defend the Celtic League title successfully this season, but also there's a massive determination within the squad to make a bigger impact in Europe. We're a young squad and we don't feel we're anywhere near our potential. Our new £27 million 20,000 all-seater stadium, which we're sharing with Swansea City, has created huge excitement amongst the players and will take us onto a different level from the other three Welsh regions. It's a venue to rank with any in Europe, but we're aware we need to provide the performances and the success to do it justice.

The recruitment policy of the Ospreys will be interesting to see over the next couple of years. There is a commitment to developing our own home-grown talent, which has to be the right way to go. The region is a rugby hotbed and there's an amazing amount of talent out there which can be identified at a young age. It's then a case of developing and honing that talent through our regional academy, plus the club sides at Neath and Swansea, and finally making sure new players are always ready to come in. But in the short-term there also has to be some recruitment of more senior players. I was disappointed to see Adrian Durston was allowed to leave at the end of the season as we haven't taken on another full-back to replace him. The departures of Elvis Seveali, Dave Teueti and Nathan Bonner-Evans have also left us short in certain areas. I think the region is right not to sign run-of-the-mill overseas players, but one or two quality international players would be more than welcome. Too many Welsh clubs in the past signed people who were no better than the local boys they were keeping out of the side. Or else they got hold of players who just weren't in the traditions of the club. Salesi Finau at Llanelli was a classic example of that. The Scarlets have always been renowned for playing attractive, skilful rugby and for being hard but fair. But Finau didn't fit into that mould. For me, he's been a bit of a cheap shot merchant – someone who goes out of his way to hurt people with head-high tackles. I'm amazed so many referees have let him get away with it. He also doesn't like it when the same treatment is dished out to him as a few players have proved over the years.

The trip to Galway to play Connacht on 10 April was now just an extension of our championship celebrations. There was even a suggestion in the Welsh media that we might put out a weakened team and not take the match seriously, just to mess up the Cardiff Blues. They were still battling for Heineken Cup qualification and needed to finish above Connacht to earn themselves a play-off against an Italian team. The rumours turned out not to be true because we ended up fielding a full-strength side and we won the game, 22–13. I was a bit surprised that all the Welsh international players were selected but I could understand it. We had never beaten Connacht and it was time to put the record straight after those three defeats. It was also important to show that our title was fully deserved and that we were clearly the best team in the tournament. Without any real pressure on us, we played some good rugby that day and scored three good tries. It did prove a huge help to the Blues and I was pleased with that. Guys like Rhys Williams, Tom Shanklin, Gethin Jenkins and Martyn Williams have become good mates in the Wales squad. I didn't want them to miss out on the Heineken Cup. That wouldn't benefit them and it wouldn't benefit Wales. I'd hope that if the tables were turned one day, and we need them to do us a favour, then Cardiff would respond and do their bit for the Ospreys.

I didn't know it at the time but my try, two conversions and a penalty took me past 500 points in Celtic League rugby. Statistics don't really bother me but it was nice to feel that I'd made a solid contribution to the Ospreys' success. After that game, we had two more matches left but these were both in the Celtic Cup. This was a kind of add-on knockout tournament that had been bolted onto the end of the season in order to provide a fuller fixture list. We wanted to do well, but it was inevitable that it would feel a bit of an after-thought after we had just won the league. I was rested in order to protect my groin injury for the Lions tour and watched the boys beat Ulster, 23–16, to reach the semi-final. That was away to the Llanelli Scarlets at Stradey Park and it turned out to be a good one to miss as we lost, 23–15. I don't particularly enjoy losing down at Stradey, so I was happy enough to be excused. I picked up the result on a text message while I was sunbathing with Charlotte on board a yacht in the south of France.

It had been a long season for the Ospreys which had begun with a friendly on 12 August and had finally ended on 7 May. We had played 20 Celtic League games, won 16, drawn one, and lost three. With the bonus points system it meant we'd won the title by seven clear points from Munster, Leinster and then the Dragons. So many players in our squad had impressed me. It had been a real group effort. But a few had stood out and really gained my respect and admiration.

Duncan Jones had begun the season as a player being tipped for the Lions tour. I'd always rated him highly as a prop, but he was desperately unlucky to get injured just before the Six Nations started. His performances for the Ospreys, though, were superb. Andy Newman, our big second row, was another who was fantastically consistent. Andy didn't feature in the Wales squad, but he was the kind of character who did it week-in and week-out for the Ospreys. Those types of players are priceless if you're going to win a league title. People like Andy and Andrew Millward just kept us going through the periods when the international players were away. Andy is 6ft 7in and almost 20 stones. Adam Jones, our prop, is almost as heavy. The two of them are big mates but when they get together in the gym there is only ever one topic of conversation. All they talk about is food. They're always discussing how many sausages they ate last night and what type they were. Or else one of them will be inviting the other around his house for a bar-beque and there'll be more lists of the mountains of food they intend to eat. It's ridiculous, but very funny if you're in the gym with them. Adam is hilarious and quite sharp. He and Duncan have taken plenty of stick over the years for their long, curly hair but they've stuck with it. It's become their little trademark and the press caught onto it in a big way with all these features about The Hair Bear Bunch. But Adam's no fool. He knows he's never been so popular with the women. That hair's not going anywhere.

Adam's workrate is tremendous. He used to carry a fair bit of excess weight but he's worked really hard on his shape and his fitness. He's always in the gym and his strength is incredible. His position of tight-head isn't one where there are lots of choices for Wales, so his emergence has been a real blessing.

Brent Cockbain is another guy who had a massive influence on the Ospreys last season. He's brought a physical edge to the pack that we were missing before he arrived. Brent's nickname is 'Disaster' because every-thing he bumps into – including team-mates – ends up in bits. Every single Ospreys player tries his utmost to avoid Brent when we're training. But you need eyes in the back of your head. He's all elbows and knees and you know that if you run into him you're going to come off worse, a lot worse. The number of people Disaster has maimed on the training field is unbelievable. On the quiet I think he's rather proud of his reputation. I'm just glad that when he's hitting rucks in matches it's normally opposition players who are on the receiving end.

We didn't see Brent for the first two months of his career with the Ospreys after he joined us from the disbanded Celtic Warriors. His son, Toby, had been diagnosed at 10 months with a brain tumour and died just a few months later. It had already been a difficult time within the dressing room because Jonathan Thomas's father had died just a short time before and many of us had gone to the funeral. Now, we were at little Toby's funeral alongside Brent and his wife, Kate. Both JT and Brent were an inspiration to me when they returned to the squad. They talked honestly and very openly about things and their strength of character was amazing. I don't know whether I could have coped as well as they did. When Brent wanted to talk about Toby then we talked, but for the most part all the players went out of their way to try and make life as normal as possible for Disaster. He was still known by that nickname and he still got stick for injuring people in training. Later on, Brent and Kate set up the Toby Lloyd Cockbain Foundation*, a charity that supports children with cancer in Wales. I was delighted to be able to donate the silver boots I wore against England for a

* www.tlcfoundation.org.uk

fund-raising event where they were auctioned. They raised £8,500. Seeing Brent deal with events in his life with such courage made me realise how insignificant most rugby players' problems are in comparison – including my own.

Brent is an Aussie who has made Wales his home and although I've got my concerns about the effects of the residency rule on the Wales team, as an individual who has chosen to make his life here I've nothing but respect for the guy. The same goes for Sonny Parker who grew up and began his senior rugby in New Zealand. Sonny was very unlucky to miss out on the Six Nations through injury because his impact on the Ospreys last season was immense. I've never played alongside a back line player as physically strong as Sonny. He's great to be with in the centre and a total professional who trains extremely hard and looks after himself. It's good to be around those players because their influence rubs off on others. There are loads at the Ospreys, but when I was at Swansea there were very few. Guys like Mark Taylor, who was a total professional and really set high standards at Swansea, were in a very small minority. It's hard to overstate the importance of that kind of influence when you're a younger player. As a youngster you take your lead from the common viewpoint inside the dressing room. If the prevailing attitude is that it doesn't matter if you're out on the beer every night, then that's the culture the youngsters will take on board. But if all young players see are professional athletes taking good care of their bodies, then they'll soon fall into line.

The Ospreys already have a strong batch of young players coming through the academy who will be the stars of tomorrow. They're hungry for success. I think that's the unspoken motivation for many senior players. The sight of some keen, young kid coming through the ranks always keeps players on their toes.

CHAPTER FIFTEEN

How Do You Want To Be Remembered?

My earliest memory of the Lions was watching Scott Gibbs on TV score a try against the All Blacks in 1993. Scott was just 21 at the time. Not only was he young and Welsh, he was from Pencoed. To see someone from my own village make that kind of impact at the very highest level of the game made a huge impression on me. I was 11 years old, sitting at home in the lounge next to my father, watching this young hero of mine smash his way through to score against the most feared rugby team in the world. It was inspiring stuff and I made up my mind. That's what I want to do.

Four years later, Scott was at it again. He was the Man of the Series against South Africa, for his defence more than anything else. I remember watching these huge Springbok players charging towards him and Scott just smashing them into the ground. A legend was born and although I didn't know it at the time, Scott would be one of the main reasons why I'd later join Swansea. But it wasn't just the matches that inspired me. I remember watching the video of the '97 tour, *Living with Lions*, and thinking: 'It would be brilliant to be part of all that – the matches, the support, the intensity of it all.' When I was with the Wales Under-16s group we were given a blank piece of paper and told to write down our goals. At the top, I wrote, 'I want to become a British Lion.' I'm not sure I ever quite believed it would happen, but it was always my goal. I think I always realised there was a big slice of luck involved with the Lions. You had to stay fit, you had to get picked, and you had to make sure both things happened at a certain time every four years. Emotionally, my dream was always to play rugby for Wales. But professionally, in terms of self-satisfaction, the personal goal was always to play for the Lions.

It seemed as though everyone was talking about the 2005 Lions tour to New Zealand from the moment the season kicked off. It was in all the newspapers, even as early on as the November internationals. There were pundits and ex-players predicting what the Lions team and the squad might be. It wasn't on my mind, though. I was just concentrating on playing well enough at No.12 for Wales to ensure I kept my place and got picked for the Six Nations. After the Ospreys beat Harlequins at The Stoop in the Heineken Cup in early December, there were a few suggestions in the newspapers that I might make Sir Clive Woodward's squad. Getting the better of Will Greenwood was seen as significant. I started wondering about my own chances around that point, but I still knew that the Six Nations would be critical. If I didn't have good form throughout that tournament then I knew I'd have no chance.

My first meeting with Woodward had come before the Wales match against New Zealand in November. Clive had decided to spend a week with us at the Vale of Glamorgan Hotel as part of an attempt to get around all four of the home countries, picking brains and swapping ideas. It was purely a watching brief, but that's the way he wanted it. He didn't speak at any team meetings. He just sat and took it all in. One morning during that week, I was on my own at breakfast when he came and sat next to me. He asked me how I'd enjoyed the World Cup experience the year before and seemed surprised when I told him I didn't get selected. Then, we talked about positional play of half-backs and centres and he told me he really liked the idea of a converted No.10 playing at No.12. He said it had been a big plus for him with England when he put Mike Catt at inside centre alongside Jonny Wilkinson as it gave the team an extra kicking option. It was something he'd be looking to do on the Lions tour. It was only a brief conversation, but I felt really encouraged by it. I felt as though I was making an impact and I was the type of player he was looking for. He also struck me as a very impressive thinker about the game and I liked the way he regarded the midfield area. All in all, he made a very good first impression.

After the victory over England at the start of the Six Nations, I allowed myself to think a little bit about the Lions. I knew I'd played well and I thought if I could hold my form over the next four games then I'd have a pretty good chance of getting selected. I couldn't be sure because I'd never gone through a Six Nations before and I didn't know how I'd cope. But I felt reasonably confident. I'd guessed the Lions would take five centres in their squad and it didn't need a rocket scientist to work out that one of them would be Brian O'Driscoll. That left four places up for grabs. As Mike Tindall was out injured and the England pair of Mathew Tait and Jamie Noon were inexperienced, that left me competing with the Irish and Scottish boys, plus Tom Shanklin. I thought Tom would go, but I fancied my chances of getting one of the other three places.

The first indication that I was in the mix came when I received a package through the post over the Christmas period. It was sent from Clive Woodward and it included lots of pictures with slogans on them. One of them said, 'How do you want to be remembered?' Another asked, 'Who says we can't do it?' I thought it was good motivational stuff and it certainly focused the mind as to the massive event that would be taking place at the end of the season. Also in the package was a multi-coloured wristband in red, white, blue and green. I tried it on. It looked a bit conspicuous so I took it off again. I decided I wouldn't wear it until I saw how many other players were wearing theirs. As it turned out, I never saw anyone wearing one, although there were rumours in the early days that some of the English boys were parading theirs.

That package had been sent out to 140 players in Wales, England, Scotland and Ireland. It was a wide spread but it had the effect of getting players to talk about the Lions. The buzz had been created and from that point of view, it had performed its purpose.

The squad for the British and Irish Lions tour to New Zealand was finally announced on Monday, 12 April, at noon. Having given the Lions organisers our mobile phone numbers, we'd all been told that we'd be informed by text message if we were in. It was the morning after the Ospreys' final Celtic League match of the season, our victory over Connacht, and we'd been out celebrating in Galway the night before. I was sitting in the departure lounge of Galway Airport, feeling slightly worse for wear. Shane Williams was on one side of me. Adam Jones was on the other. They looked even rougher than me. Nobody said much, but everyone kept checking their mobile phone. Five to 12 . . . nothing . . . 12 o'clock . . . nothing . . . 10 past 12 . . . still nothing. There were no TVs or radios around, either, but at 12.10 my mobile bleeped and there was a message. It wasn't from Sir

Clive Woodward, though. It was from Matthew Williams, a mate of mine, otherwise known as Fat Boy Roy. 'Congrats, you're in!' it said. I was just about to call Roy when my mother rang. She congratulated me as well and became quite emotional. She wished my grandfather, Trevor, had still been alive to see my name in a Lions squad. I asked her if Shane was in. Yes, she said. Adam? No. So I then had to turn to Shane and tell him he was going to New Zealand with the Lions, but tell Adam he was staying at home. I thought, 'This can't be right. I shouldn't be having to tell him this.' Adam looked a bit gutted, naturally, and then told me to ask my mother which props had been selected. Unsurprisingly, Mum didn't know.

The promised text messages from the Lions never came through, something for which they apologised when we all met up for the first time. Some people might take that as a bad omen, but in terms of organisation the rest of the entire tour went like clockwork.

My overwhelming feeling at being selected was one of massive relief. I was desperate to be included and thought I'd probably done enough. But the bitter experience of being left out of the World Cup squad by Steve Hansen in 2003 had taught me to take nothing for granted. I suppose I'd built up my own defence mechanism. I'd have been devastated if I'd been left out, but I had to expect nothing or else I'd run the risk of finding the rejection shocking as well as devastating. When my close friends and family had asked me whether I thought I was going to the World Cup, I'd said: 'I think so.' When they asked about the Lions I just replied: 'I don't know.'

Having been named in the squad, I was able to move on to the next obstacle – my groin. After the Wales match against Ireland I had come off the anti-inflammatory tablets because I'd been on them for long enough. I'd started taking them at the turn of the year so there was the risk of doing further damage to the injury. I struggled through the Edinburgh game for the Ospreys, but after the Connacht match the whole thing was becoming ridiculous. I could hardly walk. I needed to do something else to keep the problem at bay, otherwise I knew my place on the tour could be in jeopardy.

After talking it through with the Ospreys' physio, Chris Towers, with the WRU physio, Mark Davies, and with the Lions' own medical people, I decided to have a type of pain-killing cortisone injection. I went to London to see a specialist who gave me the go-ahead. The injection itself was done at the University of Wales Hospital in Cardiff and it was the worse pain I've felt since I broke my leg at 17. I'm not very good with injections at the best of times, but the needle looked about eight inches long and they sent it straight in from above my pubic bone. They then kept it there for at least five minutes – although it felt like five hours – while the contents were emptied into my groin. I watched on the screen as the anaesthetising fluid floated inside my body like smoke until it finally settled. Looking at it made me feel quite peaceful, until the pain came back again in waves. They left me on the bed for 10 minutes to recover and when I stopped feeling faint, I managed to stagger to my feet. It felt sore, but they said that would soon pass. It should then feel fine for six weeks, they said, before the effects would start to wear off. I thanked the doctor and the nurse and then limped away out of the door.

The soreness from the injection lasted a few days, but once that went it felt fantastic. I met up with the Lions for our pre-tour training camp and was under strict instructions to take things slowly. That was fine by me. The last thing I wanted to do was rush back, break down, and then find myself off the tour.

As it was I had almost put myself off the tour without any assistance from the groin injury. This was strictly to do with me and my mouth and it was my first major misunderstanding with Clive Woodward.

The 45 Lions all met up in Cardiff for our first midweek get-together towards the end of April. The venue was the Vale of Glamorgan resort, which should at least have settled any anxieties for me as it was on home turf. Sadly, I felt about as comfortable as I did waiting for the needle to go in at the hospital. It was billed as a team building exercise and tour introduction over the course of two days. It sounded daunting to me because I don't enjoy those kinds of things, but I managed to reassure myself by thinking what I would have been like a year earlier. Had it been April 2004, then I would have been ridiculously nervous. But my success against England and the whole Grand Slam experience had given me much more confidence to face people; so had being thrust into the limelight as the bloke who was going out with Charlotte Church. It meant that my profile was much higher than it had been 12 months before. The other players in the squad would know who I was and I wouldn't feel inferior, as if I didn't belong. My profile felt almost like a layer of protection that would save me from painful introductions spent trying to explain who I was.

My first impressions of the whole Lions operation was that it seemed fantastically professional. There were so many back-up staff, it was incredible. The attention to detail was mind-blowing. There were doctors, physios, kit men, legal people, a chef. Nothing had been overlooked or left to chance. All the coaches, including Clive, and the back-up staff, introduced themselves and said a few words. Then, Brian O'Driscoll stood up and he was followed by the three captains, or senior players, from the three other nations – Gareth Thomas, Lawrence Dallaglio and Gordon Bulloch. So far, so good, I thought. Soon after that, though, the weird stuff began. We were put into little groups of six or seven and asked to do role-play situations. We'd be given a number of objects, like wigs and strange masks, and were told to act out a little play that would have to include set phrases given to us beforehand. These phrases were the Lions' motivational labels, like 'The power of four' and all the rest of them. Each group had to perform their act in front of all the others. I felt a terrible sense of dread before it was our group's turn to perform. If I could have walked out then, without anyone noticing, then I would have considered it. But another part of me thought, 'Just do it. Bite your lip and do it.' I'd walked out on an international team meeting once before and I wasn't about to make the same mistake twice. What made it even worse, though, was the film crew that were recording every second of it. I felt bad enough, anyway, without some camera up my nose and the knowledge that my embarrassment would later appear on some DVD. I gritted my teeth and went along with it, but I'm not the best at hiding my feelings if I'm not enjoying something and I think it must have shown. It just wasn't for me.

I wasn't the only one who felt uncomfortable. Lots of other boys were, too. Gareth Cooper, our Wales scrum-half, was hating every minute of it. In fact, he hates that stuff even more than I do. Of course, some of the English boys were loving it. They'd probably done it before every week at public school. And some of the Irish were in their element. Obviously, I understood that the whole point of it was to make us feel uncomfortable, to take us out of the 'comfort zone'. But team building doesn't have to involve embarrassing each other. And if it was all for the good of the squad, why did the cameras have to be let in?

When all the sessions were finally over, there was a media briefing. Some reporter came over and asked me how it was going.

'Fine,' I said. Then he asked me what we'd been doing.

'Oh, just some role-playing exercises and a bit of painting.' Intrigued by this snippet, he asked if I'd enjoyed it. I thought about it. What's the point in lying? What's wrong with just saying how you feel?

'Not really,' I said. 'I felt a bit uncomfortable. In fact, a few of us did.'

That was that and I didn't think much more about it. We all checked out and weren't due to get back together again until preparation for the warm-up match against Argentina. On the Saturday night, I went along with a mate to visit his sister in London. I drove us up and we had a meal and a beer. It was a nice, pleasant evening and we were due to stay the night. At about 10 o'clock my mobile rang. I looked at the number and didn't recognise it. I thought, 'I'm not answering that. Not on a Saturday night at 10 o'clock.' A few minutes later it rang again with an answerphone message. It was Clive Woodward. He sounded angry, short with me. He was very calm but very deliberate, as though he was choosing his words carefully. He said there was a big problem with something I'd said. The Sunday newspapers had been onto him as it was all over Ceefax. He wanted me to call him back as soon as I got the message. It didn't matter how late it was, I just had to call him. I'd caused a problem and he needed to make a decision on it by the morning.

'Oh, fuck! Fuck! What the hell have I done now?' I grabbed the remote and switched on Ceefax. 'Oh, fuck! Shit! You idiot!' The story looked really bad, the way they'd written it. They'd been pretty selective in the quotes they'd used and made it out to be some massive put down of Clive and his methods. I called up the story on the internet. There was a much longer version on there with all my quotes, not just a sentence or two taken out of context.

'Well, that's not *so* bad,' I thought.

Then I thought again. 'What are you doing? Have you gone nuts?! Of course, it's bad! It's all bad! Very, very bad! You're fucked!'

My head had gone. I couldn't think straight. I was in a mess.

'Come on! Think! Think!' I looked at my watch. It was 20 minutes since he'd left the message. There was nothing else for it. I'd have to call him.

'Alright, Clive. It's Gavin Henson. Everything alright or what?'

No. Everything wasn't alright. He explained how loads of newspapers had seen the story and had got onto him for his reaction. He couldn't understand why I'd said it. He'd rung Brian O'Driscoll and Brian didn't feel uncomfortable. Why did I feel uncomfortable? I told him I thought the two days had been great but it was just that I wasn't comfortable with the role-play stuff. I was more comfortable out on the training field.

'The thing is,' he said. 'This is going to create massive headlines in the papers tomorrow. And that means I've got to make a decision on it. This is the kind of thing that's going to lose us the Test series.'

That's it, I thought. He's not going to take me. I'm going to get dropped even before we leave!

'Look,' I said. 'I'm really sorry if this has caused you a problem. I'm just not comfortable with those things and I was asked a straight question.'

He didn't seem convinced. He mentioned the Matt Dawson and Austin Healey articles that had appeared during the 2001 Lions tour.

'That's how you lose Test series,' he said.

This went on for about 15 or 20 minutes until he repeated the fact that he'd have to make a decision in the morning. He told me he'd sleep on it and call me again in the morning. I decided to call Derwyn Jones, the Ospreys team manager and a former Wales international, and explained what had happened. Derwyn told me not to worry and said that he'd call Clive and try to smooth things over. I later found out that Derwyn had given me a pretty good character reference and had insisted to Clive that he'd have no problems with me on the tour. You won't have another Dawson and Healey situation, he told him.

I couldn't stay the night in London. There were too many things racing around in my mind. Thankfully, I'd only had the one beer, so I jumped back in my car and drove back to Wales. It was around 1am when I got into bed, but that didn't stop me from waking up at six. I got up and switched on my mobile. I was desperate for it to ring. Nothing happened. The morning passed and there was still no word from Clive. That's it, I thought. He's probably making plans to call up someone to replace me. He's probably preparing a statement. By noon I couldn't handle it any more. I picked up the phone and dialled Clive's number. He was just getting off a plane in Ireland. 'Oh, Gavin. I was just about to call you. I've had a think about things and I think we can move on. Derwyn Jones called me and he's a good guy. He spoke very highly of you. I think we'll be okay. But listen, Gav. You've got to be as sharp off the field as you are on the field. Remember that.'

I told him I understood and it wouldn't happen again. We ended up on good terms and he said, 'Trust me. I won't let you down.' I told him I did trust him and we left it there.

A couple of newspapers did pick up on the Ceefax story, but they didn't make a great deal of it. There were certainly none of the 'massive headlines' that Clive had feared. I felt relieved that it had blown over and I was still on good terms with a bloke I'd never worked with before. But it did strike me as odd that he considered the incident as something that might lose us the Test series.

The Lions had one match in Cardiff before we left for New Zealand. We were to play Argentina at the Millennium Stadium so it meant a week of good, solid training in Cardiff. But as I was injured, I didn't really feel part of it. I think the same went for Tom Shanklin and the England prop, Matt Stevens. We were all having treatment with the physios, but it felt as though the real action was going on elsewhere. I realised, though, that the vital thing for me was to get the groin injury right. There could be no question of cutting corners. As it turned out, the match against the Pumas didn't exactly run to plan. As a mate of mine suggested to me afterwards, it was probably a good one to miss. The boys who played were still struggling to learn about each other's game and everything was slightly off key. Argentina played well and their team-work was obviously much smoother so it became a difficult night. Ollie Smith scored the Lions' try but although we often looked strong up front we were never able to build on it. The thing that struck me, though, was the impressive nerve shown by Jonny Wilkinson. He had a tricky penalty right at the end which he needed to put over in order to earn the Lions a 25–25 draw. He never looked like missing.

The non-playing members of the squad were allowed to watch the match with their friends, family or girl-friends, as partners had been staying in the hotel. I joined Charlotte in one of the stadium's hospitality boxes. The squad members who'd played were disappointed but everyone considered the match to be no real indicator of what was to come. Clive, too, seemed unconcerned even though the media tried to paint it as a mini-disaster. Things seemed fine between me and Clive. When we'd met up for the week, he'd even made a joke of things by shaking my hand and calling me his 'phone friend' which put me more at ease. We were back on an even keel.

I had one more day of physiotherapy on the Wednes-day and the following day we left the Vale of Glamorgan for Heathrow. I rang my parents and kissed goodbye to Charlotte at the hotel. The final press conference before departing took place at the Vale where I was given some idea of just how huge the media interest was going to be. There were dozens of reporters, camera crews and photographers and every player in the squad was made available. It was the first time I'd seen Alastair Campbell in action as the tour management's media consultant. He looked relaxed and as though he knew what he was doing. He also seemed to have a clever knack of suddenly appearing behind my shoulder whenever an interview was about to start.

How Do You Want To Be Remembered?

Later that evening we boarded our flight at Heathrow. I was looking forward to it – 25 hours of sleeping, eating and being pampered. When you feel like just resting, then I always feel being on board an aeroplane is not a bad place to be. I sat alongside Matt Dawson, Will Greenwood and Gordon D'Arcy. But there wasn't much chat. Everyone was more concerned with trying to get some sleep. I popped a sleeping tablet and prepared to nod off. It was going to be a busy 46 days ahead.

CHAPTER SIXTEEN

'Stephen on for Gavin'

My jet lag lasted the best part of a week. Perhaps it was the pure excitement of what lay ahead, but the dreaded lag seemed to have it in for me this time. I spent the first week struggling to keep my eyes open after 7 o'clock at night and then feeling wide awake at 4 o'clock in the morning. The management had tried to get the effects of the flight out of us by insisting on a fitness session as soon as we arrived in Auckland. We hardly had time to dump our bags in the hotel before we were being flogged in the gym. A few of the boys who were on the 2001 tour must have thought this was going to be another trip where all the debate was about excessive training. But it didn't turn out that way at all.

Just before we'd all met up in Cardiff, I'd become a bit bored with my hair. So I had dyed it red. But it had already started to fade by the time we reached Auckland and a few of the other players reckoned I now needed to dye it red, white, blue and green in honour of the 'power of four'. Clive admitted he wasn't sure about the red. He said his son had also dyed his hair red and almost got himself expelled from school.

We had a couple of days of gentle settling in and then began out first proper training session. I'd finally been given the all-clear on my groin and was told I could take a full part in the whole session. I was so happy at being able to sprint and stretch without any pain, I felt like a kid in the school playground. I was almost delirious with happiness and started throwing out crazy, ridiculous passes and trying outrageous things with the ball. It was just my way of reacting to the sheer joy of being able to train again. Because I was trying too hard, I dropped a couple of passes and two of my more ambitious passes were also spilled by other players. I didn't think anything of it. It was our first session on the field and I'd really enjoyed it. Just being able to run around and throw a ball felt great.

The next morning Clive called me into the team room at our hotel in Auckland. He had a tape on the TV screen of yesterday's training session. He found a bit where I'd thrown out a pass that had been dropped.

'Why did you throw that pass?' he asked me.

'I don't really know,' I said.

He then showed me another clip where I'd dropped the ball.

'What were you thinking there?' he said.

'I don't know. I just dropped it.'

He carried on through the tape, highlighting all my errors and over-ambitious passes. He wanted to know what was going through my mind. I didn't know what to say. I didn't know what he wanted to hear. In the end I told him I was just happy to be training again and I'd wanted to have a bit of fun.

'It was our first session of the tour. I wasn't really taking it that seriously.'

As soon as the words had come out of my mouth, I wanted to take them back. I thought, 'You idiot. What did you say that for?' He gave me a strange look, confused but also amazed.

'I don't want to see this kind of thing happening again in training,' he said. 'This is the kind of thing that will lose us the Test series.'

It was the second time I'd heard Clive say that. But it wouldn't be the last. If someone did something wrong, stepped out of line, or turned up late for a meeting, he'd repeat it in front of everyone. 'This is the kind of thing that will lose us the Test series; if we don't get this right, we'll lose the series,' or sometimes, even, 'This is why we're going to lose the Test series.' I couldn't get my head around that. As a player, I don't really want to hear the word 'lose'. I don't think it's a word you should hear very often. I wanted to be thinking about why we were going to *win* the series, rather than why we were going to lose it. That first training session may not have

been perfect, but it was only the first. To me, it wa
about feeling positive about training with new pla
and getting excited. Maybe, I'd got over-excited. I
I've always felt training is where you should try out ne
things. You don't get chances to try things out for th
first time in Test matches, so you have to experiment in
training.

Training may have started strangely, but everything
else about those first few days was spot on. The organisation of the tour was faultless. We'd turn up at airports
and the bus would take us right to the plane. We'd fly
somewhere and then have another bus to pick us up.
Timings were always kept to perfection. Whenever we
moved anywhere it was like a military exercise and it
usually went like clockwork. Inside the hotels, the food,
the laundry, the rooms, everything was spot on and all
you had to worry about was playing rugby. We were
given an official welcome in Rotorua, where they performed a fantastic and very scary haka and a couple of
days later we held a public training session at North
Harbour Stadium in response to the massive interest
there seemed to be in the Lions.

I quite like mixing with the public at those kind of
events. Of course, we didn't do much in training – certainly nothing that might be picked up and made use of
by anyone watching. It was all very basic stuff. That
was fine by me. After all, the whole point of the thing
was to please the fans by letting them in on our territory,

to make them feel part of it for a day. It was a PR exercise, but it seemed a good idea to me. A big crowd turned up – 4,000 fans – and after the session we all began to sign autographs. The fans were very patient and were waiting for their turn when the whole thing was suddenly brought to a very sharp end. Security guards moved in and began ushering the players away. Some of the crowd in the tunnel area started calling out: 'Please, Gavin! Sign this. Gavin, One more! I'm you're biggest fan!' The security guard was getting edgy and started signalling for me to go. But I hate walking away from things like that when people are expecting you. It's just not on. This was meant to be a meet-the-public session. I walked away and could hear how disappointed they were. So I turned around and went back to sign some more. Now the security bloke started getting really heated and began pulling me away. I was told I had to go. I walked away from the crowd and shook my head. Some of them seemed quite annoyed and so was I. If you're going to do these things, they should be done properly – not just a token effort as we'd done.

Clive was standing at the top of the tunnel, waiting. He asked if everything was okay. Not really, I said, and explained to him why I felt we'd let a lot of people down. He just couldn't understand it. 'That's life,' he said. 'It's time to go. Believe me, the Lions have done a lot of good work here today.' It didn't feel like that to me, though. It felt like a bit of a token gesture. The New

Zealand people love their rugby and really admire the Lions' traditions. They are also very knowledgeable. I just felt we'd conned them.

The team to play Bay of Plenty in the opening match of the tour was announced the following day, but Clive had told me I was in earlier in the week. He wanted to give me time to prepare mentally. I appreciated that, but something he said began to ring a few alarm bells. Although I'd played inside centre throughout the Six Nations, I had moved to full-back during a few international matches and I'd played 12, 15 and 10 for the Ospreys. I assumed my versatility might open up some extra avenues on the Lions tour. But when I asked Clive what position I'd be playing, he looked taken aback. 'You're playing at 12. I only see you as a 12,' he said. It seemed as though a few of those avenues had already been blocked off.

I had been practising with the group of four or so goal-kickers from the start of the tour, under the tuition of Dave Alred, the specialist kicking coach. There was myself, Jonny Wilkinson, Ronan O'Gara, and Charlie Hodgson. Stephen Jones would soon join us once his season had ended in France. Ronan had been chosen as the goal-kicker for the first match and I was happy enough with that. As I'd spent a few weeks nursing my groin injury, I hadn't done much goal-kicking practice over that period. Ronan obviously had done and he's a proven international goal-kicker for Ireland. It didn't bother me, as I felt I'd get plenty of goal-kicking opportunities later on in the tour.

Things went well in the build-up to that first match of the tour in Rotorua. I felt fit and pleased to be in the first Saturday team, lining up alongside the tour skipper, Brian O'Driscoll. A couple of hours before we left for the game, the phone rang in my room. It was Clive. He said he wanted to talk through a couple of things, could he come up. I was getting quite used to our little chats by now. It seemed to be his way of doing things. He sat down and told me he wanted me to be very vocal during the match, to keep talking to the players either side of me, especially Ronan. No problem, I told him. Out of the blue, he then said he had no doubts that I'd be starting in the First Test against the All Blacks. I was ecstatic, although I tried to stay calm. 'That's great to hear,' I said. After he'd gone, I felt really good. It was so reassuring to know that the head coach had so much faith in me, that he believed I was good enough. There were some players I felt were automatic selections for the Test team – like Brian and Lawrence Dallaglio – but it was fantastic to hear the coach say that I'd be starting, too.

Before the game, Gareth Jenkins spoke to everyone in the final team meeting. Gareth had been selected as the forwards coach for the midweek side and was the only Welsh coach on the trip. He's always incredibly passionate when he's with the Llanelli Scarlets and he was no different with the Lions. He spoke straight from the heart about the pride of being a Lion and became so emotional that at one stage he seemed close to tears. Some of the other players who didn't know Gareth well were uncertain quite how to take it. But no-one was left in any doubt about the history of the shirt and the great traditions of all the players who had gone before us. For me, that meant following in the footsteps of Scott Gibbs, who had worn the same No.12 jersey I was about to wear.

The first 15 minutes of that game felt like I was playing for Wales. We were adventurous and positive and we attacked them in waves, keeping the ball in hand. Bay of Plenty just couldn't cope with us and Josh Lewsey scored two great tries. Then, we suffered our first big blow of the tour. I was defending at a ruck and out of the corner of my eye I saw Lawrence Dallaglio come in and seem to slip. There was a noise, a kind of crack. It reminded me of the sound I heard when I broke my leg at 17. Instantly, I had a bad feeling, and, sure enough, Lawrence didn't get up. He'd broken his ankle and was out of the tour. We just seemed to lose all our momentum and our composure after that. The forwards no longer had the same authority. Bay of Plenty came right back into the game and although we rallied again in the second-half it wasn't quite the convincing performance it had looked in the opening quarter. We ran out winning 34–20 with Mark Cueto, Tom Shanklin,

Dwayne Peel and Gordon D'Arcy adding to Lewsey's two tries.

Lawrence's injury took all the gloss off things. He'd prove to be a massive loss. I didn't know him before the tour but in that first week I was very impressed. He had the genuine presence of a leader. Some players talk a lot in team meetings, but often they're doing it for effect. Nobody really listens. Dallaglio reminded me of Gibbsy. When he spoke up, it was always worth listening to and everyone tuned in. It was a huge setback for the squad and you could see how gutted Lawrence was afterwards by the look on his face. He stayed on the tour for a further week and gave a brilliant speech in a squad meeting just before the match against the Maori. I wasn't involved in that game, but after listening to him I felt desperate to play. Speeches never normally have that effect on me.

Bay of Plenty weren't a bad side and they had some pretty good back-line moves. At times it was a close game, but it proved to be like so many of the matches on the tour. We would struggle on occasions, but I never felt we were going to lose. I was taken off after 60 minutes and felt irritated by that. I'm not a player who's used to being taken off. The last quarter of the game is usually when it becomes loose and spaces begin to open up. That's when you can take advantage. D'Arcy came on to take my place and I sat down on the bench. I was annoyed because I felt I'd done okay, but could have done more in the final stages. I went into the dressing rooms at the final whistle and walked over to Clive as everyone was milling around.

'Everything okay?' I asked.

'Yeah, fine. You did really well tonight,' he said.

'So why did you take me off?'

He looked at me and he started to laugh. He said the game was getting tight and he wanted to use combinations of players who were used to each other. That's why he'd sent on D'Arcy to play with O'Driscoll and Ronan O'Gara.

'So I didn't do anything wrong, then?' I wanted to be clear. I needed to know what he thought.

'No. You did fine.'

It was the first time I'd ever played alongside Brian O'Driscoll and I'd been really looking forward to it. After that match against Ireland in the Six Nations, when he'd pulled my hair and tried to gouge me, I thought he might be a bit of a knob. But he turned out to be a real good guy. First impressions on the field can often be very wide of the mark. The partnership had felt good in training, but it didn't really spark in that first match. I felt it was okay, but knew it could be a lot better with more match practice. Playing alongside Ronan O'Gara also took some getting used to. I was used to outside-halves who went up in defence and made an aggressive tackle. But Ronan liked to hold his space just before the contact, so it became more of a soak-up tackle. That meant I was flying up ahead of him and getting caught too far up the field. It caused a few mix-ups. When I played with Jonny Wilkinson it felt a lot more familiar, because he likes to go up and accelerate through into the tackle in the same way as Stephen Jones does for Wales.

Clive was quite upbeat after the match and felt it was a big improvement on the display in Cardiff against Argentina. But although the first game was over there was still time for one more slip-up on my part; I'd forgotten my suit. The personal luggage was always sent on ahead of us before we travelled, but somehow I'd forgotten to hand in my suit. As everyone began to change into theirs, I suddenly realised mine was back in the wardrobe in Auckland. Knowing how strict Clive was on any lapses, I didn't want to be accused of doing something that would 'lose us the Test series', so I had to think fast. I put my tracksuit on and stood out like a sore thumb, but I had a plan.

'Where's your suit?'

'Never wear one after a game. Just a superstition of mine, but I didn't want to go against it on my first match.'

I walked out of the dressing room. Surprisingly, I think he bought it. But Bill Beaumont, our tour manager, gave me a smile and told me to remember it next time.

The next day, 5 June, the team was named for the second match against Taranaki in New Plymouth on the

Wednesday. I was surprised to learn I'd be on the bench as I was expecting to be rested. The only conclusion to draw from being in the 22 for both the first two games was that I'd definitely miss the third game against the Maori. It turned out to be the right conclusion.

Taranaki were dogged enough and actually led 7–6 at the break. We were struggling but we managed to pull clear after half-time and won comfortably enough in the end, 36–14. Geordan Murphy scored a couple of tries, but the guy who really played well that day was Charlie Hodgson who controlled everything from fly-half. Michael Owen also had a good game at No.8 and there was talk of Mike replacing Dallaglio in the Test line-up. I didn't come off the replacements' bench – but I did remember my suit. It was someone else's turn to forget something. Martin Corry was captain for the day, but when he ran out and was supposed to put our Lions toy mascot on the touchline he realised he'd left it in the dressing room.

Training was going well and I was feeling fit. My goal-kicking was good in practice and I was doing a lot of extra weight sessions on my own in the gym. One or two players used to join me, but most would use that time to rest. I've always liked to get extra weight sessions in when I can, though. It's what I'm used to at home.

The team for the second Saturday game had been named, a fixture I'd been keen to play in when I'd looked at the list of matches back in Wales. The Maori would be very tasty. Everyone knew it was going to be a really big game. But it was still hard to know what Clive was thinking in terms of his selection. It didn't look quite like a Saturday Test team, but neither did it look like a second string. Gordon D'Arcy was named at inside centre, alongside O'Driscoll, and it was their first start together. D'Arcy was the guy I considered my biggest rival for the Test No.12 shirt. He was superb in the 2004 Six Nations, but he'd missed the 2005 tournament because of injury and was still finding his way back to form. Before I'd gone on the tour, I'd had a little meeting with Lyn Jones and Sean Holley, my coaches at the Ospreys. They'd wished me luck and given me some tips. As I was leaving, Lyn had said: 'Of course, you won't make the Test team. They'll play D'Arcy. You'll be on the bench.' I don't know whether it was Lyn's genuine feeling or whether it was one of his motivational mind games. That's the thing with Lyn. You can never tell. But I felt he was correct in viewing D'Arcy as my main obstacle to a Test place.

The Maori game was Gordon's big chance, but it wasn't really the type of match to be playing in if you were still feeling a bit rusty. I felt a bit sorry for him – and for the others. It turned out to be absolutely brutal. The Maori were so fired-up. I've never seen a team as physically committed. They played as if it was the last game of rugby they were ever likely to play again. For players still getting to know each other, as the Lions boys were, it was a pretty tough day at the office. Gordon and Stephen Jones both went off with cuts and the dressing room afterwards looked like a war zone. Like all the New Zealand sides we faced, the Maori were very committed in the contact area and liked to drive through so low at the ruck. Andrew Sheridan, our prop, got sin-binned, which didn't help our cause, but the match went away from us when Carlos Spencer came on as a Maori replacement. I don't think Spencer's got the complete game but he's got a pretty good one, especially as an attacking playmaker. He always seems to have time and he set up the try that won them the match, 19–13.

At the end of every Lions game, the non-playing members of the group go into the dressing room. That's great when they've just won a game, but when they've lost it's very difficult. You don't really want to be anywhere near it. We went into the Hamilton dressing room after that match and the players looked pretty down. It was the first defeat of the tour and it had jolted everyone. The response of the coaches was to work very hard on the tackle area in training. That's where they felt we had lost it. Our rucking needed to be sharper, more aggressive and with lower body positions. That became the focus of the next few training sessions. We did plenty of drills, but I wasn't convinced. I thought we should have concentrated more on our moves with ball in hand. I've also got this fear of drills so late in the season. It's an invitation for players to get hurt. I try and shirk out of them. By that I mean, I'll perform the skill but I don't see any point in trying to do it at 100mph and risk injuries – to myself and others. But some players just can't help themselves. Blokes like Lewis Moody, Neil Back, Lewsey and O'Driscoll don't really do things by half. I prefer to be in the other camp – the players who'll wink at you and then you know they're only going in at 70 per cent. They're safer.

We had played three matches and suffered our first defeat. That was enough for the New Zealand media who begun to write off our chances. Not that I spent any time reading their newspapers, but rugby gets so much coverage on the TV out there you could hardly not be aware of their mood. We left Hamilton for Christchurch, in the South Island, for a couple of days' training, and then moved on to Wellington for the midweek game at the Westpac Stadium, where the Second Test would be played two-and-a-half weeks later. I'd been looking forward to those few days in Wellington as Charlotte was coming out to stay with me. The management had no problems with wives and girlfriends spending some time on the tour and staying in the players' rooms. Some of the boys also had their kids around for a few days, which was nice to see. Unlike previous Lions tours, every player had been given single rooms for the entire trip so there was never a problem. The management wanted to treat the players like adults and everyone respected that. At first it felt odd having a single room for a rugby tour, when I'd always been used to sharing. There was no-one to chat about game-plans and tactics with. More importantly for me, there was no-one to remind me that a team meeting was about to start downstairs in five minutes. For the first few days, every time I spent time in my room I was worried I should I have been somewhere else. Whenever my phone rang, I thought, 'Shit, what have I missed now?' The management said at the outset that if anyone felt they would rather share a room, they'd arrange it. No-one did, probably because they didn't want to seem a bit gay for requesting it.

Charlotte was on a tight schedule and only stayed with me for three days. It was a long way to come for three days but I'm glad she made the effort. It was great to have her around. We didn't want to create a lot of fuss, so we hardly left the hotel room. When I trained, Charlotte crashed out and watched films while she tried to get over her own jet lag. She's quite good at just lazing about. She was keen to know whether I'd make the Test team and I told her that things seemed to be looking quite good. At least, that's how it seemed. I was only going on what Clive had told me. When she left, the New Zealand papers claimed she'd swore at their reporters at the airport. The truth was that she was rushing for her flight and one reporter went out of her way to slow her down. Sometimes, people forget

Charlotte's only 19 years old. She attracts a massive amount of attention wherever she goes and that can be hard to cope with. Not only are people watching her every move, but there are some people who like to make life difficult for her just to provoke a reaction. She was a long way from home and feeling quite emotional as we hadn't seen much of each other in those few weeks. It was also going to be a few more weeks yet until we returned home.

The match against Wellington was my second start of the tour and was 10 days before the First Test. On most Lions tours, the Test side gets a run-out on the Saturday before the first international in order to give them a dress rehearsal. But Clive had stressed to everyone that he wanted to give his selected players a good rest going into the First Test, possibly as much as 10 days. That made the guessing games even more difficult. The Wellington match was exactly 10 days before the Test and, to me, it did have the look of a Test side. Even so, some likely Test players, like Steve Thompson and Richard Hill, weren't in it, so it was impossible to be sure. I was selected at inside centre. Jonny Wilkinson was at outside-half and Stephen Jones was on the bench.

I was excited about playing alongside Wilkinson. The guy was a real professional and training with him throughout the week had gone really well. He's very vocal on the field, he likes to clean out at rucks now and again – which suits me as I can slot in at 10 – and he's obviously a world class goal-kicker. He's also a better defender than I had imagined, when he gets his hits right. There had been a huge debate over his fitness all season, but I felt he looked fit and ready to go. We got on well and I really admired the bloke. Like me, he takes his preparation very, very seriously but he's much more obsessive than me. I like to switch off now and again, but I'm not sure Jonny *knows* how to switch off. It's 24 hours a day with him – every day.

We beat Wellington 23–6, but like most of that tour we were only convincing for patches of the game. Gethin Jenkins and Gareth Thomas scored tries and I was really pleased for both of them, but we never really put them away. I was playing opposite Ma'a Nonu, an All Black centre with a big reputation. He didn't really do much all game, so I was happy with that. I was also quite pleased with the way I'd played and felt I'd created quite a few openings. We looked dangerous in attack through the whole game. Our defence in the midfield – with me, Jonny and Brian – also held up well and they didn't manage a single try. I felt my kicking out of hand was solid, too. But once again I wasn't allowed to finish the match and I ended up feeling massively frustrated.

After 62 minutes I was taken off and they sent on Stephen Jones instead of me. When I saw Steve coming on, I thought he was about to replace Jonny – a No.10 for a No.10. After all, Steve and I were the Grand Slam partnership and we hadn't been tried together as yet.

But then I noticed it was me. Jonny was moved to centre and Steve went to No.10. I was gutted, completely gutted. I couldn't wait for the game to end. Watching the remainder of it from the bench was making me feel sick.

I walked into the dressing room and saw Clive.

'Why d'you take me off?'

'It was always pre-planned. I'd always intended to bring Stephen on in the second-half.'

'So, you're happy with what I did?'

'Yeah, you were great. You're doing fine. There's no problem with the way you're playing. I just wanted to look at Steve.'

Okay, I thought. He seems happy. He had even given me the wink as I walked off. But the next morning I was having treatment with one of the Lions physios. I told him I was gutted I'd been brought off.

'Yeah, it was a strange one, that,' he said. 'On my headset, I could hear the call to put Stephen on for Jonny. They said it three times – Stephen on for Jonny. Then, at the last minute, they changed it to Stephen on for Gavin.'

I had an uneasy feeling in the pit of my stomach. I didn't know it then, but in that split second when Clive had changed his mind over the substitution, my Test place had just gone down the drain.

CHAPTER SEVENTEEN

The Shadow

Clive Woodward wasn't the only coach I spoke to in the dressing rooms at the Westpac Stadium. The Wellington coach was John Plumtree, who had given me my first taste of senior rugby at Swansea five years before. Plum had gone back to New Zealand after leaving Swansea and had worked for a time as an analyst with the New Zealand Rugby Union. But his heart was still in coaching and he'd done very well with Wellington since taking charge, leading them to successive NPC finals. He hadn't changed. He was still the same old Plum – straight to the point and able to see through most of the bullshit. He even asked if I was out for a beer or two. I had planned to give him my Lions jersey, but, unfortunately, by the time he came into our dressing room, one of the Wellington players had already talked me into a swap. But it was still good to catch up.

We travelled from Wellington to Christchurch and

then on to Dunedin, where the next match was against Otago on the Saturday, a week before we played New Zealand. I was still running the Wellington match through my mind and decided I'd done okay. One of the problems on the tour so far had been that few players were breaking tackles, but I managed to do that a few times against Wellington and I hoped it would count in my favour.

It was colder in Dunedin, but still dry and mild compared to the weather we'd experience by the time the Test series began. Like a few other things they had up their sleeve, New Zealand were still holding back on their really bad weather. Otago played some good stuff in the first-half, but the Lions took control later on and came through to win, 30–19. The man-of-the-match was Ryan Jones, my mate at the Ospreys who had only arrived on the tour a few days before as a replacement for Simon Taylor, the Scotland forward. Ryan had been on tour himself in North America with Wales and looked fit and enthusiastic when he joined up. When his chance came, he really grabbed it with both hands and had a storming match at No.8, even impressing the New Zealanders, which takes some doing. Ryan scored one of the Lions' three tries, with the others coming from Will Greenwood and Shane Williams. But what was interesting was the way Ryan just played his own game and thrived on it. He hadn't been part of all the meetings and all the strategy. He just turned up, got his kit on, and gave it a crack. Sometimes, there's a lot to be said for keeping things simple. Mind you, I wasn't too convinced by his new habit of wearing an Alice band. Backs can get away with that kind of thing, but forwards shouldn't really do things that draw attention to their big ears and noses.

Clive was quite bullish after the game. He talked in the press conference about 'something special' building within the squad and a 'warm feeling' about the Test series. He also paid special credit to the Welsh players in the party and stressed how impressed he had been with their attitude.

It was now the countdown to the First Test in Christchurch. There was a tension in the air. Everything had been ratcheted up a notch or two. The 'business end' of the tour, as some people were calling it, was about to begin. We trained on the Saturday and the Sunday and the coaches wanted to run with Stephen Jones practising at No.10 and Jonny Wilkinson at 12. That gave me an uneasy feeling. I thought, 'I can see what's happening here.' After the second session, Jonny came up to me and seemed as though he wanted to talk.

'I think they're considering playing two 10s instead of a 10 and a 12,' he said. I nodded. He was almost apologetic and a bit surprised at the way things were going. 'I'm not really a 12. You're the 12. But it seems to me they're thinking of going with two 10s playing next to each other, instead of a normal 12.' I told him

I thought he was probably right, but said we'd soon find out.

Early on the Sunday evening, the whole squad was called into a team meeting at our hotel, the Crowne Plaza, in the centre of Christchurch. We were all a bit edgy as we sat down, no-one quite sure what to expect. Clive got up and spoke in front of everyone for five minutes. He underlined what a difficult job he'd had in selecting the side and how the whole squad had played their part. Now we were into the crucial part of the tour, he said. There were going to be some disappointed faces in a moment when he named the 22. The important thing was to stick together. The reaction of those not in the 22 was critical. If cracks appeared then that would, 'lose us the Test series.' By this stage I think I knew what was coming. I wasn't going to make the starting line-up. He was going to pick Steve at 10 and play Jonny at 12. I'd have to be content with a place on the bench. I was gutted, but I was braced for the bad news.

Then he revealed the squad of 22 for the First Test. Steve was there at No.10. So was Jonny at 12. I wasn't even among the replacements. I stared again at the seven names who'd be on the bench as Clive put the side up on the screen behind him. Nope, not there. The cover for the centre was Will Greenwood. Clive put the All Blacks 22 up next to our team, so they were side-by-side, and began telling everyone how he wouldn't want to swap any of our players in the 22 for any of theirs. But by that stage I'd stopped listening. I was in my own little world – confused, devastated, bewildered. I just couldn't believe it. I'd expected not to be in the starting line-up, but not to even be on the bench? Why? What was going on? I felt completely numb, in a daze, and in a strange way a bit panicky. This was worse than the Wales Under-16s rejection, worse than the World Cup, worse than all those other rejections combined.

What had happened? How could he have changed his mind so completely from the day of the Bay of Plenty game, the day when he'd told me he had 'no doubts I'd be in his starting line-up for the First Test'? There'd been no warning, no explanations. I'd asked him after every game if I was doing okay and he'd said, 'yeah, you're doing fine.' I just couldn't fathom it. I was in shock.

Early on, when we'd been kitted out, along with all the rest of our stuff every player had been issued with a little card, the size of a business card. On the one side was a picture of Clive Woodward and his phone number. On the other side, it just said, 'What The Fuck Is Going On?' The idea was that if anyone felt confused or angered at a team meeting they would be able to wave their card in the air and then have their say. Funnily enough, no-one had done this at any meeting so far. There had, though, been plenty of very funny suggestions among the players of what to do with the cards. The funniest was that we should photocopy them and

271

hand them out to the Lions fans. As I sat there, looking up at that squad list for the First Test, I thought, 'I wish I had my card with me. I wish it wasn't in my room. I'd wave it in the air, right now.'

In truth, though, I don't know whether I would have waved the card. No-one else had. Clive had this way of presenting things so that you felt awkward asking for explanations or putting over a different point of view. He'd always say, after every selection, that the way we respond as individual players is going to determine the outcome of the Test series. You were made to feel as though voicing any unhappiness or concerns would be seen as undermining the cause. I could see his point to a certain degree. The non-selected players have to do everything to support those in the 22. But I think the head coach should be able to have people question his decisions in meetings without being made to feel uncomfortable.

The meeting ended and we all went for dinner. I went back to my room and phoned my parents to tell them the bad news. Then I just sat there, gutted. After our misunderstanding over the role-playing sessions in Cardiff, Clive had told me, 'I won't let you down.' Later on, he'd sent me a text message saying the same thing and he'd repeated it in my personal tour folder, which all the players had been issued with. But now, when it came to the crunch, I felt he had let me down. He'd told me I'd be in the side and now I wasn't.

I'd arranged to meet a friend downstairs in the hotel lobby, so I left my room and headed down in the lift. I thought, 'Well, at least nothing else can top that this evening.' But I was wrong. While we were chatting, Alastair Campbell came across to talk to me. Much to his amusement, it seemed, I had nicknamed Campbell 'The Shadow' because he always seemed to be there, never more than five yards away from me during interviews or at press conferences after matches. I'd start talking and he'd appear just behind my shoulder, as if by magic.

'Can I have a word, Gavin?' he said and sat down. He handed me a piece of paper with a few sentences printed on it. They were under a heading that read 'Gavin Henson quotes'.

'What's this?' I said.

'We've had a chat about it and we think this is the right way to go. It says it all, really. It'll save you having to talk to the media because they're obviously bound to want to ask questions.'

I looked at the piece of paper and read the words that were supposed to have come out of my mouth. I was just stunned, amazed.

It read: '*Obviously, everyone wants to play in the Tests, so there is bound to be some disappointment at not being selected for the First Test on Saturday. But, competition was always going to be fierce and this is a squad of world-class players.*

'*The challenge for me now is to play to the best of
my ability when selected, keep challenging, and keep
learning from the experience.*'

I read it through two or three times. I thought, 'This
is ridiculous. It doesn't even sound like me. It's not what
I would say.' I looked at the word 'disappointment'.
I didn't feel disappointed. Disappointed is when you're
waiting for a train and it's delayed for 20 minutes. I
wasn't disappointed. I was devastated.

Dressed in his Lions issue tracksuit, Campbell was
sitting forward on the chair next to me. I looked up and
he was smiling. 'So. Is that okay then?' he said.

'Is what okay?'

'Can we put it out? We've discussed it with the management and we think it's the right way to play this one.
It just keeps the media happy and saves you from having
to do anything.'

'But it's not even how I feel. It's just ridiculous. Anyone could write that.'

He smiled again and said quietly: 'Go on. Just let us
put this one out. It'll be easier in the long run.'

I sat there, still staring at the page. I felt very uncomfortable. The words didn't sound as if they belonged to
me. They weren't how I felt at all. They could have
been written for any player in the squad. They were
meaningless. They sounded like something that could
have been written out before we came to New Zealand.
They probably were. But I'd just walked out of a team

meeting where Clive had emphasised the need for everyone to react in the way he was hoping for. I didn't want to cause a fuss and be accused of doing something that would 'cost us the Test series.' I also wanted to give myself a fighting chance of playing in the Second Test.

'Yeah, fine. Do what you think is best,' I said.

'Thanks, Gavin. It'll be fine.' He then got up and left.

Up to that point I'd found Campbell and his role on the tour quite amusing. I think he had, too. I'd be packing my bag in the dressing room after a game and he'd be standing in the doorway, waiting for me. We'd have a bit of a laugh about it, take the piss out of each other. But this felt different. He hadn't asked me how I felt before making up those quotes. He and the management had just decided it for themselves.

The next day we travelled to Invercargill for the midweek match against Southland. At this point, the Test team hadn't been made public. But Clive had named his side to face Southland and had stated that any player involved on Tuesday would not feature in the squad for the First Test. So it was an easy calculation to make. We had a 45-man squad and 22 of those had been named for Tuesday. That left 23 players, 22 of whom would make up the squad for the First Test. My inclusion in the team to play Southland meant that I would not be in the Test 22.

The next morning, before we left for Invercargill, we

had a training session in Christchurch and Clive asked me if we could walk back to the hotel together after the session. It struck me as a bit strange because it wasn't the usual routine at all. But he said he wanted to chat and explain his selection decision for the Test. 'Okay, fine,' I said, although it still seemed an odd thing to do because it was at least a 10-minute walk. What I didn't know at the time – and would only discover on the last day of the tour – was that a photographer had been positioned behind a car with orders from Campbell to take a picture of the two of us.

We began walking and I thought, 'This is weird. Why don't we just chat on the bus or wait until we get back to the hotel?' It seemed strange behaviour for Clive to want to do something like that in public. But I was obviously keen to hear his view of things and put my own thoughts forward. It turned out to be a slow-paced walk and Clive would also stop every now and again to emphasise a point. He began by asking me how I felt. 'Devastated,' I told him. I mentioned the quotes that had gone out and how I was annoyed by them. He told me not to worry and actually encouraged me to be perfectly honest with the media if I was asked how I felt. I thought, 'So what was the point of all that nonsense last night?'

We got onto talking about the team. I asked him what had changed between telling me I would be in the team and then leaving me out altogether. I also wanted to know why he kept taking me off with 20 minutes to go because that was normally the stage of the game when players can really make their mark. Clive told me that after watching all the games, he'd realised he needed to go for experience in the First Test. He had to select Stephen Jones at No.10 because of the brilliant season Steve had enjoyed for Wales. He wanted to play Jonny at No.12 because of his experience and the fact that Steve and Jonny offered a right and left-foot kicking combination. Okay, I thought. I couldn't argue with Stephen and it was always apparent what Clive thought of Jonny. Even before we'd left for the tour, Clive told me loads of times how the squad needed Wilkinson because of his experience in big games and how he was excited at the influence Jonny would be on me. Fair enough, I thought, I'm not going to argue about the man who won him the World Cup – even if it was fairly obvious to everyone in the squad that Jonny was not yet back to his brilliant best. But what about the bench? Why wasn't I even on the bench? Clive told me it was experience again and Will Greenwood's ability to be a good talker. He pointed out that Will was always speaking up in team meetings, while I was very quiet. He mentioned what a fantastic influence Will had been on the midweek team because of his personality. I like Will and I respect him both as a player and a person. Before every game I played on that tour he went out of his way to send me a good luck note. But I couldn't accept a coach's decision that someone had got in ahead of me because he was a better talker.

'No-one says more on the pitch than me, Clive,' I said. 'And as for team meetings, I'm the new kid here. I'm hardly going to start spouting off to guys like Will and Jonny and Jason Robinson, who've all done this before. This is my first Lions tour. In four years time, I'll be the one voicing up because I'll have the experience.' But he wouldn't have it. That's the thing about Clive. At the end of the day, it doesn't really matter what you say. He's already made his mind up. He'd decided he needed to go for experience and that was that.

We finally reached the hotel. It was a strange experience, walking along the street with the Lions coach, talking about selection. It felt odd. I couldn't help wondering why we weren't in the hotel or somewhere less public. But the real reason came out two weeks later when *The Sunday Times* described how Campbell had positioned a photographer to take a picture of Clive and I chatting together as we walked. I didn't see any photographer lurking about, or Clive looking around suspiciously, or anything like that. I knew nothing whatsoever of a picture being taken until the story came out on the day we flew home.

I suppose Campbell's intentions were to try and show through a picture that there was no rift between me and Clive, that we were still on good terms. Fair enough. I haven't got a problem with that. If Campbell had said to me what he was up to, then I'd have gone along with it if the Lions management had felt it was a good idea. If they'd said it was in the interests of the squad, then I'd have done it. I'd have played ball. After all, I went along with the suggested quotes even though I wasn't happy about it. But I didn't know anything at all about the picture stunt. When it all came out I felt I'd been used – as if they didn't trust me. I felt it was pretty sly of Campbell not to mention it to me, especially as he claimed in the newspapers afterwards that I knew all about it. I've no reason to think that Clive Woodward knew all about what was going on. He rang me a couple of days after the tour and told me that Campbell had mentioned something about a picture, but that he didn't know the details. But the whole episode has left a bit of a sour taste and I've lost any respect I had for Campbell. He was supposed to be part of a team, but in my view he was working to his own agenda.

The fact is that I get photographed almost every day of the week, either through rugby or when I'm with Charlotte. I've grown used to it. I know that pictures can serve a purpose, that they can be used to try and portray people in a positive light or in a negative one. If Campbell had come to me and explained his thinking then I would have grasped what he was trying to do. But he went behind my back and I find that hard to accept.

We trained at Rugby Park Stadium in Invercargill on Monday evening and I stayed on with the other kickers for a practice session. As I came off the field, I was approached by a reporter who asked me how I felt preparing for the midweek game instead of for the Test. I wasn't going to pretend, so I told him my honest feelings. I felt completely devastated, I said, and had felt quite shocked at being left out of the Test squad. But I had a game to get things out of my system and I still thought I could make the side for the Second Test.

I felt better after that. I'd got things off my chest and put the record straight. As the reporter walked off, Campbell spotted him and came running over. He asked me what I'd said and I told him. He then scuttled off to try and find the reporter. I went back to the hotel. I was now looking forward to the match. My groin felt fine and my kicking had gone well. I was hungry for rugby as I'd only played two games out of the first five and I'd come off after an hour in both of them. I had a text message from Lyn Jones which said: 'Two tries tonight and man of the match.' I sent one back: 'No. Three.' I was feeling confident. I've always found that. After a set-back I can always get myself up for the next game. It never affects my self-belief.

The next evening soon came around and it was time to try and make my mark against Southland. The match started well for me and I was feeling strong. I wanted the ball. I scored a try in the first half when I broke a couple of tackles and got another one in the second-half. I felt my all-round contribution was solid enough, but not a lot different to my performances in the other two matches where I'd been brought off. The only difference in Invercargill was that I'd scored two tries. Some people suggested afterwards that I looked intent on proving a point. But I honestly didn't feel like that. I was just desperate to play a whole game and enjoy myself. My only frustration was that I wasn't asked to have the goal-kicking duties, something that was to prove a major regret on the whole tour. For some reason – and I never really found out why – I was never asked to take kicks at goal during the entire trip. Of course, we had some world-class kickers in that squad. Ronan O'Gara was one of them and he struck two conversions and four penalties in that match against Southland as we completed a 26–16 victory. But I felt I could have been used as a long-range kicker, at least, in the way I'd kicked for Wales during the Six Nations. It never happened and I was never given an explanation.

Ironically, that Southland match was the one game where I really should have come off for the last 10 minutes. When I'd had the injection in my groin they'd told me the pain-killing effects would last six weeks. Those six weeks ended after around 65 minutes in Invercargill. The pain was pretty bad, but I was determined to get through the match. In the dressing room, however, things got a lot worse. I could hardly bend to get changed, the pain was so sharp. I didn't tell anyone as I didn't want the doctors to rule me out of the Second Test. So when someone asked me why I was limping, I told them it was just a knock. The truth was that I was struggling to walk.

I managed to get dressed and hobbled out the door. The Shadow was outside, waiting for me.

'You need to do the press conference,' said Campbell.

I didn't really fancy walking all the way over to the press room so I said: 'Do I have to? I've done TV and radio. Can't someone else go?'

'No. Sorry. They want you.'

I limped alongside him. It wasn't just the groin, if I'm honest. I got quite edgy in all the press conferences because I always felt if I said the wrong thing then Campbell and Clive would decide to send me home. It sounds ridiculous, but after the business with Clive before the tour I was extremely wary about saying something the management would object to. 'You need to be as sharp off the field as you are on the field,' he'd said. I took that to mean I was always on trial and that if I blurted out the wrong thing they'd find an excuse to put me on a flight back to Heathrow. In every interview I listened carefully to the question and then thought very carefully about my answer. I'd rehearse the answer in my mind, to make sure there were no lurking dangers, and then, when I was satisfied, I'd give my reply. I must have sounded like an idiot. We walked into the room and I sat on the edge of the press conference table and tried to look invisible. There were dozens of reporters with microphones and cameras pointed in the direction of me, Ronan, and Michael Owen.

'Gavin, do you think you might have done something off the field that may have cost you your place in the Test team?' asked someone.

I thought he was making a point about Charlotte's visit to Wellington, which had been cleared by the management and was no different to the visits of any of the other girlfriends.

'No. I think that's a stupid question.'

The remainder of the questions were all about my reaction to missing out on Test selection and my feelings on possibly making the Second Test. I tried to keep my answers as short as possible, so I wouldn't say anything I'd regret, and when it was over I hobbled out and onto the bus.

The next day my groin had settled down a bit, but I still needed some rest. I obviously wasn't going to be involved in Saturday's First Test but the midweek coaches were now planning their next game against Manawatu on the following Tuesday. Ian McGeechan told me he wanted me to play. I realised that my groin would be fine in a week, but I knew deep down that if I played against Manawatu there was no way the groin would have settled down again by the Saturday. I told

Geech that if they wanted to play me midweek again, that was fine. But if they had any thoughts of playing me in the Second Test then I should be rested because my injury just wouldn't stand up to two tough matches in five days. Stuart Barton, our physio, agreed with me and so the decision was taken not to consider me for the match against Manawatu. If I was put back on the anti-inflammatory pills and painkillers, then I'd be fine for the Second Test.

I liked Geech and thought he was a really good coach. He was backs coach for the midweek side and was obviously very experienced. This was his fourth Lions tour as a coach and the successful Lions team that I'd watched as a kid in 1997 was shaped by him. But although he'd done it all, he was very willing to listen. He'd always seek the players' view and let them have an input into the way we were going to play. That's why the midweek side always looked relaxed.

I found that a big contrast with Eddie O'Sullivan and Andy Robinson, who were coaching the Saturday side. With them it was always obvious that they wanted things done their way. I felt O'Sullivan was rather too negative in that he wanted us to kick for position too often, instead of keeping the ball in hand. Maybe, that was because he was used to that kind of approach with Ireland, whereas Wales play a much more fluid, handling game. I'm not against a kicking strategy if it's the best tactic you've got. It suits Ireland and there are times when we rely a lot on a big kicking game with the Ospreys. But I just felt that a kicking strategy wasn't necessarily the best thing to rely on as a way of beating the All Blacks, given the talented runners we had in that Lions squad. Our tactical approach was a bit too limited in terms of how we thought we'd beat the All Blacks. Basically, O'Sullivan, Robinson and Woodward felt we could put loads of pressure on the All Blacks through our pack, force New Zealand to give away penalties, and watch Jonny kick the goals. Tries were a bit of an after-thought. They seemed to hope that our pack was going to beat up their pack and we could then play our rugby off that. But if that's not happening, then you need an approach that's going to attack the opposition from deeper and not always through the forwards. I think maybe we suffered from not having a coach from the Wales set-up involved. It would have added a different perspective, a different way of solving the problem. As it was, we adopted the English-Irish way and it was just too negative.

The other big frustration for me was that having decided on this kicking game, they never used me as a kicker. I'm pretty proud of the distance I can kick the ball out of hand. It's what I do a lot for the Ospreys and for Wales. My stats stack up well against most players. But the Lions coaches never gave me that responsibility. I'd watch some of our kickers put the ball 30 yards downfield and think, 'I could have put it twice as far.'

Gavin Henson

But then, I've never been the best watcher. And watching that First Test at Christchurch proved to be one of the most frustrating experiences of my life.

CHAPTER EIGHTEEN

All Blacked Out

Even though I had the game against Southland to focus attention on, the week leading up to the First Test were long days for me. Every now and again I'd suddenly remember I wasn't going to be involved on Saturday and all the feelings of frustration would come crowding into my mind. Obviously, there were 23 other very frustrated players in our group, too, but my absence from the Test squad seemed to have created the biggest stir. I was aware it had been big news back at home, especially in Wales, and even within the squad itself my non-selection was a talking point. Other players told me they were surprised. One of those, Neil Back, managed to really boost my own confidence and make me even more determined to come back with a good performance against Southland. On the Monday after training, Backy – who had been named in the Test side – came across to have a word. He told me he was amazed I hadn't made the squad and said a lot of the other boys were very surprised, too. He also said he'd watched me carefully in training to see how I'd react. He felt I might be a bit subdued, but was impressed how positively I'd come out and shown lots of enthusiasm. That meant a lot to me, especially as Neil was someone with a massive status in the game who'd seen it all and was on his third Lions tour. It made me feel a lot better.

Thursday and Friday were long days as I tried to concentrate my mind and body on being ready for the Second Test. Then, Saturday arrived – a day I wasn't looking forward to at all. It's a horrible feeling watching a team you were desperate to be involved with. You want them to do well, you want them to win and you want the tour to be a success. But you also know that if they win and the players in your position do okay, then you're very unlikely to get the call yourself. The two feelings were battling inside my mind all day. It felt mentally exhausting, far worse than if I'd actually been preparing for the match itself.

If I'd had the choice then I would have stayed in my room and watched a film. But, of course, the whole squad has to go and support the Test team and so I left with everyone else in the early evening as we made our way to Christchurch's Jade Stadium. It was a filthy night, the first real heavy rainfall we'd had on the whole tour. If you were superstitious then you'd have viewed it as a bad omen.

We had a strong Lions side on paper, but there were quite a few players who hadn't yet really come to the boil, for a variety of reasons. Still, this was the night that mattered. If those boys turned it on this evening, then all the struggles of our previous games over the four weeks would probably be forgotten.

The Lions supporters ensured the atmosphere inside the stadium was electric. But if the weather was bad, then things didn't get any better when we kicked off. Brian O'Driscoll was injured in the opening minute of the match and had to be carried off on a stretcher. Our skipper had dislocated his shoulder when he was picked up and dumped over their shoulders by Tana Umaga and Kevin Mealamu. It was to become the most controversial on-field incident of the tour. To add to my mixed emotions, Will Greenwood came off the bench, the position I'd imagined I would be occupying as a worse case scenario.

Our forwards were under pressure, especially in the line-out, and we started to give away a lot of penalties. Then, another mistake at a line-out let the All Black forward Ali Williams in for a try. It didn't feel like it was going to be our night and not just on the field. Those of us who were there to add our support alongside the management were sat right up in the top tier of the stand and we were absolutely freezing. Things got worse. Clive Woodward's belief that this side would somehow gel, even though they hadn't played together as a team, just didn't happen. Daniel Carter kicked the All Blacks into a 14–0 lead and then Umaga set up Sitiveni Sivivatu for their second try. Jonny Wilkinson kicked a penalty for the Lions, but that was all we could manage. We lost 21–3 and never looked like scoring a try in the whole match. We walked into the dressing room and there were a lot of blank faces and shivering bodies. It had been a bad night.

Brian's injury cast a shadow over everything, but in truth I think most players were wrapped up in the bad result and the terrible performance. The line-out had been a disaster, but in fairness to Andy Robinson he soon put his hand up and took responsibility for that. It had been his decision to make some late changes, including the calls, as there was concern that the All Blacks had somehow worked out our previous calls. As players realised the extent of Brian's injury there was a growing feeling of resentment over what had happened. The players near that ruck said they could hear the touch judge yelling, 'Let him go! Let him go!' before Umaga and Mealamu speared Brian into the ground. But the touch judge then made no attempt to explain to the referee what had happened. Later on that night, the Lions would cite both All Black forwards for foul play, but the hearing gave them the benefit of the doubt. It's a difficult one because 'clearing out' has become such an accepted part of the game. Players often do try and grab an opponent's leg and lift it because you make him weaker and unstable. But if you keep lifting and them drop someone, then it has to be dangerous play. What really angered Brian was that Umaga never even came over to check how Brian was, even when the stretcher turned up and it was obvious his match was over.

That night, and in the days that followed, the Lions management continued to voice their unhappiness over Brian's injury. There have been suggestions since that Alastair Campbell was urging them to do this, but I've really no idea if that was the case or not. Whatever games Campbell was playing with the media weren't made apparent to me. But there was definitely a feeling among the players that we'd lost our captain through something that the New Zealanders had got away with.

After Brian was ruled out of the rest of the series, I felt pretty certain I'd come in for the Second Test. I knew the manner of the defeat would mean a re-think by Clive and the fact that we had injuries just added to my chances of coming in. But I didn't think too deeply about things at that point. I'd learnt not to count any chickens.

It was at this stage of the tour that a story appeared in the New Zealand newspapers claiming that I'd gone 'walkabout'. It suggested I'd been so upset at being left out of the First Test team that I'd disappeared from the team hotel and gone on some kind of drinking spree before the management had convinced me to come back. This is what really happened. Two of my mates were in Christchurch, following the tour. They were David Norman, 'Dai Norm' and Matthew Williams, otherwise known as Fat Boy Roy. Everyone calls him Fat Boy Roy, even his mum and dad. On the morning of the First Test they called me and we arranged to meet up in a bar opposite the team hotel. I knew I had to be off to the stadium in a short while, so I went across in my tour suit. They had a couple of beers and I had a fruit juice. I was there for a couple of hours, just catching up and killing time before the match. When it was time to go, I left the boys and joined the rest of the squad on the bus to the stadium. There were lots of supporters in and around that bar and I can only think that someone had tipped off the newspapers that Gavin Henson was 'off the tour' with his mates. The newspaper was right in claiming I was 'devastated' at being left out. But the idea that I'd skipped off the tour to go on a drinking spree was ludicrous.

I spoke to Campbell about that story, but he seemed as in the dark about it as I was. This was a busy time for The Shadow, with the O'Driscoll and Umaga business and all the press conferences, but for some reason he turned up at a team meeting following that First Test defeat. I think the players thought he was going to give some advice on media reaction to the defeat and how we should handle questions. Instead, he gave a speech about the game and told us he could tell the New Zealanders 'wanted it' more than we did. He said they'd shown more commitment than us and that some players just hadn't put their bodies on the line. 'You didn't want it enough,' he said. It was unbelievable crap. I wasn't part of that side but the idea that in a Lions Test match – the pinnacle for any player – people hadn't put their bodies on the line was just insulting. The problems went a lot deeper than that. As a player you can take that sort of stuff from ex-internationals who've been there themselves. You might disagree with them, but at least they can speak from personal experience. Where was Campbell coming from? What was his rugby experience? A lot of the boys felt very uncomfortable and angry listening to that. It was rubbish and it backfired badly.

From Christchurch we moved on to Wellington for the Second Test, but in between times there was the midweek match against Manawatu at Palmerston North. It turned out to be the easiest match of the tour by far and a good morale-booster. Shane Williams strutted his stuff and scored five tries. Martin Corry, Geordan Murphy, Jason Robinson, Charlie Hodgson, Ollie Smith, Neil Back, Gordon D'Arcy, Ronan O'Gara (2), Mark Cueto (2) and Gareth Cooper also scored and we won 109–6. We got back to our team hotel near midnight and Clive told me I'd be starting at No.12 in the Second Test. He told me the rest of the back line – Josh Lewsey, Jason Robinson, Gareth Thomas at outside centre, Dwayne Peel and Jonny Wilkinson at half-back, with Shane on the wing. I felt relieved and went to bed.

The Test team for Wellington was officially announced the next afternoon. There was a Welsh flavour to it with six players from our Grand Slam team in the starting line-up – Gareth, Shane, Dwayne, Gethin Jenkins, Ryan Jones and myself. We also now had a Welsh captain of the Lions as Gareth had taken over as skipper from Brian. I felt pleased for Alfie. It was an honour he fully deserved. Alfie was a bit mad in his younger days and those who played with him reckon they'd never have thought for a second he'd go on to captain Wales, never mind the Lions. He's incredibly relaxed and maintains that easy going feeling almost to kick-off. I like that because normally coaches go the other way and that can make players feel edgy. He's a very genuine bloke who never puts on an act in team meetings like some players do. If a coach asks Alfie a question then he'll give an honest answer, even if it might not be the answer the coach was hoping for. He's a players' captain. He can also be very funny – even when he doesn't mean to be. Before that second Test, he gathered all the players around and said: 'I've only got two words to say to you, boys. Don't fucking panic.' Nobody panicked, but it took a while for people to stop laughing.

The Welsh influence had an effect on the way we trained and prepared that week. There was still a strong emphasis on creating forward dominance, but there was more work done on how we'd attack the New Zealanders with ball in hand. We wanted to get guys like Josh, Shane and Jason into the game. Alfie also changed things a little in those sessions. They were shorter and sharper, especially the team run on the day before. We felt confident. We just hadn't performed in that first match and had given nothing away. The All Blacks had no real idea of what we might be capable of because we'd been so poor in Christchurch.

I was really excited about playing, not just about the thrill of playing in a Lions Test, but I really thought we could win. I worked out in my head how the game might go. I thought we'd get things right up front, get some momentum and then find the gaps behind. I visualised what was going to happen, that we'd turn things around and square the series. Then, we'd all be off to Auckland for the deciding Test and a chance to win the thing. I felt fit and in the mood. This was the biggest game of my life, but it was what I'd prepared for all my life as well. I was ready for it.

The Westpac Stadium in Wellington is known as The Cake Tin. It's a big, wide venue with a good surface. Conditions were fine, the Lions supporters were in fantastic voice – as they had been all through the tour – and it was all set up for a really memorable night, maybe the most memorable night of my career.

But the sad fact is that I can hardly remember any of that game as I spent most of it concussed. Since I've been back from New Zealand, people have asked me,

'What's it like to play in a Test match for the Lions?' It's actually hard to say because the memory for me is a very hazy one. That's unusual for me because I can normally remember most details of every game I've played in. I do remember our fantastic start and Alfie bursting through to score a try in the second minute. I was standing on the open side and screaming for the ball to come my way. But Alfie went the other way and it turned out to be an inspired decision as the field just opened up for him and he had a clear run to the posts. Jonny converted and we were 7–0 up. Jonny missed a penalty shortly after that. I have to admit I would have fancied that one, but I'm sure Jonny would have thought the same thing if I'd missed one. That's how kickers are.

Daniel Carter put over a couple of penalties for New Zealand before the All Blacks attacked down their right. The ball came to their wing, Rico Gear. He was quite close to the line and he's a superb finisher so I knew I had to hit him hard in order to stop him. I was pleased with the tackle. I didn't slide off him, but took him through into touch and denied them the score.

I'm not sure whereabouts on his body that I hit Gear, but I had a 'stinger'. That's the name in the game for the shooting pains you get down your arm from a heavy tackle. I'd had them plenty of times before. The arm feels numb and you have no feeling, but after a couple of minutes the feeling comes back and you can carry on. It's something that Jonny Wilkinson has suffered from quite a lot in his career. In fact, Jonny could tell what had happened straight away. 'Don't show it. Don't let them see it,' he said. 'Just get back in the line.' I did as I was told but I felt groggy. I didn't quite know where I was. There was another problem. The feeling in my arm didn't come back. It just felt loose and useless. I didn't know it then but I'd trapped a nerve and that's why I could hardly lift it above my chest.

A few moments later, the All Blacks attacked and Carter handed me off. I tried to chase him, but it felt as though I was treading water or running with lead boots on. I got handed off again and Umaga went over for the try.

A few players asked me if I was okay and I said I was fine. I thought I was fine. But I didn't really know where I was and actually felt confused. I even asked players what was going on. Jonny kicked two penalties and Carter struck one. Then, New Zealand attacked us again. Byron Kelleher made a break but should have been penalised for hanging on in the tackle. He got away with it, though, and they moved the ball from right to left. We all moved up in the back line and everyone made a good tackle. I hit Umaga but he still managed to get his pass away and Sitiveni Sivivatu finished it off after a brilliant side-step.

It was 21–13 at half-time, but my arm was still aching and my head hadn't cleared. I didn't really know what was going on or where I was. I walked into the dressing room and must have looked a bit dazed as one of our doctors asked me what the score was. 'It's 21–13,' I said. I still don't really know how I knew it, or whether someone else had just told me the score as we walked in. 'Fine,' he said. We sat down and I tried to clear my head. My senses must have been scrambled, though, because I didn't even mention my arm injury to anyone, even though I could hardly lift it.

The second-half is just a blur. I didn't touch the ball after half-time. In fact, in the entire game I think I got my hands on the ball just once, which is unbelievable for me. I was a passenger, a spectator. I still can't believe no-one really noticed and I wasn't replaced until a few minutes from the end. When I watched the tape of the game a day or so later, I was amazed at how I was allowed to stay on. I did nothing. I don't think I've ever done as little on a rugby field. The other thing that struck me was what a brilliant match Carter enjoyed for the All Blacks. He ran the show, but at the time I hardly noticed he was on the field.

It was a much better contest than the First Test, but the All Blacks were still clearly the better team and deservedly won, 48–18. Simon Easterby – who had a very impressive tour – scored our second try. The series had been lost and there must have been some pretty depressed people in the Lions dressing room after the match. But I don't remember anything that happened after the first 20 minutes, or after the final whistle. The next thing I can recall is sitting in my room back at the hotel. I felt uneasy and nauseous. I'd never suffered concussion before and so I wasn't quite sure what was happening to me. I just knew it was a sensation I didn't like. I called my parents and asked them to come over to my room. I asked them what had gone on. It was all news to me.

The next morning the doctors told me I'd suffered concussion. They also gave my arm a full examination and discovered there was some pretty bad muscle damage and a trapped nerve. They didn't need to tell me. I knew it already. I was out of the rest of the tour. Twelve months before, I'd finished the season in South Africa by getting injured on tour in a Test match. I'd had a good season, but in my last match of the campaign I'd got hurt and gave a very ineffective performance. It had rankled all summer as the last game is always the one that's freshest in the memory. I'd vowed it wouldn't happen again. But here I was in New Zealand and the whole thing had been repeated. My season had ended with an injury and we'd been hammered in a Test match that had passed me by. Now, I'd have the whole summer to stew over it, just as I had in 2004.

The last week of the tour dragged as I was told I had no more commitments, training or playing. I went to the final midweek match against Auckland – which the Lions won 17–13 – and then switched into holiday mode. All the players not in the squad of 22 for the

Third Test were allowed to go down to Queenstown for
a few days' relaxation. We were able to take wives and
girlfriends. My girlfriend had long since gone home, so
I took Dai Norm instead. Queenstown is the adventure
sport capital of New Zealand and where the original
bungy jumps were done. Shane Williams and Dai had a
jump, but Gareth Cooper and I made our excuses and
watched. I had plenty of excuses – head, arm, shoulder,
groin, but most of all a bad fear of heights and especially
of hurtling towards the ground on the end of a piece of
elastic.

The Lions lost the Third Test, 38–19, at Eden Park
in a match that won't live in anyone's memory for long.
Ten days before, I'd dreamed of playing in a Lions side
that would win in Auckland to clinch the series, 2–1.
As it was, I watched the game from the stands as *The
Sunday Times* got ready to run the story about the
Campbell-inspired picture. Once again, New Zealand
managed to score tries against us as they wrapped up
the series, 3–0. They'd scored 12 tries in the series, but
we'd managed only three. I'd had all these wishes for
how the tour might end, all these hopes, but it didn't
quite work out that way.

The tour was a great experience for me, though, and
despite some of the set-backs, I'm more than glad I made
it. I'd heard and read so much about guys like Jonny
Wilkinson, Neil Back and Brian O'Driscoll, but to be
among them was a real eye-opener. Their professional-

ism and dedication was tremendous. To watch Jonny practice his goal-kicking for three to four hours was incredible. I'd always thought my two-hour sessions were intense and committed. But Jonny's on another level. It showed me that however hard you feel you are training and practising, there's always someone prepared to go that extra yard. I'm not saying I'll be doing four-hour kicking practices next season, but I won't be so concerned about getting off the kicking field just because a coach tells me it's time to go.

I'll take confidence from the tour. In terms of overall preparation and readiness for Test rugby, as well as skill levels, I think all the Welsh players are more than a match for anything else in the British Isles. We train as hard, our back-up advice – like fitness testing and nutrition and so on – is all as good as theirs if not better. We lacked self-belief at one stage, but the Grand Slam proved those days are gone. There is nothing I would have done differently if I had the time again. I have to think that. It's the only way I can sleep at night.

Clive Woodward said many times before and during the tour that this was the best prepared Lions squad in history. He was right up to a point. The planning and the detail were awesome. We had everything we needed and the logistics of the tour were first rate. We had single rooms for the players, the travel arrangements ran like clockwork, the food was good, the laundry was taken care of; in short, there was never a hair out of place. But where it really mattered – out on the pitch – we were badly lacking. The structure of the tour was not a success. Instead of shaping the Test side through the first few weeks, and bringing it to the boil, it seemed to be thrown together at the last minute. The matches against Wellington and Otago should have been about fine tuning, but in that week before the First Test it seemed to me that we were not much further down the road than the day we landed in Auckland four weeks before.

The Test side Clive picked wasn't based on what he'd seen. It was based on what he'd remembered, mostly from two years before. He admitted he went for experience, but that's not the most important thing if players are struggling or just coming back from injuries. The tactical approach for the First Test was wrong and by the time we switched things around we just had too little time to get it right.

I felt let down because I was led to believe I'd start the First Test and I didn't. The way I was taken off in the two games leading up to that decision made me feel even more frustrated. I've still got a lot of respect for Clive, for what he achieved with England. I don't blame him at all for taking 45 players, as rugby is so physically demanding now that you cannot play two games a week. You need two squads. But his preparation of the Test team was poor. It just wasn't ready in time. I also felt his tactics and his game-plan were out-of-date, while

I was shocked to see how little actual coaching he does. He leaves that to others.

Clive's coaching methods were something new to me and left me a bit bewildered. At every coaching session he would simply stand on the sidelines, as though he wasn't really involved. Sometimes he'd come in close to see how the boys were reacting to what was going on. He'd listen carefully if a player spoke up to one of the hands-on coaches, such as Robinson and O'Sullivan, and then he'd wander off again. It was impossible to know what he was thinking or what effect he thought he was having.

The actual coaching on the field was always left to the rest of the coaching team. Clive would be more like the overseer. It was certainly unlike any coaching I'd been involved with before, but maybe that was the way he was used to with England. After all, they had won the World Cup so perhaps he felt he was using tried and trusted methods. But they were methods that felt strange to me because it complicated the lines of communication. You were never quite sure what he was after.

In team meetings, Clive would call upon each of his coaches to make their various points. Robinson would have his say, then perhaps O'Sullivan and Gareth Jenkins. At the end, Clive would briefly try and sum everything up and make the odd point himself. Perhaps he was busy behind the scenes in giving his coaches the full picture but to the players he seemed to be in more of a managerial role and not very hands-on. He was always a bit of a mystery for me. I never knew what he was really thinking. Every time he brought me off before full-time in the provincial games, I would make a point of asking him why he'd done it and what I'd done wrong. Every time, I'd get the same reply. 'You did fine. Don't worry about it.' That would simply annoy me more later on when I wasn't picked for the next game. I had nothing to go on – no idea of what I was supposedly doing wrong.

In the end, the only area he ever said I fell down on was voicing up in team meetings. He felt I'd been too quiet on the whole tour. Maybe he was right on that score, but I would have felt I was putting on an act if I'd started telling much more experienced guys like Will Greenwood and Neil Back what they needed to do. Besides, there were too many players who spoke up just for the sake of it. I lost count of the times players went on and on just because they thought it would sound impressive if they talked for a long time. They were in love with the sounds of their own voices. I'm all for players voicing their opinions. But they should be like training sessions – short and sharp and to the point.

For me, the tour failed because of a combination of factors. Firstly, Clive never really seemed sure of his best team and wasted too many games fumbling around, hoping he'd stumble on it. On previous Lions tours, I think the head coach has known early on what his best team and 22-man squad were going to be. He has then used the warm-up games before the Tests to get that squad one hundred per cent ready. But Clive only ever had a vague idea. He seemed to want to try lots of different combinations, instead of settling firmly on one group of players. Having said that, I think he was also let down by many players' performances. Far too many players under-performed when he was looking for them to demand selection for the Tests. That put too many doubts in Clive's mind and in the end he went back to what he felt he could trust – the experience of certain players who had done it for him in the past.

Secondly, there was too much concentration given to what would 'lose us the Test series' and not enough given to what would win it. Clive talked so often about certain things that would deny us the Test victories if we didn't get them right – small, off-the-field things that he had various hang-ups about, like media dealings and players' reactions to selection decisions. For me, it produced too much of a negative atmosphere when we should have been talking about all our good things that were going to be chucked at the All Blacks.

Thirdly, I think we got the basic game-plan wrong going into that vital First Test. Clive wanted a right and left-foot kicker at Nos 10 and 12, so Stephen Jones and Jonny Wilkinson played together even though it was a raw, unproven partnership without a proper No. 12. The plan was to kick for territory and then beat the All

Blacks up front by attacking their scrum and line-out. We were going to pressure them and they'd crack by giving away either tries or penalties under our pressure. It was never likely to be very pretty. In fact, Clive would often say he'd be delighted to win by one point. The trouble with that strategy was that it might have sounded fine when we left the UK, but as the tour games went on it was obvious we were not going to be able to batter the All Blacks up front because we weren't even able to do that to their provincial sides. They were holding their own in the set-pieces and then beating us hands down in the fight for loose possession.

It cried out for a change of tactics to a running game, a more attack-minded game that would utilise guys like Brian O'Driscoll, Josh Lewsey, Jason Robinson and Shane Williams. But by the time Clive went some way towards that with his Second Test selection, he'd wasted so many of the preparation games that it was probably too late. Some people might say a running game would have been too risky and played into New Zealand's hands. But, for me, the idea of going into the All Blacks' own backyard and thinking we'd scrummage them off the park was pretty risky, too. No-one does that. You have to beat them with a balanced, all-round game. I think maybe Clive felt that because England had won the World Cup that way two years before, it was the way to go again. But times had moved on. England no longer had that brutally dominant pack as we'd seen in the Six Nations, while the All Blacks had worked hard on the basics of their forward play. Clive was two years too late.

Finally, I don't think Clive and his coaches made the most of the weapons at their disposal. Lewsey looked bang in form early on and a real match-winner for us. But he was then messed about in different positions and we never got the very best out of him. Ryan Jones wasn't picked for the First Test when it was clear he was the in-form back row forward. Without wishing to sound arrogant, I'd put myself in that group of under-used players, too. I honestly believe that I'm the biggest kicker in international rugby at present. I don't think anyone can kick the ball further out of hand. If we were going to play this territorial game that required long-distance kicking, then I just couldn't understand why I was never used. It was unbelievably frustrating to see certain players kick for touch in our side, when I knew I could put it twice as far down the field. I've done it when we've needed it for Wales. I do it every week for the Ospreys. But I was never given a chance to do it for the Lions.

I should think Clive has plenty of regrets as do lots of others who were making decisions on that tour. It doesn't mean they've become bad coaches. As Clive himself often says, 'You've just got to cop it and move on.' I still have a lot of respect and admiration for Clive. More often than not, I still think he's a winner. He pays incredible attention to detail. He did on the New Zealand tour. But sometimes if you become obsessed with the small details you can lose sight of the overall picture and I think that's what happened. I think he would do a few things differently if we were to do the tour again. It's going to be very interesting to see how he now gets on in football at Southampton. It was certainly a brave move. He's achieved everything in rugby, so why not? I think he will be very good on the detail of what needs to be done and he'll definitely provide a very professional environment. I'm not really sure how soccer clubs are set up, but I would imagine Clive could be quite a refreshing change for them.

In 2009, the Lions will be off to South Africa. I'd love to be there with them. I think a 45-man squad is sensible, but I'd pencil in more games to make sure the Test team is ready. If that's not possible, then the coach has to decide on his Test team much sooner and let the midweekers prove they deserve a look-in. There is still a massive value in having the Lions and I don't agree with those who have claimed the concept is now out of date. The chance to play alongside the best of Britain and Ireland is still something that players aspire to and I'd welcome another opportunity. The thousands of fans who made the trip made it incredibly memorable. I just wish we had given them something more to celebrate.

CHAPTER NINETEEN

Crazy Chick

When I came back from New Zealand in July I needed a rest. I'd been playing non-stop rugby for 11 months and for over half that period I'd been struggling with the groin injury. It was time to put my feet up and chill out without having to worry about the next game, or whether I'd be able to get through it. The trapped nerve in my arm soon healed and my groin didn't get any worse because I wasn't putting it under any more stress. Charlotte and I went away to a Caribbean island and had a relaxing time laying on the beach, soaking up the sun. Having been apart for so many weeks it was great to be able to enjoy each other's company again.

I suppose our relationship had become more serious as the months had gone on and we both valued the chance to spend some time together. The fact that I was now into a compulsory 11-week break from rugby, combined with my injury, meant that we were able to be together a lot more and we were both very happy with that. When the season is going on, you can't just disappear for a holiday when you feel like it, so you have to make the most of your chances in the summer.

The newspapers have always taken a keen interest in Charlotte ever since she began singing and making records as a very young girl. Now she's 19 and in a relationship with a rugby player they are hardly going to back off, so the press interest is something we've both had to get used to. We can't complain. Sport and music are the businesses we've chosen to be in and they happen to attract a lot of attention. I always wanted to make it as an international rugby player and I've always been honest enough to admit that I enjoy all the attention and the hype.

But it can be hard having a relationship that is always in the public eye. There have been times when the newspapers have taken pictures of us when we happen to be facing in different directions. They've then printed stories claiming we were in the middle of a blazing row. There was one picture of us sitting on sun-loungers on the beach and because we were a few yards apart it was claimed we were not speaking and on the point of splitting up. The truth was that Charlotte had moved into the shade because she was hot. But 'Charlotte Moves Chair to Get Out of the Sun!' is not such a hot story. You just have to laugh at these things and not get upset.

In fact, we never really argue. Not at all. This is my first serious relationship but when I see some other couples, who row all the time, or go behind each other's back, it makes me wonder why they bother being in a relationship at all. Charlotte and I are not like that. We trust each other and we just couldn't get away with not being honest with each other.

We've become very close over the past few months and spend more and more time together. Our families have met a few times and Charlotte more or less lives at my place now, which is probably why it's never looked as untidy. But I can forgive her that as she leads quite a hectic life.

As a couple, it's not as if we go out of our way to crave attention. A lot of people will take that with a large pinch of salt, but it's true. As a rugby player I love all the attention that comes my way. I want rugby to be an exciting sport with big name personalities and I want to be one of them. When the spotlight is on me I feel I respond and it improves my performance as a player. But that doesn't mean I want to be spotted all the time when I'm out with my girlfriend. The fact is, though, that she's a pop star and that means she has to be out there promoting her records. We want to be together and so I go with her as often as I can. That means we'll go out to parties in London, awards nights, and other events and it's all good fun. I really enjoy most of it. But the down side can occasionally be stuff written about us in the newspapers which isn't true or is from someone with an axe to grind.

In September we went to the *GQ* magazine awards night at the Royal Opera House in London. Charlotte won the Woman of the Year Award and I was really proud of her. There were all kinds of big stars strutting about. Bob Geldof, Jay-Z, Matt Lucas and David Walliams were there but I think people warm to Charlotte because she's very natural. It doesn't matter whether she's at an awards ceremony, talking on TV, or down the Robin Hood pub in Cardiff with her mates or her family, she's exactly the same person. She gets on with everyone.

But sometimes I just can't get my head around the weirdness of it all. I always expected to do well as a rugby player, but when we go out in London, and I'm sitting alongside my girlfriend, who happens to be a pop star, in the back of a limousine with blacked out windows, riding to some nightclub where we'll be given free champagne in the VIP lounge, it does seem a bit strange. Or if we're photographed together at some big celebrity event, then it does all seem unreal. It can bring its own pressures, though, and I can now see why some couples in the spotlight find there's extra stress on their relationship. A lot of the time when we're out, I'll find there are girls who are keen to come up and talk to me. Sometimes, unless the relationship is a strong one, that can be quite hard to handle.

Crazy Chick

There's no doubt Charlotte likes to enjoy herself when she's out but she's certainly no different to most 19-year-olds and her reputation in the press has become completely over the top, to say the least. She likes to have a drink and a good time, but I don't think there's anything exceptional in that. Because of my injury I was able to let my hair down a bit over the summer and in many ways going out together at the weekends helped me to forget all the frustrations of an injury that was proving difficult to heal. After the Lions tour, I needed some nights out to keep me sane so Charlotte and I paid a few visits to clubs in London. In terms of the amount of socialising I did, there was no difference in this summer to any other. But when going out meant a few beers with my mates in Bridgend it wasn't exactly the kind of stuff that made the newspapers. Sipping champagne with Charlotte in some bar in London seems to excite a lot more interest, even though it all amounts to the same thing. I'm aware, though, that there are plenty of people who will be ready to criticise me now for my lifestyle who would have stayed quiet before. All I can say is that I'm fully aware that everything for me hinges on my performances as a rugby player. Once they start to dip, then I'm in trouble. But I've no intention of getting distracted by anything that would send me down that road. I still think I work as hard on my game as any player.

Charlotte and I had some really good nights out with

friends, too, during those weeks but by the end of the summer it was obvious to me that my groin problem just wasn't getting any better and it was starting to get me down. A number of doctors and physios had examined me and I was finally diagnosed as having suffered damage to the pubic synthesis, the joint where the pubic bones meet in the pelvis. It was explained that in some circumstances that could be a career-threatening injury. That rang plenty of alarm bells for me and made me absolutely determined to seek the very best advice and take the right course of action. The thought of not being able to play rugby again sent me into a sweat.

By the start of September it had been a full two months of no training whatsoever in order to rest the injury. But it hadn't improved at all. The pain, the soreness, and the lack of movement was still there. In the meantime, being unable to train I was starting to lose shape. On top of that, no-one seemed to be able to give me any indication of what I needed to do and how long it would take before I'd be back playing. I was getting conflicting advice from different medical people and the whole thing started to do my head in.

Then came a chance meeting with Jamie Baulch, the Welsh former 400m runner when I was working on a photo-shoot. I told Jamie about my groin problem and how depressed I was starting to feel. He quickly recommended the clinic of a German doctor based in Munich, Hans Muller-Wolfhart. This guy, Jamie explained, was the best in the business and had treated world class athletes like Colin Jackson as well as soccer players such as Michael Owen and Steven Gerrard. I thought it over and came to the conclusion that I wasn't really getting anywhere with the specialists I was seeing through the Welsh Rugby Union. Dr Wolfhart might be the answer.

I spoke to Lyn Jones, my coach at the Ospreys, and explained the situation. The doctors in this country were suggesting more rest and more pain-killing injections of the type I'd had through last season. I knew that wasn't the answer. I knew that would merely contain the problem but it wouldn't cure it. It would mean another whole season carrying the injury with the risk of breaking down at any point.

'Go and see a specialist and get it sorted,' said Lyn. So I did. I started by going for a consultation with Brian English, the surgeon for Chelsea Football Club, who works closely with Dr Wolfhart. Dr English referred me to the Munich clinic and within a couple of days I flew out to Germany with Charlotte. I was seen by Dr Ulrike Muschaweck who discovered I had a hernia problem that was stopping the pubic synthesis from healing properly. A small operation to repair the hernia was suggested and I was operated on by Dr Muschaweck the next day. The hernia problem hadn't been picked up by my doctors at home, but that was the reason why the injury simply wasn't healing. With the hernia dealt with, the actual injury should heal without a problem and I was told I could expect to be fit again within eight weeks.

It was all a bit of an awkward situation because both Wales and the Ospreys had been arranging treatment with doctors at home. But I just felt I wasn't improving under their guidance which is why I felt the need to take matters into my own hands. As it stands, I'm certain I've done the right thing. The pain I had before the operation went a day or so after I came back from Germany and I began to feel far more confident that I was making a proper recovery at long last.

At the moment, the November Tests for Wales are still a possibility, although I will just have to see how things progress. I'm certainly not going to rush back until I'm fully healed. This has been the most serious injury I've had since I broke my leg at 17 and it affected me during both the Six Nations and the Lions tour.

There are far too many important goals in my future to risk rushing back for the short-term. My Lions experience has made me anxious to be part of a successful trip next time around, although 2009 is a long way off. Before then, there is a World Cup in 2007 and that is my personal priority at present. I missed the last one and I don't want to be left behind again. Wales have two big campaigns before then and I'm confident we can build on the Grand Slam success of last season. The All Blacks arrive in Cardiff on 5 November 2005 and even if I don't manage to face them myself, I think we can beat them. They're a good side but the Lions made them look too good.

The last 12 months of my life have been incredible. If anyone had told me two years ago what was in store – a Grand Slam with Wales, a Lions tour, a Celtic League title with the Ospreys – then I would have found it hard to believe. If someone had also suggested I'd be making headlines all year with Charlotte Church, then I'd have found that even more unbelievable. But all those things have happened to me in the past year and I like to think they're only the start. There's plenty more I want to achieve on the field – World Cups, Six Nations tournaments, and success in Europe with the Ospreys. Off the field, I'd like to figure more in the marketing and promotion of the sport through the media. Charlotte also has an extremely busy year ahead with a European tour to promote her new album. I just hope we both have enough left to spend time with each other. There's no doubt in my mind I've met someone very special, someone I hope to share my life with for a long time to come. I'll admit I'm really into her and I just can't see it ending.

As far as I'm concerned, the game has only just kicked off. I'm 23 years old and the best is yet to come.

List of Illustrations

Index

Index

Index

Index

Index